Bike Repair & Maintenance

FOR

DUMMIES®

by Dennis Bailey and Keith Gates

WILEY

Wiley Publishing, Inc.

Bike Repair & Maintenance For Dummies©

Published by
Wiley Publishing, Inc.
111 River St.
Hoboken, NJ 07030-5774

www.wiley.com

Copyright © 2009 by Wiley Publishing, Inc., Indianapolis, Indiana

Published simultaneously in Canada

No part of this publication may be reproduced, stored in a retrieval system, or transmitted in any form or by any means, electronic, mechanical, photocopying, recording, scanning, or otherwise, except as permitted under Sections 107 or 108 of the 1976 United States Copyright Act, without either the prior written permission of the Publisher, or authorization through payment of the appropriate per-copy fee to the Copyright Clearance Center, 222 Rosewood Drive, Danvers, MA 01923, 978-750-8400, fax 978-646-8600. Requests to the Publisher for permission should be addressed to the Permissions Department, John Wiley & Sons, Inc., 111 River Street, Hoboken, NJ 07030, (201) 748-6011, fax (201) 748-6008, or online at http://www.wiley.com/go/permissions.

Trademarks: Wiley, the Wiley Publishing logo, For Dummies, the Dummies Man logo, A Reference for the Rest of Us!, The Dummies Way, Dummies Daily, The Fun and Easy Way, Dummies.com, Making Everything Easier, and related trade dress are trademarks or registered trademarks of John Wiley & Sons, Inc. and/or its affiliates in the United States and other countries, and may not be used without written permission. All other trademarks are the property of their respective owners. Wiley Publishing, Inc., is not associated with any product or vendor mentioned in this book.

LIMIT OF LIABILITY/DISCLAIMER OF WARRANTY: THE PUBLISHER AND THE AUTHOR MAKE NO REPRESENTATIONS OR WARRANTIES WITH RESPECT TO THE ACCURACY OR COMPLETENESS OF THE CONTENTS OF THIS WORK AND SPECIFICALLY DISCLAIM ALL WARRANTIES, INCLUDING WITHOUT LIMITATION WARRANTIES OF FITNESS FOR A PARTICULAR PURPOSE. NO WARRANTY MAY BE CREATED OR EXTENDED BY SALES OR PROMOTIONAL MATERIALS. THE ADVICE AND STRATEGIES CONTAINED HEREIN MAY NOT BE SUITABLE FOR EVERY SITUATION. THIS WORK IS SOLD WITH THE UNDERSTANDING THAT THE PUBLISHER IS NOT ENGAGED IN RENDERING LEGAL, ACCOUNTING, OR OTHER PROFESSIONAL SERVICES. IF PROFESSIONAL ASSISTANCE IS REQUIRED, THE SERVICES OF A COMPETENT PROFESSIONAL PERSON SHOULD BE SOUGHT. NEITHER THE PUBLISHER NOR THE AUTHOR SHALL BE LIABLE FOR DAMAGES ARISING HEREFROM. THE FACT THAT AN ORGANIZATION OR WEBSITE IS REFERRED TO IN THIS WORK AS A CITATION AND/OR A POTENTIAL SOURCE OF FURTHER INFORMATION DOES NOT MEAN THAT THE AUTHOR OR THE PUBLISHER ENDORSES THE INFORMATION THE ORGANIZATION OR WEBSITE MAY PROVIDE OR RECOMMENDATIONS IT MAY MAKE. FURTHER, READERS SHOULD BE AWARE THAT INTERNET WEBSITES LISTED IN THIS WORK MAY HAVE CHANGED OR DISAPPEARED BETWEEN WHEN THIS WORK WAS WRITTEN AND WHEN IT IS READ.

For general information on our other products and services, please contact our Customer Care Department within the U.S. at 877-762-2974, outside the U.S. at 317-572-3993, or fax 317-572-4002.

For technical support, please visit www.wiley.com/techsupport.

Wiley also publishes its books in a variety of electronic formats. Some content that appears in print may not be available in electronic books.

Library of Congress Control Number: 2008943495

ISBN: 978-0-470-41580-1

Manufactured in the United States of America

10 9 8 7

WILEY

About the Authors

Dennis Bailey: Dennis Bailey has been actively involved in bike repair and maintenance for over 18 years. He has worked on bikes on biking tours in the United States, Europe, and Latin America. Dennis brings a perspective on how to maintain and repair bikes, not just from within the comfort of a well-stocked bike shop or garage, but from the side of the road, where, on many occasions, he's had to put on his MacGyver hat and improvise with whatever grab bag of supplies were available at the time. You can contact him at mail@dennisbailey.com.

Keith Gates: Keith Gates started as a bicycle mechanic in 1977 when he was in high school. In 1982, after going to college, he got married and went back into the bicycle business as the Service Manager for A-1 Cycling in Manassas, Virginia. He became a partner in the business in 1984 and, in 1992, took advantage of an opportunity to buy out his partners. He has been the sole owner of A-1 Cycling since then, providing personalized service and expertise to local bike enthusiasts of all ages. You can contact him at keith@a1cycling.com.

Dedication

Dennis Bailey: This book is dedicated to Randy Cronk, who showed me that the world is best explored on two wheels.

Keith Gates: This book is dedicated to Fred Landau, who originally opened A-1 Cycling and gave me the opportunity to turn my passion into a career, and to the many people throughout the years who have helped A-1 Cycling support the Northern Virginia cycling community.

Authors' Acknowledgments

We want to express our debt of gratitude to the many people behind the scenes who made it possible to transform an idea about helping bike riders of old and young alike into something on paper on bookstore shelves. They include our acquisitions editor Michael Lewis; our project editor and copy editor, Elizabeth Kuball; our photographer, Jean Fogle; and our technical editor, Ed France.

Special thanks to Barb Doyen, our agent extraordinaire, who always has a way of matching the right people with the best project.

Dennis Bailey: Thanks to my wife, Adriana, and our daughter, Valeria, who make it all worthwhile. Additional kudos to Dave Coldiron, Aaron Plank, and Brad Graley for their timely and important contributions.

Keith Gates: Thanks to my wife, Lynn, and our children, Colin and Chelsea, and the rest of my family for their love, support, and encouragement throughout the years.

Publisher's Acknowledgments

We're proud of this book; please send us your comments through our Dummies online registration form located at `http://dummies.custhelp.com`. For other comments, please contact our Customer Care Department within the U.S. at 877-762-2974, outside the U.S. at 317-572-3993, or fax 317-572-4002.

Some of the people who helped bring this book to market include the following:

Acquisitions, Editorial, and Media Development

Project Editor: Elizabeth Kuball

Acquisitions Editor: Michael Lewis

Copy Editor: Elizabeth Kuball

Assistant Editor: Erin Calligan Mooney

Editorial Program Coordinator: Joe Niesen

Technical Editor: Ed France

Senior Editorial Manager: Jennifer Ehrlich

Editorial Supervisor and Reprint Editor: Carmen Krikorian

Editorial Assistants: Jennette ElNaggar, David Lutton

Art Coordinator: Alicia B. South

Cover Photos: © Daniela Richardson

Cartoons: Rich Tennant (`www.the5thwave.com`)

Composition Services

Project Coordinator: Lynsey Stanford

Layout and Graphics: Reuben W. Davis, Cheryl Grubbs, Christine Williams

Proofreaders: John Greenough, Joni Heredia

Indexer: Broccoli Information Management

Special Art: Photographs by Jean Fogle

Publishing and Editorial for Consumer Dummies

Diane Graves Steele, Vice President and Publisher, Consumer Dummies

Kristin Ferguson-Wagstaffe, Product Development Director, Consumer Dummies

Ensley Eikenburg, Associate Publisher, Travel

Kelly Regan, Editorial Director, Travel

Publishing for Technology Dummies

Andy Cummings, Vice President and Publisher, Dummies Technology/General User

Composition Services

Gerry Fahey, Vice President of Production Services

Debbie Stailey, Director of Composition Services

Contents at a Glance

Introduction 1

Part I: Getting Started 7
Chapter 1: Channeling Your Inner Grease Monkey 9
Chapter 2: Bike Physiology: Understanding How Your Bike Works........ 19
Chapter 3: Setting Up Shop: Repairing Your Bike at Home.................35
Chapter 4: Making like MacGyver: Handling Repairs on the Road.........53
Chapter 5: Help! When You Need Professional Assistance 69

Part II: Basic Bike Repairs 81
Chapter 6: Burning Rubber: Tires and Tubes 83
Chapter 7: Hugging the Curb: The Wheels 99
Chapter 8: Stopping Short: The Brakes... 119
Chapter 9: Taking Your Seat: Saddles and Seat Posts....................... 143
Chapter 10: Hitting the Links: The Chain..................................... 155
Chapter 11: Gearing Up: Freewheels and Cassettes........................ 173

*Part III: Shifting into a Higher Gear:
Advanced Bike Repairs* 189
Chapter 12: Holding It All Together: The Frame and Suspension........ 191
Chapter 13: Putting the Pedal to the Metal: The Drivetrain................ 207
Chapter 14: Dropping It into Gear: The Shifting System 231
Chapter 15: Turning on a Dime: The Steering System....................... 251

Part IV: Keeping Your Bike on the Road 271
Chapter 16: An Ounce of Preventive Maintenance..........................273
Chapter 17: Regular Bike Maintenance 289

Part V: The Part of Tens 299
Chapter 18: Ten (Or So) Steps to Take before You Ride 301
Chapter 19: Ten Considerations in Fitting Your Bike.......................309
Chapter 20: Ten Ways to Improve the Performance and Comfort of Your Bike ...319

Index 325

Table of Contents

Introduction 1

   About This Book...1
   Conventions Used in This Book...2
   What You're Not to Read...3
   Foolish Assumptions..3
   How This Book Is Organized...3
      Part I: Getting Started...3
      Part II: Basic Bike Repairs...4
      Part III: Shifting into a Higher Gear: Advanced Bike Repairs............4
      Part IV: Keeping Your Bike on the Road 4
      Part V: The Part of Tens..5
   Icons Used in This Book 5
   Where to Go from Here..5

Part 1: Getting Started 7

   Chapter 1: Channeling Your Inner Grease Monkey 9

      Starting down the road of bike repair and maintenance...........................9
      Before, During, and After Your Ride 10
         Before you ride...11
         While you ride 12
         After you ride 12
      Making repairs 12
      Performing Maintenance 15
         Monthly maintenance..15
         Annual maintenance...16

   Chapter 2: Bike Physiology: Understanding How Your Bike Works 19

      Gross Anatomy: Identifying the Parts of a Bike..............................20
      Getting Your Bearings..23
      Don't Screw This Up: The Threading System 24
         Tightening enough, but not too much 25
         When fasteners come loose..26
         Shopping for threaded fasteners 26
      Considering How Cables Control a Bike.......................................27

Gearing Up 29
Making Sure You Don't Get Derailed 30
The Quickest Release in the West 32
Other Bike Parts to Keep in Mind 34

Chapter 3: Setting Up Shop: Repairing Your Bike at Home 35

Tools of the Trade 36
Assembling your bike-tool starter kit 37
Specialized tools for advanced bike jobs 43
Setting Up Shop 48
Considering how much space you need 48
Factoring in ventilation 48
Looking into the light(ing) 49
Wrangling a workbench 49
Focusing on storage 49
Banking on a bike stand 49

Chapter 4: Making like MacGyver:
Handling Repairs on the Road 53

When You Can't Call AAA: Handling Your Own
Bike Repairs on the Side of the Road 54
Repairing a bent rim 54
Replacing a broken spoke 55
Fixing flats and torn tires 57
Repairing a broken chain 57
Extracting a jammed chain 58
Dealing with the derailleur 59
Knowing When You Should Walk Home 63
Inspecting Your Bike after an Accident 64
Looking for looseness 64
Checking the alignment 65
The All-Purpose Repair Tool: Duct Tape 66

Chapter 5: Help! When You Need Professional Assistance 69

What to Look for in a Bike Shop 69
Shopping at Your Bike Shop 72
Buying a bike 72
Buying accessories 76
Recognizing the Repairs You Need Help With 78
Repairing frames 78
Installing a new headset 78
Truing a wheel 79
Working on suspension 79

Part II: Basic Bike Repairs 81

Chapter 6: Burning Rubber: Tires and Tubes. 83
Why Flat Tires Happen to Good People.................................. 84
Fixing a Flat.. 85
    Grabbing yourself a wheel.. 85
    Removing the tire or at least half of it............................ 87
    Finding the puncture... 90
    Patching the tube... 91
    Inspecting the tire.. 93
    When it's more than just a flat...................................... 93
Ready to Roll!... 94
    Putting on the tube and tire.. 94
    Attaching the wheel.. 96
    Coming to a screeching halt: When you get
       another flat right away.. 97
A Pound of Cure: Preventing a Flat 97

Chapter 7: Hugging the Curb: The Wheels. 99
The Spin on Wheels.. 99
    Shopping for new wheels... 100
    Caring for your wheels.. 101
    Inspecting the wheels for problems................................ 102
    Taking off a wheel... 103
    Repairing dents in the rim... 106
    Installing the front and rear wheels 106
Hubba-Hubba: Working on the Hubs 107
    Overhauling the hubs.. 108
    Reassembling the hubs 111
    Adjusting a hub 114
I Spoke Too Soon: Working on the Spokes............................. 115
    Replacing a spoke.. 115
    Truing a wheel.. 116

Chapter 8: Stopping Short: The Brakes 119
Types of Brakes 120
Inspecting the Brakes... 123
Removing and Installing Brakes and Brake Pads 124
    Removing brakes and brake pads.................................... 125
    Installing brakes... 128

Adjusting Brakes..130
    Adjusting brake-pad position...130
    Centering and tensioning brakes..132
    Silencing those squeaking brakes!...136
    Using the brake quick release..137
    Replacing brake cables...138

Chapter 9: Taking Your Seat: Saddles and Seat Posts 143

Saddle Up! Types of Saddles 144
    Material 144
    Function 145
    Gender...146
Removing and Installing a Saddle...147
Adjusting the Saddle Fore, Aft, and Height 150
    Angling for the right angle 150
    Fore and aft, to and fro..151

Chapter 10: Hitting the Links: The Chain 155

A Chain Is Not a Chain Is Not a Chain: Types of Chains 155
Recognizing What Can Go Wrong with the Chain 158
    Getting down and dirty 158
    Stuck in a rut: Stiff links...158
    Wear and tear...160
Caring for Your Chain 163
    Keeping it simple: Cleaning and lubricating your chain...............163
    Going deeper: Giving your chain a heavy-duty cleaning 165
Replacing a Chain 167
    Unchain me! Removing the chain 167
    Measuring your new chain 169
    Reassembling your chain..170

Chapter 11: Gearing Up: Freewheels and Cassettes 173

The Dirt on Freewheels and Cassettes 173
    What's so free about a freewheel?..174
    The best things come in packages: The cassette 175
Inspecting Your Freewheel or Cassette...176
Cleaning the Freewheel or Cassette..176
Lubricating the Freewheel or Cassette..177
Removing a Freewheel or Cassette 178
    Removing a freewheel...178
    Removing a cassette...179
    Removing individual the cogs on a freewheel or cassette 183
    Removing the free-hub body...186
Installing a Freewheel or Cassette...187

Part III: Shifting into a Higher Gear: Advanced Bike Repairs 189

Chapter 12: Holding It All Together: The Frame and Suspension 191

I've Been Framed: Your Bike's Frame 192
  What to look for in a frame.. 194
  Types of frame materials 195
  Inspecting your frame 196
  Maintaining your frame... 199
Suspended in Disbelief: The Suspension............................... 201
  Types of suspension.. 202
  Tuning the suspension.. 202
  Maintaining the suspension... 206

Chapter 13: Putting the Pedal to the Metal: The Drivetrain 207

Putting the Pedal to the Metal 207
  Shopping for new pedals 208
  Identifying worn-out pedals.. 209
  Removing pedals.. 209
  Overhauling the pedals 211
  Installing new pedals 213
Crank It Up! Working on the Crankset and Bottom Bracket 214
  The crankset... 215
  The bottom bracket... 223

Chapter 14: Dropping It into Gear: The Shifting System 231

Demystifying Derailleurs 231
  The rear derailleur.. 232
  The front derailleur 241
  The derailleur cable... 246
Gear Shifters... 248
  Removing shifters 250
  Installing shifters 250

Chapter 15: Turning on a Dime: The Steering System 251

Gimme a Hand: Types of Handlebars.................................... 252
Delving Deeper: Handlebar Options.................................... 253
Taping Your Handlebars... 255
Getting Your Head around This: The Headset.......................... 261
  Inspecting the headset... 261
  Adjusting your headset... 262
  Overhauling your headset 263

Part IV: Keeping Your Bike on the Road 271

Chapter 16: An Ounce of Preventive Maintenance .... .273
Before You Ride 274
    Assembling an emergency tool kit 274
    Giving your bike the once-over: A pre-ride inspection 276
While You Ride 278
After You Ride 278
    Cleaning your bike 278
    Giving your bike a lube job 282
    Storing your bike 287

Chapter 17: Regular Bike Maintenance .... .289
Monthly Maintenance 290
    Surveying your bike for structural damage 290
    Kicking the tires 290
    Cleaning your bike 291
    Giving your bike a lube job 291
    Tightening up 292
    Checking the brakes 292
    Examining the chain, cogs, and chainrings 292
    Protecting your saddle 293
    Inspecting the suspension 293
Annual Maintenance 293
    Deep-cleaning the chain 294
    Truing the wheels 294
    Replacing cables and housing 295
    Overhauling the hubs 295
    Overhauling the headset 296
    Overhauling the pedals 296
    Overhauling the bottom bracket 297
    Cleaning the rear derailleur 297
    Replacing the brake pads 297
    Replacing the handlebar grips or tape 298
    Waxing the frame 298
    Checking your accessories 298

Part V: The Part of Tens 299

Chapter 18: Ten (Or So) Steps to Take before You Ride .... .301
Take a Road Safety Skills Class 301
Adjust the Handlebars 302
Adjust the Saddle 303

Check Tire Pressure 304
Check the Brakes 304
Look for Looseness 304
Check the Wheels 306
Grab Your Toolkit 307
Wear Your Helmet and Gloves 307
Improve Your Visibility...308
Stock Your Emergency Gear 308

Chapter 19: Ten Considerations in Fitting Your Bike.............309
Considering Crank Arm Length 310
Going for Gearing..310
Resisting the Temptation to Tilt Your Saddle 311
Setting the Saddle Height 311
Looking at the Saddle Fore and Aft 311
Choosing the Right Saddle Type...............................313
Sizing Up the Frame...314
Focusing on Frame Dimensions...............................315
Positioning Your Handlebars 316
Getting a Handle on Handlebar Style 317

**Chapter 20: Ten Ways to Improve the Performance
and Comfort of Your Bike 319**
Upgrading Your Wheels and Tires 319
Ramping Up Your Rear Derailleur 320
Beefing Up Your Bearings.....................................321
Pumping Up Your Pedals......................................321
A Shoe-In: Choosing the Best Shoes for the Job 322
Saddle Up! Taking Your Saddle to the Next Level 322
Upgrading Your Handlebars...................................322
Boosting Your Brake Levers 323
Taking Your Clothing up a Notch 323
Embracing Your Inner Geek with a Cycling Computer 324

Index **325**

Introduction

· ·

Welcome to *Bike Repair & Maintenance For Dummies,* where the often confusing and complex world of caring for your bike just got a whole lot easier. We've written this book to tell you not only what your bike needs to stay in great condition but also how to take care of the repair and maintenance yourself. It doesn't matter if you're planning to work on your kid's single-speed bike or overhaul an expensive road bike, the same repair and maintenance principles found in this book apply.

Maybe you picked up this book because you're planning on making biking a larger part of your life. With the price of gasoline these days and the health benefits from exercise, riding your bike makes a lot of sense. Or maybe after biking for a number of years, you've decided that your trusty two-wheeled companion could use a little better care. Good idea. You don't want a wheel or something coming off the next time you round a tight curve. Whatever the case, if you're interested in attending to the health of your bike and you want a simple and easy-to-understand guide to do it, you've found the right book.

Yes, working on bikes can be challenging — but it doesn't have to be. A lot of books written on the topic are thick, technical manuals written by hard-core bikers for hard-core bikers. Peel away the jargon and the arcane discussions and you're left with some basic procedures that anyone with a little hand-eye coordination, the ability to follow simple directions, and a willingness to get a little grease under the nails can do.

About This Book

We know that many books on bike repair and maintenance are competing for your attention. But we offer the following compelling reasons why this book stands apart from the rest. If you're still not convinced, we're not above bribes and begging — but we're confident we won't have to go that far.

✔ **It's in plain English.** This book is not another one of those dense tomes full of technical language that require a degree from a bike-mechanic school to understand. Those are better left for when your only other source of entertainment is watching paint dry. In *Bike Repair & Maintenance For Dummies,* our goal is simple: If someone with zero bike knowledge can understand the concept, we've succeeded.

Dennis approaches bike maintenance and repair through the lens of a bike rider, having toured thousands of miles on three continents. Keith is a bike-shop owner who, over the years, has worked with thousands of customers, most of whom are *not* bike experts. Together we combine our biking knowledge with a penchant for communicating in everyday English to help you care for your bike.

✔ **It's a reference.** You can read this book cover to cover if you want. But we know that you're busy and that your goal is not to become a bike mechanic — at least not anytime soon. So you can also use this book as a reference guide — and we've written it with that goal in mind. You can pick it up whenever you're having a specific issue with your bike and turn right to the section that explains how to handle it.

✔ **It's comprehensive.** Just because this book is written in easy-to-understand language without a lot of biking jargon doesn't mean it's not comprehensive. We cover every part of the bike and all the maintenance and repair procedures that you'll likely ever need.

✔ **It's objective.** We're not trying to promote or sell bikes or a line of parts. Our goal is to make you as knowledgeable as possible so that you can repair the parts on your bike and, if needed, know how to replace them.

Conventions Used in This Book

Every book has its own conventions, and this one is no different. To make the most of the information we provide, keep your eye out of for these conventions:

✔ Terms we're using for the first time are in *italics.* Plain-English explanations or definitions of these terms are nearby, often in parentheses.

✔ When we give you steps to follow in a particular order, we number the steps and put the action part of each step in **bold.**

✔ Web addresses are in `monofont`. *Note:* When this book was printed, some Web addresses may have needed to break across two lines of text. If that happened, rest assured that we haven't put in any extra characters (such as hyphens) to indicate the break. So, when using one of these Web addresses, just type in exactly what you see in this book, as though the line break doesn't exist.

One last thing: We're writing this book as a team, but when one of us has something to say, we use our first names (see the preceding section for an example of this convention in action).

What You're Not to Read

You're not on the hook to read the whole book. You can jump around to find the information you need, and leave it at that. You can also safely skip *sidebars* (text in gray boxes) — sidebars are interesting, but they're not essential to your understanding of the topic at hand. Finally, you can skip anything marked by a Technical Stuff icon (for more on icons, see "Icons Used in This Book," later in this Introduction).

Foolish Assumptions

So that we could tailor this book to your needs, we made a few assumptions about you:

- You like to bike or are thinking about making biking a part of your life.
- You or a member of your family owns a bike and you're interested in caring for and maintaining it.
- You'd like to find out how to do some of your own bike maintenance and repair so you won't have to take your bike to the shop every time you have an issue or call someone for a ride if you break down on the side of the road.
- You have little or no experience in using tools on your bike.
- You may be a seasoned bike rider who wants some additional tips and tricks to keep your bike in top condition.

How This Book Is Organized

As soon as you look at the table of contents you'll notice that the book is divided into five parts. Here's what you can find in each of them.

Part 1: Getting Started

Part I is your Bike Repair and Maintenance 101 class. Before you jump into chapters on working on your bike, you may want to take the time to get to know the names of the different bike parts and how they work together — you find all that information in this part. Here we also describe some basics for setting up a bike shop at home. Then just to whet your appetite for repair and maintenance, we discuss how to handle breakdowns on the road and tell you which repairs are better handled by a professional.

Part II: Basic Bike Repairs

If bike repair is a new endeavor for you, the repairs in this part will probably be the ones you attempt first. Here we cover the more basic bike repairs that anyone with a little concentration and elbow grease (be prepared to get dirty!) can do. We fill you in on tires and tubes, including probably the most frequent bike repair, the flat tire; wheels and hubs and the mysterious art of wheel truing; freewheels and cassettes (we tell you how you can tell the difference between the two); saddles and seat posts, including how to get the most comfortable fit for your bike; everything you need to know about brakes to keep them in working order and guarantee a sure stop every time; and the chain and why this hard-working part of your bike deserves more respect and attention than it normally receives.

Part III: Shifting into a Higher Gear: Advanced Bike Repairs

This is the part of the book where you earn your advanced degree in bike repair. These procedures are a little more advanced and some require specialized tools, but they're still very doable. Here, we cover the frame and suspension, the pedal, the crankset, the bottom bracket, the steering system, and the shifting system.

Part IV: Keeping Your Bike on the Road

If your bike has treated you well, this is the part of the book where you learn how to return the favor. If you want to greatly extend the life of your bike, increase your riding comfort, and improve safety, performing maintenance on your bike is the way to go. In this part, we discuss preventive maintenance, including how to perform a pre-ride inspection, how to care for your bike while you're riding, and how to store your bike when you're done for the season. We also tell you the regular maintenance you should perform on your bike, and we recommend setting up a schedule for monthly and annual maintenance.

Part V: The Part of Tens

This is the part that all *For Dummies* book are known for — the cool lists of things in the back of the book. We've included a list of ten steps to take before you ride, ten ways to improve the fit of your bike, and ten things you can do to enhance comfort and increase performance when you ride.

Icons Used in This Book

Throughout the book, you'll find icons in the margins that alert you to specific kinds of information. Here's what each of the icons means:

Whenever we have a particularly useful suggestion that'll save you time or money or just make your repair and maintenance a little easier, we flag it with this icon. (We wanted to flag this whole book with a big Tip icon, but our editor said no.)

This book is a reference, which means you don't have to memorize it — there won't be a pop quiz Monday morning. But occasionally we do tell you something that's important enough that you'll want to commit it to memory. When we do, we mark it with this icon.

When you see this icon, listen up. Bikes are precisely engineered machines, and sometimes you need to perform a certain procedure in a particular way or with a specific tool — or risk danger to you or your bike. Heed these warnings where they appear to keep yourself — and your bike — out of trouble.

We love bikes, and sometimes we can't help but share some information that's especially technical but that you don't really need to know. When we do, we mark it with this icon. If you're the kind of person who likes knowing all the details, read these paragraphs. But if you're more of a just-the-facts kind of a person, you can skip these paragraphs — no harm, no foul.

Where to Go from Here

This book is a reference, which means you can dive in wherever you want. If you're brand-new to bikes and you don't know your derailleur from your down tube, turn to Chapter 2. If you're itching to set up your own workshop in your house or garage, head to Chapter 3. If your bike is riding fine and you want to keep it that way, go to Chapter 16 and do a bike inspection so some part of your bike doesn't fall off on your next ride. Use the table of contents and index to find the information you need.

Finally, send us an e-mail with some feedback or a photo showing us your greasy bike hands as proof that you're caring for your bike. You can e-mail Dennis at mail@dennisbailey.com and Keith at keith@a1cycling.com.

Part I
Getting Started

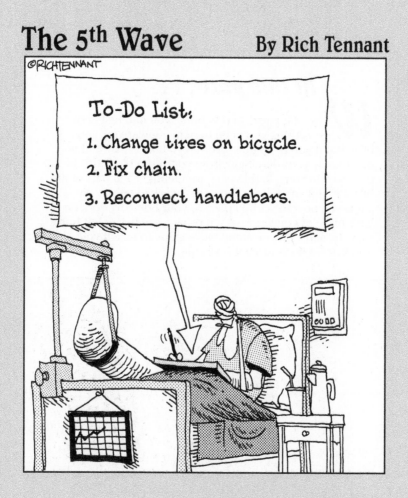

In this part . . .

Within the pages of this book, you find just about everything you need to help you care for your bike. But if you're completely new to bike repair and you don't know your derailleur from your drivetrain, this is the place to start. In this part, we identify each part of the bike for you and tell you how they work together. We show you how to set up space in your home to work on your bike, let you know which repairs are better left to the experts, and give you some basic steps to take if you break down on your next bike ride.

Chapter 1

Channeling Your Inner Grease Monkey

In This Chapter

▶ Entering the world of bike repair and maintenance

▶ Caring for your bike before, during, and after you ride

▶ Making emergency, basic, and advanced repairs

▶ Performing monthly and annual maintenance

*J*ust as you'd bring along a map if you were heading off for a trip on your bike into an unfamiliar area, you should have a roadmap for your venture into the world of bike repair and maintenance. The journey you're about to take or have already started can be fulfilling and bring lifelong rewards as long as you have a guide to help you get where you're going. We've written this book to be your guide — to take the mystery out of bike repair and maintenance.

In this chapter, we open up the roadmap and examine all the different routes that are possible when it comes to caring for your bike.

Starting down the Road of Bike Repair and Maintenance

When it comes to bike repair and maintenance, the starting point is knowing the various parts of a bike, their function, and how they work together (see Chapter 2). When you know the various parts of the bike, you know

✔ How bearings reduce friction when you ride

✔ How to tighten threads an appropriate amount

✔ Why cables for brakes are different than shifters

  ✔ What combination of gears is best for your bike

  ✔ How springs drive derailleurs

  ✔ How to make sure a quick release wheel doesn't become dangerous

When you've figured out all the parts of your bike and how they work together, you're ready to get started on your journey. But wait! First you need a shop where you can work (see Chapter 3). Working on a bike doesn't require a lot of space, but it helps to have a location where you can operate comfortably. You'll want enough space for tools, a drop cloth to protect the floor, good ventilation, and lighting.

If you're serious about bike repair and maintenance think about two major additions to your shop:

  ✔ A workbench with a flat surface where you can work

  ✔ A bike stand that will hold your bike off the ground

Good news! You don't have to run out to the store to start your tool set. Many of the tools you need are probably in your house. If you have a variety of wrenches, Allen wrenches (hex keys), screwdrivers, pliers, and a hammer, you'll be able to perform a number of basic procedures on your bike. As you move into more advanced procedures, you'll need some specialized tools.

You may want to wait to buy a specialized tool until you have to actually per-form the procedure it's used for. For example, you may need a crank extractor to remove a crank arm. Instead of running out to the store and buying a crank extractor right now, wait until you do your annual maintenance on your bike and actually need that tool.

When you do decide to purchase tools — such as a chain tool, chain whip, freewheel tool, or spoke wrench — you need to decide whether to buy them on the cheap or invest in a more expensive brand that will likely last longer than your bike. In Chapter 3, we give you some options.

Finally, to keep the moving parts of your bike in good working order, pur-chase an all-purpose lubricating oil. Focus on lubricating your chain and the pivot points in places like the brakes and derailleurs. Having a cleaner around when you're working on your bike is just as important. Look for an environmentally friendly product, such as a citrus degreaser.

Before, During, and After Your Ride

Bike repair and maintenance involves more than caring for your bike while you have it stowed away at home. It's an ongoing process that'll involve action before, during, and after your ride.

Before you ride

The before-you-ride part of the trilogy deals mostly with the preventive maintenance steps you should take, which not only help your bike but increase the safety of each ride.

One of the best things you can do to improve your safety is to do a pre-ride inspection and maintenance check:

- ✔ Using a gauge, check that your tire pressure is equal to the recommended level on the tire's sidewall. (See Chapter 6 for more information on tires.)
- ✔ Inspect the brake to make sure the pads are not worn and they tightly grip the wheel when you squeeze the brake levers. (See Chapter 8 for more on brakes.)
- ✔ Look and listen for looseness in the handlebars, headset, wheels, and other part. (See Chapter 16 for more information on inspecting your bike.)

Whether you have a brand-new bike or a 20-year-old clunker, things go wrong when you ride. Your best bet is to be prepared and bring a toolkit along with you to help you if you get into a jam. Here are some steps you should take to prepare your toolkit (see Chapter 4 for more information):

- ✔ Have a small tire pump mounted to your frame.
- ✔ Include everything you need to repair a flat, including a patch, glue, tire levers, and spare inner tube (in case you blow a tube).
- ✔ Include some hand tools, such as Allen wrenches, screwdrivers, a spoke wrench, and pliers. These will allow you to make adjustments as you ride.
- ✔ Pack away a rag to wipe the grease off your hands when you're finished.

If you're planning an extended trip, you'll want to add some tools to your kit. These include a spare foldable tire, a chain tool, chain links and rivets, extra spokes, spare cables, lube, and the all-purpose MacGyver tool, duct tape. (See Chapter 4 for more information.)

While you're preparing for a possible roadside emergency, don't forget the following:

- ✔ Cellphone
- ✔ Identification
- ✔ Money
- ✔ Energy bars
- ✔ Rain jacket
- ✔ Sunglasses

While you ride

Although you may not think about riding as a time for bike maintenance, there are things you can do while you ride to care for and maintain your bike. If you get into the habit of doing these things, you'll extend the life of your bike and stay safer:

- ✔ Keep your tires properly inflated while you ride to improve rolling resistance and absorb shock.

- ✔ Pay attention to the road in front of you.

- ✔ Walk your bike over curbs and other objects.

- ✔ Raise yourself out of your seat and use your arms and legs like a horse jockey to absorb an impending blow.

- ✔ Shift into lower gears before you reach the steeper sections of inclines to put less strain on the chain and derailleurs.

- ✔ Look out for any creaks or loose parts on the bike before they're in need of repair.

For more information on safe riding practices, turn to Chapter 16.

After you ride

The trilogy of maintenance activities is completed with the after-you-ride phase. Dirt acts as a major abrasive against your bike and, as it works its way into the internal parts, it starts wearing out bearings and other components. After you ride is a great time to combat this enemy by washing your bike. Wet it down — but make sure you don't spray water directly at the hubs or bottom bracket. Use a brush and soap to scrub down your bike. Use degreaser to break up any difficult-to-remove grease.

Remember to always lubricate your bike after drying it — particularly the chain, derailleurs, brakes, and cogs. When you're finished, wipe off any excess grease so that it doesn't attract additional dirt.

For more information on washing and lubricating your bike, turn to Chapter 16.

Making Repairs

If you're lucky, you'll never have to repair your bike anywhere but in the comfort of your own shop at home. But nobody's that lucky. The fact is, if you ride long enough, sooner or later you're going to break down on the side of the road and have to make a repair, like one of the following:

- ✔ **Fixing a flat tire:** A flat tire is the most basic of emergency repairs (see Chapter 6).

  Practice patching a tire before you have to — that way, if you get a flat on the road, you'll be able to fix it without stressing out.

- ✔ **Dealing with your wheels:** If you hit something with your wheel, the rim may bend or a spoke may break. You can repair both issues on the side of the road, depending on the severity of the damage (see Chapter 7).

- ✔ **Coping with the chain:** Your chain may act up on you while you ride. In some cases, a chain may jump off the smallest chainring and become jammed between the chain stay and the chainring. Worse, the chain may even break. To fix the chain, you'll need to have a chain tool and an extra link or two available, or else you'll be walking home (see Chapter 10).

- ✔ **Dealing with the derailleur:** The fact that derailleurs stick off the side of your bike make them vulnerable to being hit or knocked as you ride, which may bend or damage them. Depending on the situation, you may need to adjust the derailleur, reposition it, or remove it (see Chapter 14).

Some repairs you won't be able to make when you're on the road — mainly because specialized tools are needed. These include a loose crank, loose pedals, problems with the bottom bracket, or a bent frame. If any of these happens while you're on the road, your best bet is to call it a day, because riding could cause greater damage to your bike or lead to an accident.

Emergency repairs are the ones no one wants to deal with. Much more preferable are all the repairs you can do in your shop at home. Some of these repairs are simpler to perform than others. If you're new to bike maintenance and repair, try these basic repairs before attempting the more advanced ones:

- ✔ **Repair flat tires.** Flat tires are the main source of problems with tires and tubes, and you'll have to learn how to remove a tire, find the puncture in the tube, patch the leak, and reinstall it. After you've done it a few times, it's pretty easy. (See Chapter 6.)

- ✔ **Overhaul hubs.** Central to maintaining your wheels in good working order is caring for the hubs. Overhauling them at least once a year will keep your wheels spinning smoothly. (See Chapter 7.)

- ✔ **Change brake pads.** Few things are more important than being able to stop on your bike when you need to. Learn how to adjust your brakes and changes the pads, and you'll be in good shape. (See Chapter 8.)

- ✔ **Adjust saddles and seat-post position:** This is where you can make adjustments that your butt will thank you for. Choosing the right saddle and then adjusting it to the right fit will make riding a more enjoyable and comfortable experience. (See Chapter 9.)

- ✔ **Replace chain.** The hard-working chain is one of the most exposed parts of your bike and, as a result, it needs a lot of care. After it has given you a few thousand miles, you'll need to replace it. (See Chapter 10.)

✔ **Replace cassettes and freewheels.** Over time, the teeth on the cogs of cassettes and freewheels will wear out causing your chain to skip gears. With a couple of tools and a little bit of effort, you can replace them yourself. (See Chapter 11.)

In reality, advanced repairs are not that advanced — they're just a little more complicated than basic repairs. In some cases, you'll need a specialized tool or two and you'll have to be careful to follow the directions step by step. With a little concentration and determination, you too can be a hard-core grease monkey who knows how to handle just about any repair on your bike, including the following:

✔ **Maintain the suspension.** Although you'll be limited to the kind of frame repairs you can perform, you can handle the maintenance and repair of suspension. In some cases, you'll need to make an oil change or adjust the air pressure depending on what type of suspension you have. (See Chapter 12.)

✔ **Overhaul the pedals, crankarms, and bottom bracket.** The pedal, crankarms, and bottom bracket are part of the drivetrain of your bike and work to transfer force to the rear wheel. They absorb a lot of force and should be overhauled every year. You'll need one or more specialized tools for this job. (See Chapter 13.)

✔ **Adjust the shifting system.** Most modern-day shifters are highly calibrated mechanisms that only require minor adjustments and maintenance. Most of your work supporting the shifting system will come from keeping the rear and front derailleurs in good working order. (See Chapter 14.)

✔ **Overhaul the steering system.** Handlebars, stem, and headset give you the smooth steering you expect of your bike. The bearings inside the headset take a pounding from the road so do this component a favor and adjust it frequently and overhaul it annually. (See Chapter 15.)

Even the most gung-ho grease monkeys should take some of the most difficult procedures to the pros at their local bike shop. Your local bike shop will have the expensive tools and, more important, the experience to handle these procedures properly. The following repairs should all be handled by a pro:

✔ **Repairing frames:** Frame repair is beyond the scope of what most people can accomplish at home. Some bike shops even recommend that you go to a frame specialist for many jobs or replace the frame altogether.

✔ **Fitting a headset:** Adjusting or overhauling a headset is an easy job that you can perform at home or on the road. But when you're installing a new headset, it's time to head to your local bike shop to leverage their experience and specialized tools.

✔ **Truing a wheel:** Truing is complicated stuff. You need specialized tools (such as a truing stand, a spoke tension meter, and a dishing tool) and a lot of practice.

✔ **Working on suspension:** There are many different types of front and rear suspension and all repair work on them should be done either by the manufacturer, your local bicycle store, or a specialty bicycle suspension repair facility.

Performing Maintenance

In bike repair and maintenance you have two options:

✔ You can focus on the maintenance so that your bike will need fewer repairs.

✔ You can ignore maintenance and end up having to do more repair work.

We prefer the former. If you do, too, here are the maintenance activities you should be performing on a monthly and annual basis.

Monthly maintenance

Put your monthly maintenance on the calendar for the months you ride and it will soon become a habit and normal part of your life.

Here are the steps you'll take during your monthly maintenance:

✔ **Check for structural damage.** Visually inspect your frame for signs of stress and structural damage, paying particular attention to areas where the frame is welded and hard-to-see sections such as the underside of frame tubes.

✔ **Inspect the wheels and tires.** Are they spinning straight? Are the tires worn, cut, or torn and are the spokes tight?

✔ **Clean your bike.** Dirt is your number-one enemy so if you don't have the time to clean your bike after every ride, make sure you do it monthly, especially if you've been riding on a regular basis.

✔ **Lubricate your bike.** You take your car for an oil change every 3,000 miles — make sure your bike gets a lube job every month that you ride to extend the life of its movable parts.

✔ **Check for tightness.** Even if they're tightened properly, fasteners such as nuts and bolts have a way of working themselves loose over time. You don't want something to fall off while you ride, which could be dangerous or cause you to lose a part, so check to make sure everything is tight as a part of your monthly maintenance.

✔ **Check the brakes.** When a squirrel runs out in front of you is not the time to discover that your brake pads are worn out. Check the brake pads for wear, confirm that the cable clamp has the cable securely in place, and give your brake levers a firm squeeze to confirm that the brakes evenly and firmly grab the rim.

✔ **Examine the chain, cogs, and chainrings.** Don't let your chain wear out because it'll shorten the life of your chainrings and cogs. Measure the chain to confirm that 12 links measure 12 inches and, if not, replace the chain or soon you'll be replacing the much more expensive cogs and chainrings.

✔ **Protect your saddle.** If you have a leather saddle, you'll need to pay attention here. Leather saddles are great, but they require a little extra work, including a regular leather treatment to clean the leather and replenish the leather's natural oils.

✔ **Focus on your suspension.** If you have suspension on your bike, inspect all suspension pivot and linkage bolts for correct tightness. If you have suspension forks, check your owner's manual for instructions on how to care for them.

For more information on monthly maintenance, including instructions on how to do all these things, turn to Chapter 17.

Annual maintenance

Do you yearn to ride your bike in the middle of those cold winter months? Do the next best thing and become reacquainted with your bike by giving it an annual overhaul:

✔ **Deep-clean the chain.** Soak the chain in a environmentally safe degreaser to get a deep clean in between the links, rollers, and pins.

✔ **True the wheels.** All those bumps over the course of the year are going to affect the tension of your spokes and, as a result, your wheel alignment. Take the time to bring it back into true.

✔ **Replace cables and the housing.** Inspects your cables and the housing in which they run. If you notice any kinks, rusting, fraying, or a buildup of dirt and grime, it's probably time to install new ones.

✔ **Overhaul the hubs.** Overhauling the hubs annually is especially important if you have traditional hubs with loose bearings. If you have sealed bearings, you probably can go a few years.

✔ **Overhaul the headset.** Yearly maintenance is a good time to inspect, clean, adjust, and overhaul the headset.

✔ **Overhaul the pedals.** Pedals are another component that utilizes bearings. As with the hubs, if you want them to continue spinning smoothly, give them an overhaul.

✔ **Overhaul the bottom bracket.** The bottom bracket is the center of your drivetrain. All the revolutions of the bottom bracket add up over the course of a year, so do your bike a favor and overhaul or replace the bottom bracket.

✔ **Clean the rear derailleur.** The focus here is on removing the derailleur so that you can clean the dirt where it builds up most, on the two jockey wheels.

✔ **Replace the brake pads.** Keep an extra set at home. They're cheap and easy to install, and when you install a fresh pair, they give you peace of mind.

✔ **Replace the handlebar grips or tape.** Need to add a little pizzazz to your bike after a long year of riding? Inject some color and life as well as some comfort for your hands by replacing the handlebar tape or grips.

✔ **Wax the frame.** If you take apart your bike for the annual overhaul, take advantage of easy access to a clean frame and give your bike a good waxing.

✔ **Check your accessories.** Don't make the mistake of discovering that you're missing an important accessory — like a patch kit, tool, or extra batteries for your light — when you have an emergency. Take a quick look at your accessories and confirm that everything is there.

For more information on annual maintenance, turn to Chapter 17.

Chapter 2

Bike Physiology: Understanding How Your Bike Works

In This Chapter

▶ Identifying the different parts of a bike

▶ Understanding the role bearings play in reducing friction

▶ Uncovering the importance of threads and how to protect them

▶ Discovering how cables control the bike

▶ Exploring how gears work and the supporting role of the derailleurs

▶ Finding out about quick-release hubs

▶ Identifying other bike parts

*I*n this chapter, we lay the foundation for all the bike repair and maintenance procedures that follow in this book. If you understand this chapter, not only will you be able to impress your buddies and the local bike-shop staff with your newly gleaned knowledge, but you'll have greater insight into the inner workings of a bike, which is invaluable when you sit down, tool in hand, and begin to work on it.

If you really want to become self-sufficient in bike repair and maintenance, it's not enough to know how to perform certain procedures. You need to have an understanding of the inner workings of a bike. Think of it this way: Cardiologists haven't just studied the heart — they've learned how the entire body works. After all, the body is a complex set of interacting systems. To operate on the heart, a doctor has to understand interactions between the heart and the circulatory, nervous, and other systems.

Now, we're not saying that a bike is remotely comparable to a body in terms of complexity, but it does contain its own systems. If you understand how gears work, how bearings reduce friction, and how cables transfer power to breaks and derailleurs, you won't just be a certifiable bike geek — you'll have greater insight into how to maintain and repair your bike properly. If you have to change a cable, you'll have more confidence performing the job if you understand how that cable interacts with the shifters, brake levers, derailleurs and brakes than if you see it in isolation. Awareness of how your bike functions may also serve you well when you're broken down on the side of the road and trying to diagnose a problem or improvise a solution.

Although the bike is a mystery to many people, much of its technology and mechanics were engineered in the last century. Unlike your iPod, which will probably be outdated in six months, your trusty bike can last years and years and still perform as well as newer models. If you take care of your bike, you should be able to have many, many years together. But as with any relationship, it takes hard work and effort. Take the time to learn a little bit about how your bike works, and you'll be rewarded with many years of enjoyable time together.

Gross Anatomy: Identifying the Parts of a Bike

Figure 2-1 identifies the different parts of a road bike, and Figure 2-2 illustrates many of the same parts — and a few differences — on a mountain bike.

Not all bikes are the same, and some parts vary from bike to bike —road bikes are different from racing bikes, which are different from touring bikes and mountain bikes. A road bike has thin tires, light weight, and is built for smooth, pavement riding. Somewhat similar in appearance to a road bike is a racing bike; racing bikes are designed with expensive, lightweight materials and with a premium on aerodynamics (for example, with handlebars that are positioned lower than they are on a road bike). A mountain bike is easy to spot with its thick knobby tires, suspension, and heavy disk brakes to support riding on trails and rough terrain. A touring bike looks very similar to a road bike but usually has a wider wheelbase, a greater range of gears, and racks to carry pannier bags.

These two diagrams give you the basics on two of the most popular types of bikes, road and mountain bikes; for information specific to your specific bike, check out the manual that came with it.

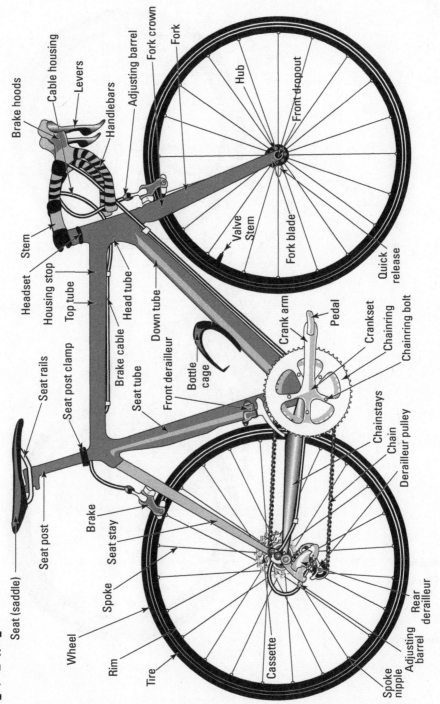

Figure 2-1:
Parts of a road bike.

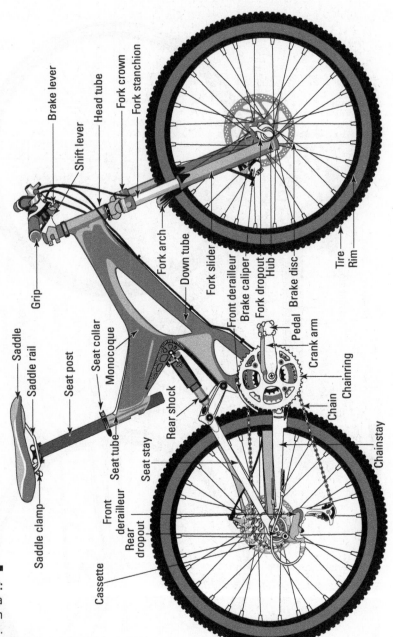

Figure 2-2:
Parts of a
mountain
bike.

Getting Your Bearings

Of the three major forces which work against you as a cyclist — air resistance, gravity, and friction — it's friction that our tireless little friends the ball bearings are designed to overcome.

Bearings are one part of the bike that has changed little over the last century. In fact, the first use of bearings goes back thousands of years. Ever since the wheel was invented, humans have looked to bearings to help with the problem of friction from a moving part rubbing against a nonmoving part.

Bearings, like those shown in Figure 2-3, are hardened steel balls designed to reduce friction among the moving parts of a bike. When your wheel rotates smoothly around its axle, it's the bearings that enable this to happen with minimum resistance and friction. Bearings are found in many parts of a bike including the wheel hubs, pedals, bottom bracket, and headset.

On some more expensive bikes, bearings are made of ceramic, which has a number of properties that improve the reduction of friction.

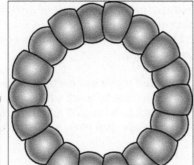

Figure 2-3: Bearings from the bottom bracket.

Bearings are an amazing feat of engineering, designed with a precision to millionths of an inch. When examining them, you should see a smooth, rounded, and shiny surface. If the bearings are dull or chipped with tiny divots, they need to be replaced.

Although it would appear that the round shape of bearings is all that's required to reduce friction, the fact is that bearings still require significant lubrication for reliable performance. In many cases, bearings inside the parts of your bike are packed in water-resistant grease specially designed for bearings.

If you perform a procedure that requires bearings to be installed, make sure the parts are clean before you pack the bearings in grease. Grease can become contaminated with grit and break down over time.

You may wonder how these little metal balls are kept in place. They're secured with something called a *race*. A tried-and-true race design, still popular after more than a century, is the cone-and-cup. In this design, a ring of bearings sits in a cup and is secured in place by a cone, which is screwed onto an axle or spindle.

The cone is typically adjusted to be tight enough so that there is no side-to-side looseness and the part (that is, the hub) rotates smoothly. Over-tightening could cause unnecessary force to be applied against the ball bearings, leading to wear and tear — not to mention the fact that it could make it much harder to pedal.

Bearings will either be in a "cage" or retainer ring, or be set as independent "loose" bearings. (Also, retainers are typical for all bearings on a bike, and perform inferiorly to loose bearings. The only benefit they have is convenience in building the bike).

One of the modern advances in bikes is the use of sealed bearing cartridges, which eliminate the need for adjustment or lubrication (less work for you!) and prevent grit and other contaminants from entering. Buy a bike with cartridges and you'll save yourself the hassle of playing with tubes of grease and chasing bearings across your bike-shop floor.

Your inner gear geek may be disappointed if you use cartridges, because bearings are cool, shiny little balls that are fun to work with. Dennis feels like he hasn't really worked on a bike until he's juggled a few bearings in his hands and packed them in some fresh grease. But even so, cartridges do require less work.

Don't Screw This Up: The Threading System

If you're like most people, you probably think you know the basics of how threads work, but we promise you'll be surprised by how much science there is to the basic concept behind a nut and bolt.

Why is this important? Of all the activities you'll perform while working on a bike, tightening and loosening threads on a bike is at the top of the list. Improperly handle something as seemingly innocuous as a nut or a bolt, and you could irreversibly damage the threads of an expensive component on your bike.

Threaded fasteners are the unsung heroes of the biking world. Although they're essential to keeping your bike together as it rolls on down the road, they're so inconspicuous that people rarely notice them. About the only time they come to your attention is when something on your bike starts making a rattling sound, usually due to a fastener being loose.

Fasteners are heterosexual partners. They consist of a male part (such as a bolt) and hollowed female part (such as a nut), as shown in Figure 2-4. Male and female parts, designed to work together, are cut with complementary matching grooves that allow them to be threaded together.

Different fasteners are designed to handle different amounts of force. The bolt used to hold the water-bottle cage in place would not provide enough force to secure a crank.

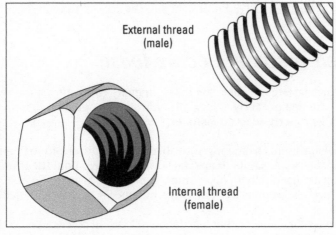

External thread
(male)

Internal thread
(female)

Figure 2-4:
Male and female threads on a nut and bolt.

Tightening enough, but not too much

The one thing you need to know about fasteners — and never forget — is this:

> Never over-tighten a fastener.

When Dennis learned this concept, it was like a revelation. He had always assumed that the rule was: The tighter, the better. If someone had shared this all-important rule with him earlier, he could've saved himself from ruining a number of fasteners.

Fasteners stretch and flex when tightened, which gives the joint force to stay in place. Over-tightening the fastener can cause it to stretch to such a degree that the joint becomes damaged.

You don't have to freak out the next time you have to tighten a nut or bolt. The general principle is to tighten it a bit, and then check it: If there's still some play in the part, tighten it a little more.

If we've made you paranoid about over-tightening, you can always purchase a torque wrench. Bike mechanics use these in order to apply exactly the right amount of force when tightening a fastener.

If you've made like the Incredible Hulk and ended up damaging a thread, the folks at your local bike shop may be able to recut it using a tool called a *tap*. Of course, this assumes that the damage to the thread was minor and that there's still enough undamaged thread remaining. If not, the thread may be irreversibly damaged.

Clean and lubricate all threads before tightening them. For smaller fasteners, a liquid lubricant will do the job. For thicker fasteners (such as the thread of a bottom bracket), a heavier lubricant such as grease is recommended.

When fasteners come loose

Sometimes a fastener will come loose. In many cases, this is the result of not being tightened properly. (Normally, vibration is not enough to overcome the force of a properly secured fastener.)

To prevent threads from loosening, bike manufacturers sometimes use devices such as locknuts or special washers to help hold the thread in place. Washers are used to help distribute the pressure around the bolt's nut or head. They also reduce friction as the nut and/or bolt is tightened.

To increase the chances that a fastener will stay in place once it's tightened, use a thread-locking compound. When this compound is applied to a thread, it hardens and expands, helping to keep the joint secure.

Shopping for threaded fasteners

When you're shopping for threaded parts, keep in mind that threads are classified in a number of ways. One is according to the diameter from one side of the thread to the other. Threads are also measured based on how many threads are contained within a fixed length. Usually you will see measurements such as $1/2$ inch x 20 tpi. The first number refers to the thread diameter, and the second number refers to the number of threads per inch. The important thing is not that you memorize what the two numbers mean but that you know that, if you have to buy a bolt, you'll need to take a measurement like this when you go shopping. If you have a bolt in hand and need to buy another one, take it to your local bike shop. Just by eyeing the threads, the bike-shop staff will be able to help you.

For bolts, you commonly see an *M* before the measurement to represent millimeters. For example, the M5 bolt of a water-bottle cage is a 5mm bolt.

It's not as important to know what the numbers describing a thread mean as it is to make sure the measurements of the old and new fastener match.

Considering How Cables Control a Bike

Despite the important role of bike cables, they rarely get the respect they deserve. They usually play second fiddle to their sexier companions, the shifters, brake levers, derailleurs, and brakes. The truth is, improperly installed or worn-out cables can prevent even the best derailleurs and brakes from functioning properly. When a squirrel jumps out in front of you while you're hurtling down a hill on your bike, you're not only counting on your brakes to grip the wheels and slow you down, but you're depending on your cables to transfer the force from your clenching grip to the brakes.

Although cables have long been used to transfer force when pulled, bike cables are unique in that they have to transfer force around the curves and corners of a bike. The design of the cable with an inner wire supported by a stiff outer housing made of steel and covered plastic makes this possible.

Most bike cable housings have a liner made of plastic, nylon, or Teflon. This liner sits between the wire and the housing to help reduce friction. In older cables, wires didn't have such a liner; because they came into contact with the housing, they required grease for lubrication.

In order to save weight and reduce the amount of friction, many bikes are designed to use cables with the inner wire exposed. The cable housing runs along a portion of the frame until it comes to a stop. The cable housing is fed into the narrow opening in the stop, which allows only the inner wire to pass through. To ensure a snug fit in the stop, a small metal cap, called a *ferrule*, usually covers the end of the housing. From here, the wire continues on until it comes to another stop, facing in the opposite direction, where the cable housing begins again.

Not just any cable housing can be used with a bike. For index gears, you use a different style, higher-quality, non-compressing cable housing. It's made with separate wires running parallel inside the housing and is held together by plastic.

Higher-quality cable housing for shifting shouldn't be used for brakes, because it may not be able to handle the higher force applied during severe braking.

Less flexible non-compressing "gear" housing, though more expensive, is a different style and not necessarily higher quality. The only real benefit is that the index adjustment holds better than conventional housing. The failure rate of this housing is significant, and many people use brake housing for derailleurs anyway, although that usually means an additional adjustment to get the indexing correct.

The main consideration in the design of how cables work on a bike is eliminating friction so that force can be consistently transferred to the brakes or derailleurs. Cables that are too long create unnecessary friction and lead to a soft or spongy response. Cables that are too short may create kinks in the housing or limit your ability to fully turn from one side to the other.

Setting cable housing to the right length is important. If you're replacing cable housing, measure them against your original housing. Keep them a little longer than you think you need — you can always trim off some extra length. If you cut your own cable housing, use cable or diagonal cutters.

After cutting the cable housing, examine the ends to see if any burrs were created. If so, you can recut the cable housing or file them down. After cutting the cable housing, you may have to open up the end of the housing with a tool, such as an awl.

If ferrules came with the cable package, attach them to the end of the cable housing. They protect and support the cable housing and help keep it in alignment with the stops.

You can buy cables in kits with inner wires, housing, and metal ferrules all included.

When running cables around a frame, you should try to avoid bends when possible. If you can't avoid bends, make them as gradual as possible (as shown in Figure 2-5). If you're replacing cables, use the cable path that was designed for the bike — an engineer took time to think this through.

For maintaining your cables, lubrication is useful to prevent rust. Use silicon, mineral oil, or a synthetic lubrication, and coat the cable before inserting it into the housing. Lubrication is also necessary for the parts that come in contact with the cables including adjusting barrels and anchor bolts, both of which have threads that need to be protected.

Don't use grease to lubricate your cables — it creates too much friction and the dirt and dust from the road or trail will stick to the grease, causing even more problems.

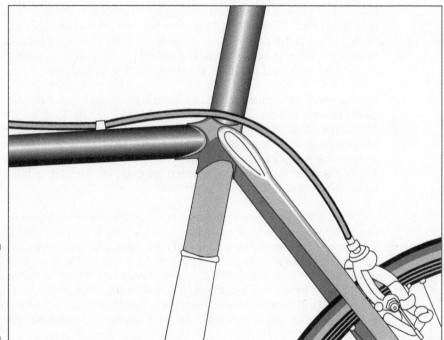

Figure 2-5:
A gradual
bend in
a cable
is best.

Gearing Up

If your biking experience goes back as far as ours does, to when you climbed onto a tricycle for the first time and pedaled off to conquer the world, you may remember what it was like to ride with one gear. Cruising down the sidewalk at your parent's side was pretty easy — at least until it started sloping uphill. You had to apply more and more force to keep your bike moving, until finally your little legs gave out and your parents had to turn around to head home.

Why was riding a tricycle uphill an impossible task? When a bicycle has no gears, each time you rotate the pedals, the rear wheel also rotates one turn. You rotation of your pedals will move your wheel one rotation (the full circumference of that wheel.) The force required to move that one rotation is much greater if you're pedaling uphill. The idea behind gears is that the distance the wheel travels for each rotation of the pedals can be lengthened or shortened, allowing you to apply a consistent amount of force, regardless of whether you're on an incline or decline.

Gears rely on the combination of the size of the front chainrings and the sprockets on the rear wheel of a bike. By switching between different sizes of chainrings and sprockets, gears allow you to use the same amount of force when pedaling, regardless of the terrain. Most bikes have two or three chainrings with 22 to 52 teeth between the largest and smallest chainring. On the rear cluster of sprockets, they have 11 to 32 teeth. Based on where the chain sits on the chainrings and sprockets, the rotation of the pedals will cause the rear wheel to have a different number of rotations.

For example, if the chain sits on a chainring with 44 teeth and a sprocket with 11 teeth, the gear ratio is 4 (44 ÷ 11), which means that, for every rotation of the chainring, the rear wheel will rotate 4 times. A higher ratio is ideal for going downhill or pedaling with the wind at your back. If the chain is on a chainring with 22 teeth and a sprocket with 32 teeth, the ratio is 0.69 (22 ÷ 32). A low ratio such as this is needed for climbing up a steep hill. (Is your head spinning as fast as your gears yet?)

The total number of gears on a bike is calculated by multiplying the number of chainrings by the number of sprockets. If your bike has 3 chainrings and 9 sprockets, you're riding a 27-speed bike. On a bike with more gears, you'll have a wider range of lower gears for going uphill and higher gears for going downhill. This also makes the changes in gear ratios much smaller, allowing you to more easily find a comfortable gear in which to pedal. Dennis's touring bike has 27 gears and gives him great flexibility whether he's huffing and puffing going up the side of a mountain or screaming down the other side at 50 mph.

When you're buying a bike, keep in mind the following gear tips:

✔ Choose a bike that has high enough gears to support faster speeds without your legs spinning at an uncontrollably fast number of revolutions.

✔ Choose a bike that has low enough gears to enable you to climb hills.

Whenever possible, avoid gears that cause the chain to cross from the front to the back at an angle. For example, avoid locating the chain on the smallest chainring in the front and smallest cog in the back. This causes the chain to stretch and wear out and is bad for the sprockets.

Making Sure You Don't Get Derailed

Anyone who has ridden a bike up a windy mountain pass or into a stiff headwind appreciates the ease of shifting into the appropriate gear with a click or twist of a shifter. The mechanism that makes shifting a nearly effortless activity is the *derailleur*.

To look at a derailleur, you'd think that it's the most high-tech part of a bike. In reality, derailleurs are simple devices designed to move the chain between the different gears. Both the front and rear derailleurs are designed with a cage through which the chain runs. When you change gears with your shifter, the derailleurs force the chain to one side or the other until the chain falls or is lifted onto the chainring or sprocket next to it.

The front derailleur consists of a cage that, in a side-to-side motion, moves the upper part of the chain — the part that transmits power to the rear wheel. Because the upper part of the chain is under the force of your pedaling, it wants to stay in place. It's more difficult to shift when you're applying a lot of power and moving slowly.

Its more advanced partner, the rear derailleur, both pushes the chain from side to side and pulls it tight. The rear derailleur is designed to serve two main roles: moving the chain between the sprockets and keeping the chain under tension.

The mechanism controlling the rear derailleur is a hardened spring hidden inside. This spring is constantly pushing the derailleur away from the bike and toward the smallest sprocket. The cable attached to the bike's shifter opposes the force of the spring. When the shifter pulls the cable, the cable overcomes the spring and moves the chain toward the bike and onto the next sprocket. When the shifter releases the cable, the derailleur again moves away from the bike. Tension of a second spring provides the resistance, which takes up any chain slack.

Rear derailleurs have a common design (see Figure 2-6). They have a cage that holds two pulleys in the familiar S-shape. The top pulley is the *jockey pulley* (also known as the upper jockey wheel); it guides the chain into what's called the *cage*. The bottom pulley is the *tension pulley* (or lower jockey wheel); it's designed to keep tension on the chain and take up slack.

Derailleurs are designed to maintain the appropriate amount of space between the jockey pulley and the rear sprockets as the derailleur moves back and forth. The derailleur also move its arm back and forth with each shift to keep its cage centered under the sprocket on which the chain sits. Usually, one or more screws are utilized to control the amount of lateral movement and spring tension.

The rear derailleur cage that connects the jockey pulley and the tension pulley has a length that varies depending on the amount of chain slack needed to be taken up. Models with longer cages are designed to support larger, lower-geared cogs and longer chains; they're typically found on bikes with three chainrings. Rear derailleurs also have a maximum tooth capacity, which specifies the largest cog onto which it can shift a chain. Short cage derailleurs are found on racing bikes; they offer quicker shifting and higher ground clearance, the latter of which is important when cornering in tight curves.

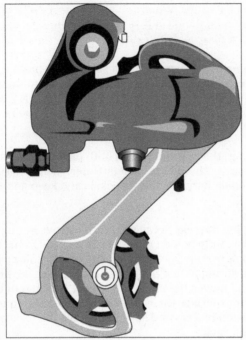

Figure 2-6:
A rear
derailleur.

The Quickest Release in the West

On a cold day in the middle of a race in the Italian Alps in 1927, engineer and racer Tullio Campagnolo's hands were so cold that he had trouble removing the wing nuts that held his wheel in place. This experience is supposedly what led him to invent the quick-release lever, something that has made lives easier for scores of bikers ever since.

Anyone who has ever had to remove a wheel on a bike without the benefit of a quick release knows just how much of a convenience Campagnolo's contribution has been. Whether you're taking off a wheel to quickly change a flat or to throw your bike into the car, the quick-release mechanism is virtually indispensable to biking.

The basic design of the modern quick release (shown in Figure 2-7) still resembles the original. It's made of a long rod with a lever-based cam mechanism on one end and a serrated edged nut on the other. When the nut begins to tighten and the lever is lifted, the cam clamps down on the wheel hub.

Make sure to clamp the lever as snugly as you can. Do not rotate the lever like a wing nut — that's what the quick release replaced, and you won't be able to get it tight enough to secure the wheel.

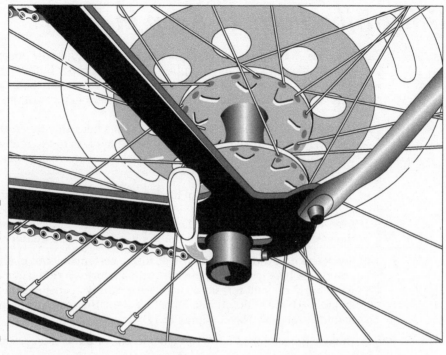

Figure 2-7:
A quick release on a wheel makes a biker's life much, much easier.

Working with quick releases takes a little practice, especially when you're learning how to tighten the nut just enough so that there's the right amount of play in the lever to enable it to tighten in the closed upright position.

Properly tightening quick-release hubs is important, because if they aren't tight, they could come loose and the wheel could fall off. Today, most bicycles have front forks that utilize a secondary wheel-retention device to keep the wheel from disengaging if the quick release is incorrectly adjusted. Secondary retention devices fall into two basic categories:

- ✔ The clip-on type is a part that the manufacturer adds to the front wheel hub or front fork.

- ✔ The integral type is molded, cast, or machined into the outer faces of the front fork dropouts.

Ask the people at your local bike shop to explain the secondary retention device on your bike.

Secondary retention devices are not a substitute for correct quick-release adjustment.

Other Bike Parts to Keep in Mind

Earlier in this chapter, we cover important bike parts and how they work together as different systems to support the bike's proper functioning. Here we want to take a moment to mention some other very critical bike parts or "systems" that are discussed in great detail in other chapters of this book:

- **Drivetrain:** Considered the transmission of a bike, the drivetrain is the system for transferring power from the rider's legs to the rear wheel. It includes the pedals, cranks, bottom bracket, chain, chainrings, and cogs. (See Chapter 13.)

- **Steering system:** Consisting of the front fork, the handlebars, the stem, and the headset, the steering system enables you to balance and turn a bike. When you turn the handlebars, bearings within the headset allow the system to pivot within the frame's head tube. (See Chapter 15.)

- **Suspension:** Although a bike will absorb a certain amount of shock as you ride, a bike with a suspension system improves riding comfort and handling in difficult terrains. There are a variety of suspension types including those built into the forks, the stem, the rear part of the frame, and the seat post. (See Chapter 12.)

- **Brakes:** Brakes (see Chapter 8) fall into one of three categories:

  - Rim brakes have brake pads that rub against the wheel rim when the brakes levers are squeezed. A cable connects the brake lever to the brakes.

  - Disk brakes operate on the hub. Heavier than rim brakes, they offer better performance in wet conditions. Some disk brakes use a hydraulic system, whereas others depend on cables.

  - Hub brakes are similar to disk brakes except the brake pads are pushed outward against the inside of a cylindrical drum inside the hub. Included in this family are the good old coaster brakes.

- **Wheels:** Usually consisting of an aluminum or steel rim, connected to a hub by spokes, the wheel is connected to the frame by either a quick-release mechanism or nuts threaded onto the axle. Some modern rims and wheels are made with carbon fiber and other high-tech materials. (See Chapter 7.)

- **Frame:** The frame is what holds everything together. In one way or another, all parts are connected to the frame. A frame consists of a top tube, down tube, seat tube, head tube, seat stays, and chain stays. The geometry of a frame is important, because it greatly impacts the handling of a bike. Most issues with frames require professional care; in many cases, buying a new frame is easier than replacing a damaged one. (See Chapter 12.)

Chapter 3

Setting Up Shop: Repairing Your Bike at Home

In This Chapter

▶ Finding out about basic and specialized bike tools

▶ Getting clear on lubricants, degreasers, and cleaners

▶ Setting up a workshop for your bike at home

▶ Finding a bike stand that suits your needs

*W*orking on your bike can be fun. In fact, you don't know what fun is until you're covered in more dirt and grime than your local auto mechanic and your significant other puts on gloves and changes clothes just to kiss you. Actually in most cases, the average bike-repair and -maintenance job won't leave you looking like a grease monkey — and even if it does, there's nothing quite like the satisfaction gained from fixing your own bike.

Even if the part-time role of bike mechanic isn't your dream job, there are many benefits to doing your own work:

✔ You'll be amazed at how much you'll learn about how your bike works — things you never would have known just from riding it.

✔ You'll discover tricks for maintaining your bike so that repairs are kept to a minimum.

✔ You'll become so in tune with your bike that you'll figure out ways to tweak it to give yourself a better ride.

✔ When you break down, you'll be able to diagnose the problem quicker than Lance Armstrong can put on a yellow jersey.

Even if your goals for maintaining and repairing your bike are slightly less ambitious, you'll always have one of the best excuses for getting out of household chores — you're busy working on the family's bikes.

In this chapter, we fill you in on the tools you need to get started — and tell you about a few more tools useful for some advanced procedures. If you're looking to take it to the next level, we explain how to set up your own bike workshop, which will be the envy of your neighbors — at least those who know that the Tour de France isn't a trip through Bordeaux to sample the year's Beaujolais.

To buy or not to buy

Buying bike tools is kind of like stocking your kitchen with cooking supplies. There are certain tools you'll need no matter what. If you're cooking, one of the tools you need is a spatula. But when you're buying a spatula, you have lots of options. You can buy a cheap, plastic model, knowing that you'll save some money — even though it may not be the most comfortable to hold and probably won't last very long. Or you can invest a little in your purchase and buy a spatula that's ergonomically designed for your hand and made of material guaranteed to last and covered by a long-term warranty.

The same is true for bike tools. A full spectrum of options is available, ranging from cheap, all-purpose tools (which you can adapt for use on a bike) or custom-made, high-quality products designed specifically for working on bikes.

Obviously, cost is a major consideration when buying tools. A number of companies — including Park Tool (www.parktool.com) and Pedro's (www.pedros.com) — make high-quality bike tools. They offer products made of durable materials that are comfortable to use and designed to work with high-end bicycle components. There's something to be said for investing in quality tools that will last — not the least of which is impressing your buddies.

If you're on a budget, however, you can buy many brand-name tools on the cheap from bike-tool manufacturers such as Spin Doctor,

Performance, and the extremely inexpensive Chinese-made Lifu tools, which cost from $30 to $200. If you need basic tools like screwdrivers, wrenches, or pliers, you can find them in the hardware section of stores like Wal-Mart.

Keep in mind that working on a bike doesn't mean going to the toolbox, grabbing whatever looks handy, and giving it a try. Although some of the tools that you may have in your house today will serve you in certain jobs (such as a screwdriver, adjustable wrench, and pliers), a number of bike parts require specialized tools. To find and purchase these tools, you can visit the manufacturers' Web sites and see where the products are sold, or visit your local bike shop.

Some tools are designed for particular jobs that you may perform rarely or never at all. For example, if you plan on doing a yearly overhaul of the bottom bracket, you'll need specialized tools that can't be used for any other purpose. Most of the year, they'll be sitting around in your workspace gathering dust.

If you join a local bike club, you'll find lots of opportunities to borrow the tools you need, saving you from having to buy tools that you won't get much regular use out of.

Start by acquiring a basic set of tools. At a later date, if your goals become more ambitious, you can always add tools as needed.

Tools of the Trade

If you were tired of eating out every night and decided to learn how to cook, you'd want to make sure your kitchen was stocked with all the necessary cooking supplies. The same applies to bike repair and maintenance. If you're interested in taking care of your bike, you need some basic tools in order to be successful. If you're really serious about becoming a gourmet chef of the biking world, and want to handle advanced repairs and maintenance, you'll need to buy some additional tools. First, we start with the basics.

Assembling your bike-tool starter kit

If you're looking for a basic set of tools to allow you to start caring for your bike, everything in this section is what I recommend. (See Figure 3-1 for an illustration.) You probably already have some of these tools in your house; other tools you'll be able to buy with very little cost and from a variety of sources.

Buying tools in sets will save you money as compared to buying them individually. Buying a tool sets will also give you more options when it comes to working on different parts of your bike.

Wrenches

When working on a bike, you'll find yourself grabbing wrenches a lot. You have many options when it comes to wrenches, including open-ended, box, and combination (see Figure 3-1).

Many people keep an adjustable crescent wrench (refer to Figure 3-1) around the house because of its flexibility; you can use one on a bike, although you're better off using non-adjustable wrenches when possible, because they tend to fit more snugly to a nut or bolt. If an adjustable wrench slips while tightening or loosening, it could cause damage to a nut or bolt — not to mention your knuckles.

When shopping for wrenches look for sizes 7mm to 17mm and every size in between to give you enough coverage for nuts and bolts on a bike.

Wrenches should fit securely over the bolt or nut before turning. If you aren't sure which wrench to choose, select the wrench that fits the most tightly.

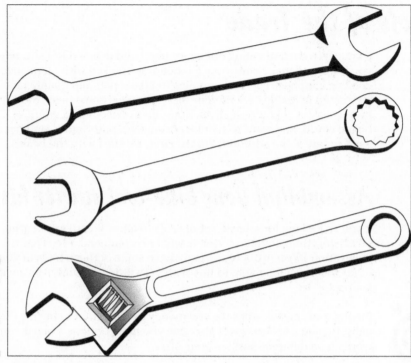

Figure 3-1:
Wrenches
come in
many
varieties.

Screwdrivers

What would a toolbox be without a trusty screwdriver or two? Both flathead and Phillips screwdrivers are necessary for working on a bike. You should have a range of sizes for the various screw heads found on a bike.

In general, the largest screwdriver that can fit a screw head is preferable.

Allen wrenches

Allen wrenches (also called hex keys) are the L-shaped tools used to tighten recessed bolts (see Figure 3-2). You use sizes 4, 5, and 6 the most.

Instead of buying a set of Allen wrenches, consider purchasing a mini folding tool — an indispensable and handy little tool that contains Allen wrenches and sometimes screwdrivers, wrenches, and other tools. It's perfect for taking with you when you bike.

For Allen wrenches, sizes between 4 and 10 mm are usually sufficient.

An Allen wrench should be fully inserted into the socket before turning.

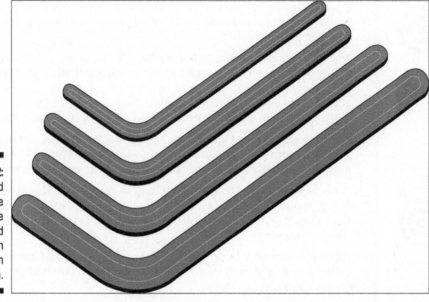

Figure 3-2:
Recessed
bolts have
to be
tightened
with an
Allen
wrench.

Hammer

Sometimes you need a hammer to tap part of a bike, such as when loosening a seat post or removing the pin that holds a crank. A small hammer or plastic mallet will ensure that you can control the blows while avoiding doing damage to your bike.

Pliers

Pliers come in handy for pulling cables, although they shouldn't be used for *cutting* cables. If you plan to cut your own cables, use a cable cutter designed for this activity.

Never use pliers to loosen or tighten nuts and/or bolts — they'll damage the edges.

Tire tools

If you ride your bike often enough, eventually you'll need to work on your tires — whether that means keeping them properly inflated or repairing them when you get a flat. Here are all the tire tools you need:

  ✔ **Pump (see Figure 3-3):** If you haven't already purchased one, you'll want to buy a bike pump that matches your valves — either Presta or Schrader (see Chapter 6 for more on these types of valves). Some of the better-quality pumps will handle both types of valves.

If you have two or more bikes — with both types of valves — you can find a pump that is reversible, allowing you to switch back and forth between types of valves.

Smaller pumps designed to fit on a bicycle frame are convenient for taking with you on trips — although, they require more pumping to fill a tire, because they're designed only for emergency repairs on the road and not for routine maintenance inflations. Having a larger pump at home or even an air compressor will make pumping tires a breeze.

✔ **Pressure gauge (see Figure 3-4):** To take the guesswork out of filling your tires with air, you can use a pressure gauge. This will help you inflate tires to the proper pressure as indicated on the sidewalls.

Many higher-quality pumps have a built in gauge. With the gauge on the pump, you won't have to search for it at the bottom of your toolbox every time. Plus, you don't have to go back and forth, between pumping and checking pressure.

✔ **Patch kit:** Sooner or later, you'll have to patch a leak and unless you want to buy a new tube each time, you'll want to keep a patch kit available at all times. A patch kid includes

- Patches

- An abrasive to rough up the surface of the tube to improve adhesiveness

- Glue

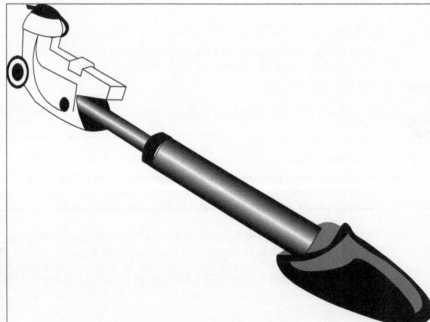

Figure 3-3:
A tire pump is essential to maintaining proper pressure in your tires.

Figure 3-4:
A pressure
gauge
eliminates
all the
guesswork.

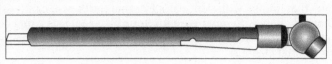

✔ **Tire levers (see Figure 3-5):** Tire levers are usually made of stiff plastic and are used to pry a tire off a wheel rim. You'll probably need three levers, although on some mountain bikes the tires are loose enough that one or two may suffice.

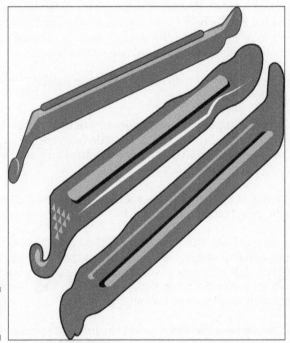

Figure 3-5:
Tire levers.

Lubricants, cleaners, and degreasers

Lubricants, cleaners, and degreasers aren't technically "tools," but they're essential to properly repairing and maintaining your bike. With so many moving parts causing friction, a bike requires proper lubrication — including specially designed oils and greases — to reduce this friction and help prevent rust and corrosion.

The same qualities that give oil and grease their lubricating properties and enable them to stick to external parts are also what attracts dirt and grime. This means that, unlike with your car's internal parts, you can't wait 3,000 miles for an oil change. Regular care for your bike requires using cleaners to remove surface dirt and degreasers to cut through heaver grime that's too strong for normal cleaners.

We cover lubricants, degreasers, and cleaners in the following sections.

Lubricants

If you're an average rider, an all-purpose lubricating oil designed for bikes will be all that you need. You can use oil to lubricate pivot points such as brakes and derailleurs, as well as to keep the chain lubed.

Some riders use a lubrication specially designed for a chain. Manufacturers offer a number of quality lubes that are designed with different conditions in mind. A dry wax-based lube is best for dry, summer-like conditions. For the rainy season, a wet lube is the choice for many riders — although a wet lube is messy and attracts dirt and grime, it holds up well to water.

For a great description of use of chain lubes, see *Urban Bikers' Tricks & Tips,* by Dave Glowacz (Wordspace Press).

Liquid lubricants can be applied from an aerosol can or a plastic squeeze bottle. We prefer to drip a lubricant out of a bottle because we can control the flow. Spray cans are much more difficult to control and can over-lubricate parts.

When you need to loosen a seized part — such as a seat post that won't budge — use a light, penetrating oil like WD-40.

WD-40 should not be used as a chain lubricant. Although WD-40 works wonders in getting tight parts moving again, it's a solvent that will strip away existing lubrication. Although it may *appear* to be lubricating while it's wet, as soon as it evaporates, your chain lubrication will be gone. Also keep WD-40 away from shifters, because it may damage the inner parts.

In addition to oil, grease is needed to support the internal moving parts of your bike, particularly those that depend on bearings to reduce friction. Bearings in the hubs, bottom brackets, headsets, and pedals are packed in grease. When these are overhauled, the grease needs to be replaced. Grease also protects the threads found on the same parts and lubricates and prevents rust from forming on the gear and brake inner wires

Grease is often sold in a tube. Be sure to keep the lid on at all times to prevent contamination.

Buy only grease designed for bikes. Grease for automobile bearings will be too heavy and thick and will gum up your bike.

Cleaners and degreasers

The simplest way to clean a bike is to rinse it off with water after a ride. This will dislodge any loose dirt, sand, or grit lodged in the bike's parts.

When washing your bike, use a light mist spray to avoid directing water into bearing areas, such as hubs or the bottom bracket, where it can break down bearing grease.

A mild soap (such as dish soap) will remove dirt and grime, although it won't be strong enough to clean grease-laden parts such as the chain rings, cogs, and chains, as well as the insides of hubs, bottom brackets, and the headset.

Although solvents such as gasoline, kerosene, and paint thinner will cut grease and oil, we don't recommended that you use them because they're highly flammable, they emit toxic fumes, and they're very harsh on your bike.

Commercially available degreasers are designed to not harm bike components — or you. Many of them are biodegradable and environmentally friendly. Citrus-based degreasers are among our favorites — they're made from oil extracted from orange peels. A number of green cleaners are also available — not only will they clean your bike, but they don't give off the toxic fumes associated with typical solvents.

Specialized tools for advanced bike jobs

In a chef's personal kitchen, some cooking tools (like knives or bowls) are multipurpose and can be used for a variety of recipes; other tools (like pastry bags or pasta machines) are very specialized. Unless those more specialized tools are in the kitchen of someone who makes pastries or pasta from scratch, they're likely going to remain stored away most of the time.

The same is true of many specialized bike tools: They're designed for specific procedures (such as extracting a crank or removing cogs), activities that you'll either perform infrequently or leave to your local bike shop.

Companies like Park Tool sell hundreds of different types of these tools, many of which are designed to work with specific makes and models of bike components. When shopping for a particular tool, make sure you identify the one that's designed to work with *your* bike component. If you aren't sure, your local bike shop will be able to advise you.

Here's a list of specialized tools you may have a need for if you want to take your repairs up a notch:

✔ **Chain tool (see Figure 3-6):** If you plan on replacing or repairing a chain, you'll need this tool. It's used to break or connect a chain by pushing a pin through the chain links. Some chains, such as SRAM Master Link, do not require a chain tool to be removed and reinstalled. A chain tool is still needed for installing a new chain in order to cut it to the proper length.

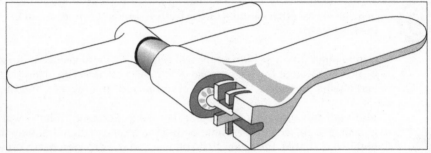

Figure 3-6:
A chain tool.

✔ **Crank puller (see Figure 3-7):** Many bikes require this special tool, which threads into the crank to pull it off the bottom bracket. In these situations, you'll also require a socket set or a dedicated crank bolt tool (usually 14mm or 15mm).

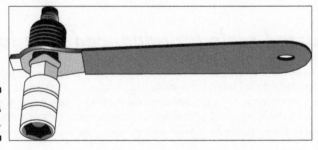

Figure 3-7: A
crank puller.

✔ **Cone wrench (see Figure 3-8):** You use a cone wrench if you're going to overhaul or make an adjustment to the bearings of your wheel hub. There are a number of standard sizes (usually 13mm for the front and 15mm for the rear), so be sure to check your wheel specifications. It's good to have two of each size.

Figure 3-8:
A cone
wrench.

✔ **Chain whip (see Figure 3-9):** A chain whip is used to hold the cogs in place while removing a cassette. Two of these can be used together to remove individual cogs from a freewheel.

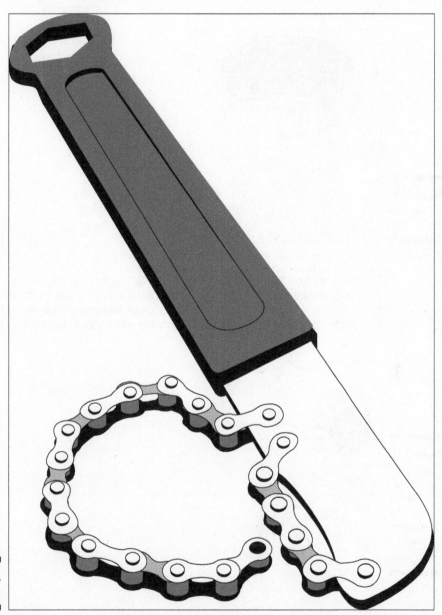

Figure 3-9: A chain whip.

✔ **Freewheel tool (see Figure 3-10):** A freewheel tool is required for removing the cassette from the rear hub. As always is the case with any specialized tool, be sure to buy one that fits your bike's particular make of freewheel or cassette.

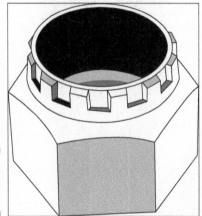

Figure 3-10:
A freewheel
tool.

✔ **Bottom bracket tools (see Figure 3-11):** Depending on the type of bottom bracket on your bike, you'll need one or more tools. Review your owner's manual or check with your local bike store to identify the manufacturer and model — this'll determine what tools you need.

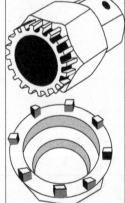

Figure 3-11:
The bottom
bracket
tools you
need vary
depending
on the bike
you have.

✔ **Headset tool (see Figure 3-12):** To work on the headset, you need two large, flat, open-ended wrenches. These come in different sizes, so be sure to check the owner's manual and buy ones the fit your headset.

Figure 3-12:
A headset
tool.

✔ **Spoke wrench (see Figure 3-13):** Also called a *spoke key* or *nipple spanner,* this wrench is used to tighten, remove, or install a spoke. Although spokes may all appear the same to an untrained eye, they require the right-size spoke wrench to prevent damage to the nipples.

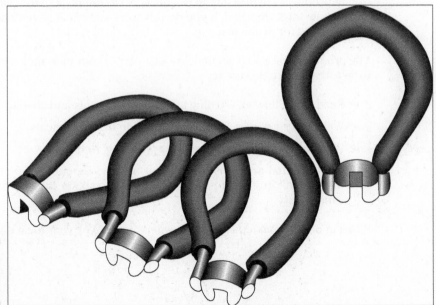

Figure 3-13:
A spoke
wrench.

Setting Up Shop

Working on a bike doesn't require a lot of space, but it is convenient to have a location set aside in your house where you can comfortably organize your tools, handle individual bike parts, and have enough space to move around without bumping into anything. If you're planning on doing your own bike repair and maintenance, you may want to start thinking about where to do it.

Considering how much space you need

Although it'd be *nice* to have an individual room in which to set up your own bike shop, most people don't have that much extra space. Fortunately, you don't *need* a large space. You just need an area that's long enough and wide enough to hold your bike and possibly a workbench, with enough space in between that you can operate comfortably. Part of a basement or garage can be a solution, or even the corner of a room.

Factoring in ventilation

Look for a space with proper ventilation. Vapors from cleaners and degreasers can be irritating to some, so unless you want to be seeing colors and taking a ride on a magic carpet instead of a bike, you need access to plenty of fresh air.

Not all products are pleasing to the nose. Go to the back of the bike shop and you'll know what we mean. If you do this work in a small unventilated area, you're asking for problems.

The products that you'll accumulate as a part of your bike shop should be used with caution. Be sure to

- ✔ Read and follow all warning labels both for tools and chemicals.
- ✔ Wear rubber gloves to protect your skin from chemicals.
- ✔ Wear safety glasses when cutting, grinding, or drilling.
- ✔ Use tools that are designed for your bike's components. Forcing a tool that doesn't quite fit a part could cause it to slip or break, which can cause injury.

When in doubt, consult with your owner's manual or your local bike shop.

Looking into the light (ing)

Also pay attention to lighting. Extra lighting can be helpful so you don't strain your eyes while working on small, intricate parts. A droplight hung from the ceiling will give you the ability to move the light as needed, to reach those poorly lit parts of your bike.

Wrangling a workbench

You'll need a flat surface for many repair and maintenance procedures. You may need to lay out parts, cut a cable, or steady a hand when setting bearings. This is where a workbench comes in handy. In fact, what would a shop be without a workbench? You wouldn't have a kitchen with a counter, would you?

Look for a bench with enough flat space to lay out your tools and parts, and one that's solid enough that if you need to strike something with a hammer or attach a vise, there'll be enough support.

Because clutter can build up quickly, maintain some space under the workbench to stow away trash, rags, cleaning cloths, and spare parts. This will go a long way toward keeping your space organized and impressing your housemates enough that they'll actually visit or bring you a drink once in a while.

Focusing on storage

To organize your tools, you'll want either a toolbox (to put your tools in) or a pegboard (to hang your tools on). Most hardware stores supply long and short hooks that work with pegboards.

If you're working with a pegboard, trace the outline of each tool onto the board with a marker, and you'll always remember what goes where. This technique will also keep you from misplacing a tool and blaming it on the kids.

Banking on a bike stand

If you're serious about doing your own bike repair and maintenance, and you've invested in the right tools for the job, you may want to think about buying a bike stand (see Figure 3-14).

Working on a bike when it's suspended off the ground is much easier. You can raise, lower, and rotate the bike to get exactly the position you want. Plus, you're not hunched down over your bike — your back will thank you for that when you're finished.

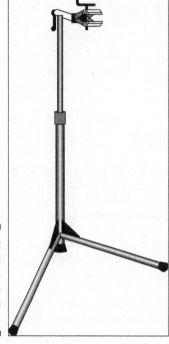

Figure 3-14:
A bike stand
makes the
job of bike
repair much
easier.

A number of different types of bike stands are on the market. Prices range from under $100 to several hundred dollars. The best stands have adjustable heights and allow you to rotate the bike 360 degrees. Some are freestanding, while others attach to a wall or worktable (which can be useful in tight spaces). Some models are foldable for easy storage when you're finished — useful if you're short on space. In general, the more-expensive models have designs that provide greater stability, which is useful when applying leverage to your bike.

If you don't have the money for a stand, you can get creative and suspend your bike with hooks connected to the ceiling. Although many jobs are much easier if your bike is immobilized by a stand, you can do most jobs with a suspended bike.

When clamping your bike to the bike stand, consult the owner's manual for your bike. Most bikes can be clamped at the seat post or frame, but some bike manufacturers recommend that you avoid clamping or over-clamping the frame. This is especially true for carbon-fiber bikes, which should never be clamped in traditional stands.

Some bikes can be turned upside-down and supported by the handlebars and saddle. If you do this, be careful to move the shifters out of the way so that they aren't damaged. The clamps that hold the shifters in place can be loosened with an Allen wrench and tightened when you return them to their original position.

Working on bikes can get pretty messy. You're dealing with bottles of oil, tubes of grease, dirt, grime, and cleaning solutions. After some procedures, you'll feel like someone should spray you off with a hose before you leave the shop. To protect your floor and to facilitate cleaning up afterward, always place a mat, dropcloth, or extra piece of carpet or flooring under your bike. You'll be thankful you did.

Repair and maintenance tips

If you've just embarked on a journey of bike repair and maintenance, you're on course for an adventure of learning, self-sufficiency, pride, and satisfaction. We want your journey to be full of enjoyment, not one that makes you want to pull your hair out with frustration. Follow these tips, and you can avoid lots of unnecessary problems:

✔ **Take safety precautions when you work.** Wear safety glasses to protect your eyes and rubber gloves to cover your skin. (Gloves will also keep your hands clean. Trying to get dirt and grease off your hands and out from under your fingernails can be a chore.) If you're using chemicals in an enclosed space, limit your exposure by wearing a mask and limiting your exposure time. Better yet, don't use chemicals in an enclosed space, period. Make sure that you always work in an area with proper ventilation.

✔ **When you take something apart, note the order in which you disassembled it.** This tip will save you all kinds of time when you try to reassemble it. You can scratch notes on a piece of paper or line up the parts in sequence on a flat surface.

✔ **Before reassembling a component, thoroughly clean its parts.** Also clean the part of the bike you removed it from.

✔ **After you finish lubricating a part, wipe off any excess lubrication.** This will help keep dirt and grime to a minimum.

✔ **Be careful when tightening parts.** Too much force and you could strip the threads. If you aren't sure, under-tighten the part, check it, and if it's loose, tighten it a little more.

✔ **Never force a part that doesn't want to cooperate.** This advice is especially true for threads. Always check to see that the threads match, use grease on the threads, wait for the grease to penetrate the threads, and tighten slowly when you begin — to make sure you don't cause any damage.

✔ **When following the instructions in this book, keep in mind that many procedures may vary depending on the component, the bike, and the manufacturer.** We give you guidelines for basic bike maintenance and repair, but you may need to tailor them to your individual bike. When in doubt, follow your bike owner's manual.

✔ **Don't feel as though you have to do everything yourself.** If you aren't sure about how something works, you're better off taking the time to look for the answer in the owner's manual or asking staff in your local bike shop. Otherwise, you could end up damaging your bike or hurting yourself. *Remember:* Even the best the bike mechanics ask for help sometimes.

Chapter 4

Making like MacGyver: Handling Repairs on the Road

In This Chapter

▶ Making emergency repairs on the side of the road

▶ Identifying problems that make your bike unsafe to ride

▶ Inspecting your bike after an accident

▶ Using duct tape as an all-purpose repair tool

*I*n a perfect world, your bike would never break down mid-ride. You'd be able to anticipate and prevent any malfunctions before they happened. Unfortunately, you can't predict when your bike is going to give out, cause you problems, or be involved in a collision that makes it unrideable. The only thing you know for sure is that there's always a chance that one day you'll be broken down on the side of the road and need to make an emergency repair if you have any hopes of finishing your ride.

When it comes to emergency bike repairs, your best bet is to be prepared. There's no AAA or OnStar service that'll come to your rescue if you break down. Plus, it may happen in an area where there are few bikers to help you out, and you may not have a friend or family member available to pick you up. Nothing is worse than planning a nice, long bicycle ride and ending up taking a not-so-nice, long hike while pushing your bicycle. In times like these, you'll be thankful that you took some time to read this chapter.

In this chapter, I explain the importance of keeping the appropriate tools with you to make repairs, fixing common sources of bike breakdowns, being able to identify those repairs that make your bike unsafe to ride, and getting creative and improvising a solution with whatever materials you can round up in order to hold your bike together until you can get it home.

When You Can't Call AAA: Handling Your Own Bike Repairs on the Side of the Road

Your bike can break down in numerous ways — in this section, we cover the most likely scenarios. If you know how to handle the repairs in this section, you'll be able to ride with confidence, knowing that there's nowhere you can't go on your bike.

When you ride, always keep a set of tools available so that when emergency strikes, you're prepared to deal with it. (See Chapter 16 for a list of tools you should bring along when you ride.)

Repairing a bent rim

Even if you do your best to avoid objects in the road, sooner or later a pot-hole will sneak up on you and you won't be able to avoid it. If your tires are inflated properly, your wheels *should* absorb the blow and you shouldn't have a problem. But if you hit one of the bottomless potholes that some cities are infamous for — the kind that look like they were left by a landmine — or you crash into a curb or some other immovable object, you may end up damaging your wheel so much that you can't ride. If your wheel is bent or "tacoed" and it won't roll even if the brake is removed (like the one in Figure 4-1), you may need to bend it back into shape in order to make the trip home.

Although the wheel may be beyond repair and will probably have to be replaced, your immediate goal is to return it as close as possible to the original shape so that it'll spin and clear the brakes.

Here's how to repair a bent wheel to get you back home:

1. **Remove the wheel from the frame.**

2. **With the tire on the wheel, grab the sides of the wheel with both hands, with the bent part facing away from you.**

3. **Find something like a curb where you can support the wheel at an angle with the hub elevated on the ground.**

4. **Using your weight, try to forcefully press down on the wheel against the direction of the buckle.**

   Repeat this a few times — that may be enough to correct the bend. If not, continue to Step 5.

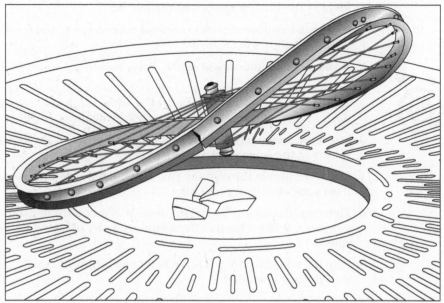

Figure 4-1:
A bent rim.

5. **If the previous step is not enough to return the wheel to a round shape, try hitting the bent part of the rim against the ground.**

   Hit it several times, like a blacksmith shaping a piece of metal, until it begins to resemble a round wheel again. Start with a soft blow and increase the intensity with each blow, after examining the rim for results. This is a last-ditch effort if all else fails.

Have the rim replaced after you get home.

Replacing a broken spoke

Wheels are amazing things: Even though they have rims that are suspended by, on average, 28 to 36 thin metal spokes, they can take a tremendous amount of punishment. A wheel gets its strength from the equal or balanced tension spread across its spokes. Remove a spoke, and this tension becomes unbalanced, causing the wheel to spin out of alignment or true, and potentially making the wheel unsafe to ride on.

The only permanent solution to a broken spoke is to replace it and retrue the wheel. But if you break a spoke while you're riding, follow these steps to get yourself home:

56 Part I: Getting Started

1. **Identify the broken spoke and remove it.**

   If you can't remove the spoke, wrap it around one of the neighboring spokes, as shown in Figure 4-2.

2. **If you have a replacement spoke, first remove the wheel and tire.**

   If you don't have a replacement spoke or can't replace it, loosen the two spokes that are adjacent to the broken spoke. This will help balance out the tension in the wheel and bring it somewhat back into alignment.

3. **Insert the spoke through the hub hole and weave it through the other spokes in the same form as the rest of the spokes.**

4. **Insert the nipple through the rim, and tighten it using a spoke wrench from your emergency tool kit.**

5. **Tighten the spoke to a tension where it makes a similar sound when you pluck it like a harp as the sound made by plucking the rest of the spokes.**

6. **Spin the wheel to see if it has a bend and adjust the spoke tension to straighten it if needed.**

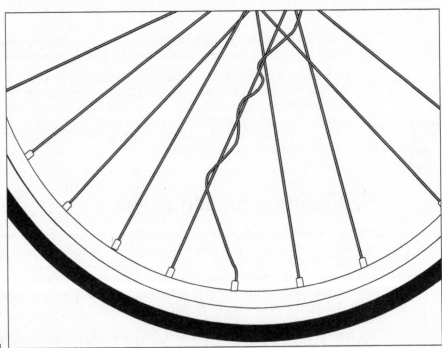

Figure 4-2:
A broken spoke wrapped around another spoke.

Fixing flats and torn tires

You should always have your patch kit available when you ride, because sooner or later a flat will sneak up on you. (For instructions on how to change a flat, see Chapter 6.) It's also good to have a spare tube on hand in case a tube blows out and can't be patched.

Before you reassemble the wheel, don't forget to inspect the tire and tube for the sharp object that caused the flat. Otherwise, you might be stuck on the side of the road repairing a flat in another five minutes.

If you have a torn or ripped tire, you'll want to fix it as soon as possible or risk blowing the tube — especially if the tube has started protruding out through the tear. Bike stores sell tire boots, which you can use to reinforce the inside of the tire where the cut is located. If you don't have a tire boot, there are a number of alternatives that'll do the job. Dollar bills, duct tape, food wrappers, plastic cut from a soda bottle — you're only limited by your imagination. (To repair or boot a tire, see the steps in Chapter 6.)

Repairing a broken chain

A broken chain is a pretty infrequent event, though as newer chains are manufactured to be narrower this occurrence is becoming increasingly more common. When a chain breaks, the outer plates on one of the links are twisted and/or ripped off, causing damage to the link and possibly to your bike. You can repair the chain in an emergency, but as soon as you get home, you should replace it.

To repair a broken chain:

1. **Remove the chain from the bike and, using a chain tool from your emergency tool kit, remove the affected link or links.**

   Follow the instructions in Chapter 10 for using the chain tool.

2. **If you have extra links, use the chain tool to connect the extra links to the chain, replacing the damaged links.**

   If you don't have extra links, you can shorten the chain by removing the faulty links and reconnecting the chain. However, you most likely won't be able to shift into the gears when the chain is in the larger cogs in the rear and the largest chainring in the front.

3. **Reconnect the chain using the chain tool and following the steps in Chapter 10.**

   Examine all the rivets and links to be sure that there are no other weaknesses in the chain.

Extracting a jammed chain

A jammed chain (like the one shown in Figure 4-3) can be one of the most annoying malfunctions when you're riding. A jammed chain often happens when the front derailleur shifts the chain too far inward and over the smallest chainring. It can also be caused by a worn chainring not grabbing the chain properly or mud clogging the chain and chainring.

Figure 4-3:
A jammed
chain.

Dennis has had this happen to him while shifting into his smallest or "granny" gear during a steep climb. Trying to stop pedaling when you're on a sharp incline on a bike loaded down with pannier bags is awful — it takes all your energy not to fall over and become fresh roadkill.

The best thing to do when you hear a loud, grinding sound when you shift is to stop pedaling immediately. If you continue to apply force to the pedals, you could further jam the chain and make it even more difficult to remove.

To extract a jammed chain:

1. **Try pulling on the chain to separate it from the chainstay and chainring.**

   Be careful not to twist it — you don't want to damage the chain in any way.

2. **If pulling on the chain is not enough to free it, try rotating the cranks backward while you pull the chain.**

   This is often enough to spring the chain loose. If not, move to Step 3.

3. **Insert a screwdriver between the chainring and chainstay and, using it as a lever, gently pry open the space.**

   This should allow you to slide the chain out (if not, move on to Step 4). Check the chainrings for any damage caused using this method and straighten as necessary.

4. **Separate the chain with a chain tool.**

   Note: This step should only be used as a *last resort,* when all the preceding steps fail.

Dealing with the derailleur

If the front derailleur gets hit or the chain gets stuck when you try to shift, the derailleur can become twisted or bent. If the derailleur moves out of place by twisting on the seat tube, you'll want to move it back into place.

Follow these steps to adjust the position of the front derailleur:

1. **Loosen the derailleur clamp bolt, which keeps it attached to the seat post.**

   Usually a 5mm Allen wrench or 8mm box wrench will do the trick.

2. **Position the derailleur so that its cage is parallel with the chainrings and only 1mm above the top of the largest chainring.**

3. **Retighten the clamp bolt.**

   See Chapter 14 for more details on installing a front derailleur.

If the derailleur is bent or damaged, you'll need to remove it and continue your ride without it. Follow these steps to remove the front derailleur:

1. **Remove the screw at the back of the front derailleur cage.**

2. **Separate the cage and remove the chain.**

3. **Bypass the derailleur and place the chain on the chainring that will best serve you on your ride home.**

4. **Remove the clamp bolt holding the derailleur to the seat tube, disconnect the shift wire, and detach the derailleur from the bike.**

   You'll need to move the shift wire into a position out of the way or completely remove it.

Like the chain, the rear derailleur is a very exposed part of the bike. It sticks out and has very little protection. If you brush up against or hit something while you're riding, you can easily bend or damage it. A bent rear derailleur frequently is the result of a bike that falls over on that side.

Most mountain bikes use a replaceable derailleur hanger that is designed to fail before the expensive derailleur itself would. In this case, buy your bike's replacement hanger, and keep it with you when you ride.

Although modern rear derailleurs are precise instruments that are sensitive to the slightest adjustments, if you're in a jam and a bent rear derailleur is causing your from finishing your trip, you can try manually bending it back into place. You can do this by inserting an Allen wrench into the mounting bolt and pulling upward while you pull the S-shaped cage away from the bike using your other hand, as shown in Figure 4-4.

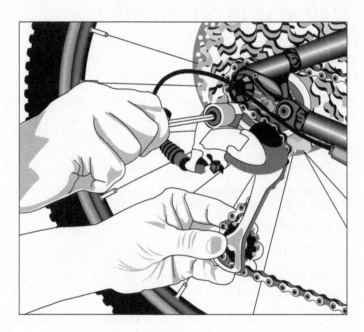

Figure 4-4:
Unbending
a bent rear
derailleur.

If you straightened out the rear derailleur enough to ride home, you may want to take it to your local bike shop to be properly tuned. Bike mechanics use a special rear derailleur hanger alignment tool to properly position the derailleur.

If the rear derailleur is damaged beyond repair and won't shift or allow you to continue biking, you'll need to bypass the derailleur and turn your bike into a single speed. If this happens to you, follow these steps to get back on the road:

1. **Use a chain tool to separate the chain.**

   See Chapter 10 for more information on separating and reconnecting a chain.

2. **Decide on a gear that is appropriate for your ride home.**

   We recommend that you pick the middle chainring on triple-chainring bikes or the smallest chainring on two-chainring bikes and the middle cog in the cassette. Leave the rear derailleur on the bicycle.

3. **Hold the chain together to determine if there is any overlap in the two ends.**

   If there is, you'll need to remove some links in order to keep enough tension on the chain.

4. **After removing the additional links, reconnect the chain.**

   Spin the cranks a few times to be sure that there is enough tension on the chain and that it won't come off the chainring. If it doesn't, you should be good enough to finish your journey.

If a cable is old, worn, or frayed there is a chance one may break while you're riding. If it's a cable for the derailleurs, you'll be limited in the number of gears you can use, but you'll still be able to ride home.

If the front derailleur cable breaks, the lack of tension will move the derailleur to the left and position the chain on the smallest chainring. If you have a triple chainring and want to use the middle chainring, pull the derailleur over the middle chainring and tighten the L-limit screw (shown in Figure 4-5) to keep it in place. For more details on adjusting the front derailleur, refer to Chapter 14.

In the case of a rear derailleur cable break, the derailleur will move the chain to the smallest cog on the cassette. If you're comfortable riding in this gear, you can finish your ride. However, if you need a more appropriate gear, you'll need to adjust the rear derailleur. Keep in mind that there is only a limited amount of adjustments with this method and you might only be able to use one of the three smallest cogs. To make the adjustment, follow these three steps:

1. **Place the chain on one of the larger cogs.**

2. **Use your hand to push in on the rear derailleur.**

3. **Tighten the H-limit screw (shown in Figure 4-6) to keep the derailleur in place.**

   Keep in mind that you may have to fine-tune the position of the derailleur so that the chain runs smoothly.

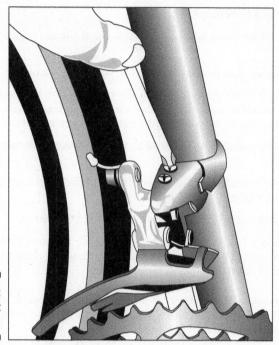

Figure 4-5:
The L-limit
screw.

Figure 4-6:
The H-limit
screw.

Knowing When You Should Walk Home

Certain repairs probably shouldn't be attempted while you're on the road. In some cases, you probably won't have the tools with you. In other cases, the chance of a malfunction happening makes continued riding a dangerous proposition.

Here are some situations when you should put away your emergency tool kit and start walking home:

✔ **When your brake cables have broken:** If you break a brake cable, you'll be limited to half your brakes. Not only will you have reduced braking power, but applying only the front or rear brakes could cause you to have an accident. Squeeze too hard on only the front brakes and you wind up being thrown head forward over your handlebars. Do the same with the rear brakes, and you could skid out. When your front or rear brakes are out, your best bet is to walk your bike if possible or ride it home *very slowly*.

✔ **When your crank is loose or has fallen off:** If the crank has loosened or fallen off, it may be best to call it a day. The crank must be tightened with a significant amount of torque and this tightening is best done with the proper tools (including a torque wrench) and with the bike supported by a bike stand if possible.

✔ **When your pedals are loose:** Pedals can be secured with the proper wrench, but if you don't have one available, you should walk your bike home. Riding with a loose pedal will damage the crank and could lead to an accident if the threads give out.

✔ **When you have a problem with the bottom bracket:** Working on the bottom bracket requires specialized tools that most riders wouldn't consider taking along on a ride. If the bottom bracket comes loose or falls apart, don't continue to ride.

✔ **When your frame is damaged:** A damaged frame is usually the result of an accident. If you've had an accident, you should immediately inspect the bike, paying particular attention to the frame. Besides looking at the frame from different directions to determine if it's bent, you should inspect the frame close up, looking for cracks, especially in any welded sections, as well as cracks, bubbles, or ripples in the paint. (See the following section for more on what to do after an accident.). A damaged or bent frame undermines the integrity of the bike and increases the chance of an accident.

Inspecting Your Bike after an Accident

Even if you're the world's safest and most cautious biker, there's always a chance you could end up in an accident. When you're on a bike moving forward on two thin wheels, you're completely exposed. Add in the fact that you'll end up biking on busy roads, crowded bike paths, or the ever dangerous off-road trails, and you increase the odds that you'll have a crash eventually.

Always wear a helmet, wear biking gloves, and keep a cellphone and identification with you at all times.

If you do end up in an accident, the first thing you should do is make sure you're okay. The shock of being involved in a collision may keep you from realizing that you're injured. If after checking yourself out, you're lucky enough to have nothing more than a scratch or two, the next thing to consider is the state of your bike.

Most modern bikes are designed with components and materials that can resist certain types of impact. However, in the case of an accident, you'll want to thoroughly inspect your bike before getting back on it to ride. Something may have come loose or the collision may have caused a weakness in the frame or some other part of the bike that may become apparent later on down the road.

Looking for looseness

One of the simplest ways to identify if there is a problem with your bike after a crash is to check for looseness. Spend a few minutes to make sure that all the parts of your bike are still securely fastened and in place as they should be. You're much better off finding a potential issue at this point rather than discovering it when the part falls off your bike.

To check for looseness, perform the following steps:

1. **Straddle the front wheel pinching it between your thighs.**

2. **Grip the handlebars and try to twist them side to side.**

3. **Straddle the frame, squeeze the brakes, and try to rock the bicycle back and forth.**

   If there is play in the handlebars or stem, it could mean either that the clamp bolts need to be tightened or you have a loose headset, something that could be dangerous at high speeds.

4. **While straddling the bike, use the handlebars to lift the front wheel off the ground.**

5. **Drop the handlebars and let the bike hit the ground.**

   If you hear any jingling or rattling, it could mean that something on the bike is loose. Repeat the procedure to isolate the location of the noise.

Checking the alignment

If your bike was involved in a collision, there's a chance that something has been bent or broken and caused your bike to be out of alignment. Unless you visually inspect your bike, you may not notice that there is a concern. This is especially important with the frame, which helps keep you balanced, influences the bike's handling, and provides stability. A crash can impact the integrity of the frame and make riding your bike a risky proposition.

An important factor in how well a frame can hold up to a collision is the material it's made of. Different frame materials offer varying levels of strength. Frames made of steel and steel alloys are amazingly strong, as are titanium frames. Aluminum frames, on the other hand, while having the benefit of being lighter than steel, are also weaker and fatigue over time. Carbon, which is a popular choice these days for frames, is made of up fibers that are arranged into a pattern, which gives significant strength to the material; however, carbon can be prone to breakage where the different tubes of the frame are connected.

To perform an alignment check from the front of the bike, perform the following steps:

1. **Stand in front of your bike with the wheel between your legs and the handlebars in your hands, as shown in Figure 4-7.**

2. **Eyeball the various angles of the frame.**

   You should confirm that the head tube is parallel with the seat tube and that the top tube is in the same plane as the down tube.

3. **Look down at the forks to confirm that they're evenly spaced around the wheel.**

To perform an alignment check from the back of the bike, follow these steps:

1. **Have someone support your bike while you stand behind it.**

2. **Visually confirm that the seat tube and the head tube are in alignment.**

3. **Check to see that the seat stays are straight.**

4. **While you're visually examining the frame, look at other parts of the bike, including the cranks and pedals and the front and rear derailleurs.**

   The rear derailleur should be hanging straight down and be positioned under one of the cogs.

Figure 4-7:
Checking
alignment.

The All-Purpose Repair Tool: Duct Tape

If you pack the emergency repair kit described in Chapter 16, you should be able to handle many of the basic emergencies that may strike when you ride. However, at some point, you may find yourself in a situation where a part of your bike needs repairing or replacing and you don't have the tools to do the job, but you still need to keep riding. This is when you need to put on your MacGyver hat and get creative. A piece of wire on the side of the road may be good enough to secure a loose bottle cage. A PowerBar wrapper could be used to boot a tire. Really the only limit to bike repair and maintenance — at least as a temporary fix — is your imagination.

Perhaps the most valuable of the multipurpose materials you can use to fix your bike is duct tape. Serious bikers always leave a roll in their bag for special emergencies. Duct tape is strong and secure, resists water, and can get you out of a number of jams. Here's a list of some of the things you can do using duct tape and a little old-fashioned ingenuity:

- Hold a torn saddle together
- Keep a loose saddle post from coming off
- Secure a bike pump to your frame if the mounting bracket breaks

- ✔ Repair rips or tears in clothing, pouches, and pannier bags

- ✔ Attach a flashlight to your bike or helmet

- ✔ Hold together a cracked helmet at least until you can get home and replace it

- ✔ Hold together frayed cable ends

- ✔ Boot a torn tire

- ✔ Secure a broken buckle on a shoe

- ✔ Hold a bottle on a bike if the cage falls off

Any and all repairs, patches, and fixes using duct tape are temporary and must be replaced at the earliest possible time.

Chapter 5

Help! When You Need Professional Assistance

In This Chapter

▶ Knowing what to look for in a bike shop
▶ Buying a bike at your local shop
▶ Recognizing which repairs are better left to the experts

*I*f you're serious about making biking a part of your life, you'll want to have people you can call for help when you need it. You'll want someone you can trust to help you buy the right bike, fit it to your body style, and accessorize it as needed. You'll want someone to turn to when it comes time to make complicated repairs. You'll want help if you're looking for a biking group or a new trail or you want to add some biking clothes to your wardrobe. In other words, you need a local bike shop.

Usually owned and operated by hard-working people whose zeal for biking is only matched by their desire to share it with others, local bike shops are some of the best resources you can find to support you with your biking needs. In this chapter, we discuss the bike-shop experience, including what you can expect to find when visiting one, what you should look for, and how to choose one that's right for you. We also tell you how to get the most out of your bike shop, including using them to shop for a bike and to handle the most challenging repairs.

What to Look for in a Bike Shop

Bicycle shops can sometimes be intimidating — especially if you're new to biking. You walk in and the store is crowded with bikes and bike parts. Bikes are hanging from the ceiling, accessories cover the walls, there may be bike videos playing and posters of bikers hanging on the wall. But the fact of the matter is: Most bicycle-store employees are bikers with a passion for biking who love to share their knowledge of and excitement for the sport.

Although most areas have several bicycle stores, they aren't on every street corner. In fact, depending on where you live, there may be only a few in your area. Even so, you should visit each shop to get a feel for which store is right for you.

Talk with other bikers for recommendations for local stores and then visit a couple of stores to meet the staff and check out their product line. Knowing a bike shop staffed by people who understand your needs and are knowledge-able enough to help you with any issue will go a long way toward improving your overall biking experience.

Take the time to get to know the staff at the shop you like — they'll be a great source of information, helping with everything from places to ride to how to find group rides. They can offer advice on the newest and coolest parts and accessories. And they can even give you advice if you want to do some of the adjustment and maintenance yourself.

In fact, a good bike-shop staff members will *encourage* you to do your own work. A bike shop shouldn't be about making customers dependent on their services in order to get more business out of them. It should be empowering its customers so that when they have problems, the customers can handle it themselves.

Here are the main features you may want to look for in a bike shop:

✔ **Customer service:** Most bicycle stores take a lot of pride in customer service, and strive to have the best customer service possible. Usually, when you first walk into a store you can feel what the level of customer service is going to be. If you're greeted shortly after entering, if the staff members are easily identified with uniforms, if they have adequate hours, if the store is clean and well lit, and if there's a good assortment of merchandise displayed in an inviting way, these are sure signs of a store that cares about its customers.

✔ **Year-round service:** One of the best times to take advantage of the services of a bike shop is during the winter season. Instead of hanging your bike up for the winter hibernation, think about using this time to do annual maintenance and upgrades. The benefit is that, because most people aren't riding as much, bicycle stores aren't as busy and can spend more quality time with customers advising and servicing their bicycles. During peak season, the bicycle stores are sometimes backed up and you may not be able to get an appointment if you need one.

One benefit of year-round service is being ready for spring. Nothing is worse than sitting in your garage or basement on a beautiful spring day with grease on your hands working on your bicycle instead of being out on the road or trail — all because you haven't worked on your bike during the winter.

Most bicycle stores will offer a limited-time warranty on the repair work they perform so make sure to ask the next time you visit.

✔ **Expertise:** You want to find a bike shop with expert staff. Talk with the staff and get a feel for whether this job is just a part-time one for them to make some extra money or whether they do it for the love of biking. The best staff are those who exude a passion for biking and who love to share their excitement for bikes with others.

If an employee doesn't have the experience or knowledge, he should be able to ask another employee for the answer. The bicycle industry has many different service classes for mechanics, and there should be at least one staff member with this kind of training. Of course, a mechanics class doesn't replace years of experience working on bikes.

✔ **Women and family friendly:** Some bike shops are staffed by hard-core male bikers who are interested in racing, top-end bikes, working on bikes, and other riders who share their interests. When it comes to the needs of women and families, most of these guys are pretty much clueless. Unless you fit that same description, look for a bike shop with a staff that includes a mix of men and women who can relate to women's biking issues (such as clothing, riding interests, and how to fit a bike to the physiology of a women). If you have kids (or you think you might in the future), you also want a bike-shop staff who can assist families with their biking needs. Fitting bikes to children is as important as fitting them to adults. For example, a child's saddle should be positioned so that he can place both feet flat on the ground. In addition, children should ride in a more upright position so that they can more easily keep their eyes on the road ahead.

You don't have to worry about which brand of bike you have or which brands the store sells. Most bicycle stores will work on all models and brands.

✔ **Turnaround time:** When you do have to take your bicycle into the bicycle store, remember you aren't the only one who is desperate to have their bike ready to ride this weekend. Sometimes you can get your bicycle fixed while you wait, and other times you may have to leave your bike for a few days while they order that special part or repair the other bicycles brought in before yours.

Some bicycle stores allow you to make an appointment so if your bicycle is still rideable, you can continue putting on those miles until they're ready to work on it.

The cost of doing business

Like any business, every bicycle store is in the business to make money. This doesn't mean the owners and employees are driving around town in their Lamborghinis, wearing Rolex watches, or drinking Dom Perignon. Selling bicycles is a hard business to be successful at — it involves a high overhead, low profit margins, and a constant need for trained and educated staff. Plus, staying in tune with the bicycling industry and the evolving technology behind it is a constant challenge.

In most cases, you'll find that employees and owners choose to work in the biking industry because they have a true love and passion for the sport. They enjoy working with and helping people discover and develop the same love and passion for biking.

For a bike-shop owner, it's satisfying and rewarding to see a family out on the trail having some real quality time, knowing that they've outfitted them with bicycles and/or accessories. It's equally rewarding to talk with the person who started as a recreational cyclist and is now addicted to biking and rides or commutes to work every day.

These are a few of the reasons that drive many of the people who work in your local bicycle stores. Keep this in mind the next time you're shopping for that cool new bicycle part or accessory upgrade. They need to make a little profit so they can continue to pay the bills and be there the next time you need something.

Shopping at Your Bike Shop

The most significant benefit you'll get from working with a bike shop is the obvious: They can help you buy the bike that's right for you. Sure, you can use the Internet to find a bike, and save some money. But if you shop online, you're missing what only a bike shop can provide: the personal touch and customer service. The hands-on, face-to-face service of a bike shop is invaluable when you're searching for the right bike. Plus, the folks at your local bike shop can help with sizing and the assembly of your bike.

When you shop at your local bike shop, you're building a relationship that will benefit you when you need additional support.

Buying a bike

Whether you buy a bike online or at a bike shop, it'll need some initial adjustments and an inspection. The benefit of buying from a bike shop is that they can make these adjustments when you buy it.

Plus, when you buy a bike from a local bike store, they won't just put the pedals, seat, and handlebars on your bicycle and send you off. They'll disassemble your bicycle first. They'll take many of the parts off and double-check and fine-tune them before assembling and checking everything and making the final adjustments.

When you arrive to pick up your bike, they'll go over the bicycle with you, making sure it's fitted and adjusted to your personal riding style and comfort. They'll go over its function, show you how everything works, and give you riding tips.

After you've put some miles on your bike, the gear and brake cable will stretch and need adjustment, the spokes will settle into place and need truing, the bearings will loosen up and need adjustments — and all of this can be done for free by many shops. They know that this initial break-in period is the must critical time for the best performance and extended life of your bicycle, so they want to take care of it for you.

Use the Internet to research the bikes you're interested in. Almost all manufacturers have very user-friendly Web sites that can help you when you walk into your local shop and start trying out different bikes.

Here are some of the major bicycle manufacturers and their Web addresses:

- **Cannondale:** www.cannondale.com
- **Fuji:** www.fujibikes.com
- **Gary Fisher:** www.fisherbikes.com
- **Giant:** www.giant-bicycles.com
- **Kona:** www.konaworld.com
- **Raleigh:** www.raleighusa.com
- **Schwinn:** www.schwinnbike.com
- **Specialized:** www.specialized.com
- **Trek:** www.trekbikes.com

When you're looking for a bike with the help of a bike shop, they'll help you figure out which type of bike is most suited for your needs. There are many different types of bikes available, each with their own benefits:

- **Road bikes** are built for smooth pavement riding and fast speeds. They're lightweight for easier acceleration and top speeds. They have thin, higher pressure tires (for less rolling resistance) and dropped handlebars (to support a bent-over riding position for better aerodynamics).

✔ **Mountain bikes** are built for riding on trails and rough terrain. They have higher-performance brakes for long and steep descents; thick, knobby tires for better traction in steep and/or loose terrain; and suspension for more control and comfort.

✔ **Hybrid bikes** are all-purpose bikes that combine features of a road and mountain bike. They weigh more than road bikes but less than mountain bikes. Their tire circumference size compares to a road bike, and the tire width is wider than on a road bike and narrower than on a mountain bike. A hybrid bike gives you a little of the performance of a road bike and the comfort and durability of a mountain bike. They have flat handlebars for a comfortable upright riding position.

✔ **Touring bikes** are built to carry heavier loads across long distances. They have mountings for bike racks to carry your gear, a wider frame (for stability), wheels with more spokes (to support the additional weight of gear and for greater durability on long, hard rides), and a greater range of gears for wide variety of elevation changes.

✔ **Cruiser bikes** are designed for leisurely riding. They have very few (if any) gears. They're built for an upright riding position, with a wide saddle. They have fat, soft tires for a super-comfortable ride. Some cruiser bikes have coaster brakes (in which you pedal backward to stop).

✔ **Recumbent bikes** are designed for riders who want a reclined riding position. On a recumbent bike, you can't stand to pedal up hills and stretch your legs on long rides; you're limited to that one, reclined position for your entire ride. Recumbent bikes are good for riders with back problems. Some have coaster brakes (in which you pedal backward to stop).

Recumbent bikes are more difficult for drivers of cars to see than the other types of bikes are.

✔ **BMX bikes** are built to ride off-road on a dirt track or to do tricks. They have small frames for quick handling, tricks, and jumping. They're made of very durable components and have foot pegs or extensions off the frame for performing stunts.

Before you buy a bike, be sure to test-ride it — and test-ride a variety of other bikes, too. It's hard to get a feel for a bike unless you compare it against other bikes. You can do all the research online, read all the bicycle magazines, talk with the staff at the bicycle store, talk with your neighborhood or office bicycle guru, but until you ride the bike, you won't know for sure if it's the right one for you.

You should always wear a helmet when riding a bike — and, easy as it is to overlook, this is especially true when you're test-riding. You're more likely to have an accident on a bike and in territory that you're not familiar with.

When test-riding, find a location with enough space so that you can observe how the bike handles at lower and higher speeds. Riding the bike at different speeds will allow you try out a range of the gears. If you can, ride it uphill so that you can use the higher gears. Here's some of what you should feel on your ride:

- ✔ Shifting between gears should be smooth and almost effortless.
- ✔ The bike should ride in a straight line and the wheels shouldn't wobble.
- ✔ The bike should be easy to handle and smooth in the turns.
- ✔ The brakes should grip the wheel firmly and slow you down or stop you smoothly.
- ✔ Your arms should comfortably reach the handlebars without being too bent or locked out.
- ✔ You should be able to easily grip the shifters and brakes without having your wrists in an awkward position.

A test ride will also give you an idea of the quality of work and service the bicycle store will offer you after the initial purchase. Before they send you out on a test ride, the folks at the bike shop should:

- ✔ Check all the nuts and bolts on the bicycle.
- ✔ Make sure the brakes and gears work properly.
- ✔ Check the tires for proper air pressure.
- ✔ Set the seat and handlebar position for you.
- ✔ Inform you of the proper gear and brake operations.
- ✔ Give you ridings tips, such as what to look and feel for on your test ride.

Shopping for a used bike

For many people, buying a used bike is the way to go. Sometimes you can find a great deal when shopping for a used bike if you know where to look and what to look for.

Many times, you can find a newer used bike at a significant discount. You may come across someone who recently purchased a bike and, for whatever reason (she's moving, he needs the money) — has to sell. A bike is just like a car in one way: The moment it's sold for the first time, it depreciates in price. Buy a bike after that initial sale, and you could be getting a real steal.

Not all bike shops sell used bikes, but those that do will have usually inspected the bike and made any necessary repairs before selling them. So if your local bike shop sells used bikes, that's a great place to start.

(continued)

(continued)

Beyond bike shops, you can shop at flea markets and garage sales; peruse the classifieds in the local paper; or check the Internet. Sites like eBay (`www.ebay.com`) and craigslist (`www.craigslist.org`) offer a wide variety of bikes. The advantage of craigslist is that you can shop in your town and likely take the bike for a test-ride before you buy.

You can tell a lot about a bike and how it was maintained just by looking at it. If there is rust and corrosion in the chains or cables, if the paint is worn and chipped, if the tires are starting to rot, this could be a sign that the bike was neglected and may not be worth the investment.

If you're going to test-ride a used bike that isn't being sold by a bike shop, be careful. The owner may not have maintained the bike and, in the worst-case scenario, something may come loose or fall off, causing you to crash. Before you ride, perform the pre-ride inspection from Chapter 16. In particular make sure that:

✔ The brakes work.

✔ There is no looseness in the handlebars or headset.

✔ The pedals and cranks are secure and the bottom bracket is not loose or binding.

✔ There are no bad links in the chain and the cog and chainring teeth are not worn.

✔ The wheels are attached properly and there is air in the tires.

✔ Assume that you'll have to do some repairs or tune-ups on the bike, and evaluate the bike to diagnose just how much repair is needed. You can get a great deal if you're willing to do some of the repair yourself, but don't take on too much — the bike may not be worth it.

✔ Check all bearing surfaces, the bottom bracket, the headset, the hubs, and the pedals. If these are in bad shape, an overhaul may not be sufficient and those parts may be shot.

✔ Inspect the drivetrain. Are the chain and the cogs/chainrings in good shape, or are they significantly worn? A blown-out drivetrain could be prohibitively expensive to repair.

✔ Are the wheels true? Are the rims in good shape, or are they worn on the braking surface? What is the quality of the brand of the wheels? This information helps determine the value of the bike.

✔ Are the cables still usable? When you shift or brake, is there resistance from friction and corrosion, or are they smooth? Replacing cabling can be a pain.

✔ Is the frame free from rust and dents?

Buying accessories

Bike shops are great when it comes to helping you find the right biking accessories. Staff in many bike shops use much of the equipment they sell, so they can talk to you about what works well and will fit with your budget. When you've found a bike shop you trust, the staff can even advise you if they think that a more expensive product isn't worth the additional cost or if a cheaper product is cheaper for a reason and should be avoided.

Here are some accessories you may want to consider buying:

✔ **Helmet:** For safety reasons, a helmet should be at the top of your list. The bike-shop staff can help you find a helmet that fits properly and doesn't move around on your head. They can also help you adjust the straps to fine-tune the fit.

Sizing is very important. A $20 helmet sized properly will protect you better than a $150 helmet that doesn't fit or is not adjusted properly.

✔ **Lock:** If you're ever going to leave your bike alone for more than a minute or two, you'll want a lock. The folks at your local shop can help you find a balance between a lock that's difficult to cut and one that doesn't weigh too much.

✔ **Gloves:** Biking gloves will reduce vibrations and provide protection if your fall off your bike. Bike-shop staff can help you decide whether to get gel padding, full fingers, or cutoffs, and how tight the gloves should fit. They may suggest rolling your gloves off rather than pulling at the fingers (which can prematurely tear the stitching).

✔ **Bike pumps:** You'll need two pumps: a mini bike pump to mount onto the frame and a larger pump to keep in the house. You may also want to consider a CO_2 cartridge system for quick and easy tire inflating. They're a little more expensive than traditional tire pumps, but they'll get you back on the road fast.

✔ **Lights:** Bike lights will keep you safe if you get caught out after dark. The folks at your bike shop can offer suggestions on what types of bulbs are best for both front and rear lights, whether rechargeable batteries are the way to go, and where to mount the lights.

✔ **Computer:** A computer will track statistics regarding each of your rides and provide motivation when you ride to exercise. Staff can help you decide if you need extra features such as a heart monitor, altimeter, and wireless connection.

✔ **Shoes:** Biking shoes designed to work with clipless pedals will significantly improve your pedaling efficiency. Staff will advise you on whether to buy stiff road biking shoes or ones designed for walking, as well as talk to you about the best type of material and whether the shoes will work with your pedals.

✔ **Clothes:** Bike clothes can keep you cool in warm weather, warm in cool weather, and dry in wet weather. Staff will help you find properly fitting clothing for the right season and provides padding and wicks moisture where you need it the most.

Recognizing the Repairs You Need Help With

With this book in hand, a few tools, and a healthy dose of confidence, patience, and determination, you can do just about everything needed to maintain and repair your bike. There are only a few situations in which you may have to step aside and let the professionals in your local bike shop handle the load. In this section, we fill you in on when to leave it for the pros.

Repairing frames

In general, all frame repair should be handled by professionals — either your local bicycle store or a professional frame builder/repair facility. Most local bicycle stores can handle minor frame alignment issues if they have the proper tools and experience. If your bike has any frame-integrity issues — such as cracks, dents, or stress marks in the paint — they should be inspected, repaired, or replaced by a frame specialist.

If you need to have your frame repaired by a specialist, you may as well have an extra set of fasteners attached for an extra water bottle, bike rack, or tire pump. You may even want to get the cool new paint job you've been dreaming of.

Installing a new headset

Adjusting a headset is an easy job that you can perform at home or on the road. Overhauling a headset is also a job you can perform at home. However, installing a *new* headset is a job probably best saved for the professionals at you local bicycle store.

There are several specialty tools required to remove the old headset and then install the new one: a fork race removal tool, a headset cup removal tool, a fork race setting tool, and a headset cup pressing tool. Plus, you need the knowledge to use these tools properly. Most bike shops will have the tools and the expertise to put them to use.

Truing a wheel

The basic concept of straightening a rim by adjusting spoke tension is easy. The problems begin when you get into concepts that the professionals call *dishing* or *rounding* or when you have to straighten a rim that has a flat spot or a bend in it and the spokes are all tensioned differently. This is where significant expertise is required.

Even with a truing stand, spoke tension meter, dishing tool, and spoke wrench, you still need the knowledge and experience to make everything come together properly. The big advantage of having your wheels trued by a professional is that they'll stand behind and warranty their work. Just because you get the wheel perfectly dished, rounded, and straight doesn't mean the wheel will hold up the first time you go for a ride.

Working on suspension

There are many different types of front and rear suspension and all repair work on them should be done either by the manufacturer, your local bicycle store, or one of the specialty bicycle suspension repair facilities.

Most of the manufacturers have programs set up so you can ship the suspension part back to them where they'll repair it and ship it back to you for a nominal charge. A couple of independently owned repair facilities provide the same service. The advantage of going through your local bicycle shop is that you don't have to pay the shipping costs, although there are certain repairs for which the bicycle store may also have to send the part back to the manufacturer for service.

Refer to your owners manual for the proper oils and lubricants and the routine maintenance you can and should be performing yourself on your suspension parts.

Part II
Basic Bike Repairs

The 5th Wave   By Rich Tennant

@RICHTENNANT

"Listen, thanks. I'll return them as soon as
I get the wheels fixed."

In this part . . .

Although a bike is not very complicated, some of the procedures required to repair and maintain it are more challenging than others. In this part, we cover some of the simpler procedures, including those involving the wheels, tires and tubes, freewheels and cassettes, brakes, and chain. But don't make the mistake of assuming that simple means you can skip it. Some of the information in this part is essential to maintaining your bike (for example, regularly caring for your chain will prolong its life and the lives of all the components the chain comes in contact with).

Chapter 6

Burning Rubber: Tires and Tubes

In This Chapter
▶ Preventing flat tires
▶ Removing a wheel, tire, and tube
▶ Patching a punctured tube and fixing a tire
▶ Putting the tire, tube, and wheel back together again

*W*hy does it always seem like a flat tire comes at the worse possible time? You're out riding your bike — enjoying the scenery, concentrating on working up a sweat, or hustling to get to your destination on time — when suddenly your trip is interrupted by that irksome troublemaker, the flat tire. It starts as an slow, inconspicuous leak of air — it grabs your attention only when the tire is completely flat and an abrupt stop to your trip is the only option.

If you're new to biking or you've been fortunate enough to have avoided tire and tube problems so far, rest assured: Sooner or later, you'll find yourself on the side of the road, tube in hand, searching for that pesky leak.

Instead of trying to figure out how to remove a tire and patch a tube the first time it strikes, practice fixing and changing a tire before you actually need to. When you're sitting at the side of the road is not the time to figure it out.

In this chapter, I take the mystery out of fixing a flat by explaining step by step how to remove a tire, find the puncture, patch the tube, and reassemble the wheel. Follow these instructions, and the next time a flat tire tries to derail your trip, you'll be back on your bike in no time.

Why Flat Tires Happen to Good People

When it comes to flat tires, the universe does not play favorites. The next victim of a flat could just as easily be Lance Armstrong on an expensive racing bike in the French Alps as a little old lady from Kansas on a utility bike with a loaf of bread in her basket. Given that none of us is immune, the best you can do is understand what causes flats, try to limit the chances of having one, and be able to recover from one if you're on the losing end of this game of chance.

Before you figure out how to handle flat tires, you need to know the parts of the bike involved:

- **Wheel:** The wheel includes the rim, spokes, and hub.
- **Tire:** The tire sits between the rim and the road and is made of interwoven fabric and rubber.
- **Tread:** The tread is the rubber-coated part of the tire that comes in contact with the road.
- **Tube:** The tube is an inflatable balloon that fills up the inside of the tire as it expands.
- **Valve:** The valve is a metal connector that can be opened and closed to inflate or deflate the tube.

When it comes to flats, the tube plays a leading role. The tube provides the cushion of air between the road and the rider, allowing for a smooth, efficient ride. When the tube is damaged in some way such that it can no longer maintain air, a flat is the result. Tube damage can be caused by any of the following:

- **Sharp objects:** Objects such as glass or a nail can pierce a tire and tube.
- **Low tire pressure:** When your tire pressure is low, it's easier for an object to penetrate the tire rather than bounce off.
- **The tube getting caught between the sharp edge of the wheel rim and the tire:** When this happens, the result is something called a *pinched flat* or *snakebite puncture*.
- **Tires wearing out:** When your tires wear out, they lose their capacity to protect the tube.
- **Tubes losing their integrity:** If you've patched your tubes multiple times, they'll be more prone to damage.

Fixing a Flat

If you plan on doing a lot of biking, you'll probably end up fixing flats regularly. You have two options for recovering from a flat:

✔ **Install a spare tube.** Although this method is a quick, surefire way to get back on the road in a matter of minutes, the cost of tubes can add up after a while.

Note: In the cases described below, you'll *have* to replace the tube:

- After you' have patched a tube a dozen or more times, the integrity of the tube starts to break down, leaving you more vulnerable to additional flats or a complete *blowout.* (A blowout is a rip or tear in the tube that cannot be patched and requires the tube to be replaced).

- A damaged stem valve also requires the tube to be replaced.

✔ **Patch your existing tube.** This option is a cheap, reliable fix — and it's the method we recommend. Before long, you'll be a biking veteran proudly showing off the patches on your tube as if they were badges of honor.

In this section, we walk you through the entire process of fixing a flat, with a focus on patching your tube. We also tell you how to replace a tube, in case you really need to.

Grabbing yourself a wheel

Before you can even think about fixing a flat or addressing any other tire or tube issue, you need to be able to remove the wheel from the bicycle frame. Fortunately, bike manufacturers have made the lives of bike riders easier by introducing things such as quick-release hubs and brakes. In the case of bikes without the quick release, don't fret — a wrench will do the trick.

In the following sections, I walk you through loosening the brakes and removing the wheel, regardless of how your bike was made.

Loosening the brakes

Because brakes are typically designed to sit close to the wheel rim, their location normally prevents the wheel from being removed if the tire is fully inflated. If you want to remove a wheel, you first have to open the brakes so there's room for the tire to fit through the brake pads.

Many bikes have a quick release built into the brake, which quickly enables the cable to slacken and the brakes to spread. The quick release may vary depending on what type of brakes your bike has:

- **Cantilever brakes:** If you have cantilever brakes, squeeze the brake arms together with one hand to create slack in the cable and, with the other hand, lift the loose end of the cable out of its pocket. Release the breaks and they'll pop open.

- **V-brakes:** If you have V-brakes, pinch together the top of the brake arms to loosen the cable. Pull the rubber boot back to expose the cable Carefully pull the cable out of the narrow slot in the cable holder, and release it to open the brakes

- **Side-pull brakes:** For side-pull brakes, look for a small lever on the caliper where the cable is attached. Pull the lever upward and release the brakes just enough to allow the wheel to pass. In some models, you have to look for a button on the lever and push it to release the tension on the brakes.

Worst case, if you can't release the brakes to allow the tire to past through the brakes, let the air out of the tire; this will give you the clearance needed.

Taking off the wheel

After the brakes are loosened, you're ready to remove the wheel. To remove a wheel, follow these steps:

1. **Shift the chain to the smallest cog in the back, so that the chain and derailleur have more slack and are out of the way.**

   If you're removing both wheels, remove the front wheel first, because it's the easier of the two.

2. *For wheels that use axle nuts:* **Use the proper size wrench to loosen one side slightly and then the other, alternating until the wheel is free.**

   Avoid loosening one side all at once, because this could lead to problems with the bike's hub bearings. If you have two wrenches, you can undo both nuts at the same time.

3. *For quick-release wheels:* **Pull the lever away from the bike.**

   The initial release of the lever may be enough to free the front wheel. If not, hold the nut opposite the lever with one hand and rotate the lever a few times to loosen it.

All newer bicycles have some type of safety retention device to hold the front wheel in the frame, even if the quick release is opened or the axle nuts have been loosened. If your front fork has a clip-on type of safety retention device, disengage it. If the safety retention device is molded, cast, or machined into the front fork dropouts, loosen the tension, adjusting it enough to allow removal of the wheel.

If you've successfully taken off the front wheel, you're ready to remove its more challenging counterpart — the rear wheel. Unlike the front wheel, which practically drops off the bike after you release it, the rear wheel has the chain and derailleur wrapped around its cogs. To free it you need to:

1. **Loosen the nuts or the quick release for the rear wheel in the same way as you did for the front.**

   This time you may need to give the wheel a stiff blow from the rear of the wheel toward the front of the bicycle to jar the axle loose.

2. **Move the wheel away forward and downward from the derailleur to let the chain fall off.**

   If this doesn't work, you may have to get a little dirty and lift the chain off the cog with your hand.

Don't be afraid of the chain, derailleur, and cogs when you remove the rear wheel. The chain and rear derailleur will stay attached to the bicycle frame and the cogs will stay attached to the rear wheel. You won't affect any of the adjustments.

Removing the tire or at least half of it

The tire is easier to remove if you release any remaining air from the tube. You release the air from the tube through the valve. There are two main types of valves (see Figure 6-1):

- ✔ **Presta valve:** A Presta valve is thin and all metal. Many road bikes use Presta valves, which can handle greater pressure and leak less than Schrader valves.

- ✔ **Schrader valve:** The Schrader valve is fat, like what you'd see on a car tire. Schrader valves are easier to pump up than Presta valves; you can fill them up at a gas station.

Some bike pumps are designed for either Presta or Schrader valves while some are reversible and work with both. If you aren't sure what you need, ask for help in your local bike shop.

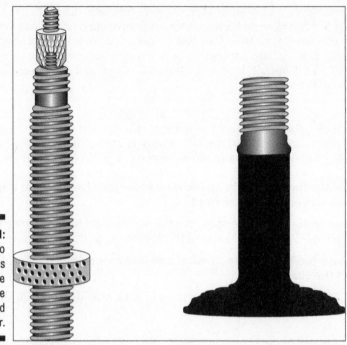

Figure 6-1:
The two
main types
of tire
valves are
Presta and
Schrader.

If you're putting air in a tire at a gas station, be careful not to overfill it — the tire could explode.

If you have a Presta valve, unscrew and press down on the tip of the valve. If you have a Schrader valve, insert the tip of a tire lever into the center of the valve while squeezing the tire to allow air to escape.

Then, using the tire levers, try to lift one side of the tire off the rim while leaving the other side in place. Here's how:

1. **Pinch the tire all the way around the rim to move the edge (or *bead*) of the tire away from the rim.**

2. **Slide the flat end of the first tire lever between the rim and the bead of the tire under it.**

   Make sure to use tire levers, not flathead screwdrivers — screwdrivers have sharp edges that can puncture the tire. In a pinch, the handles of silverware can work.

3. **Pull the lever down so that the bead rises up and over the rim.**

4. **Hook the bottom of the lever to a spoke to keep it in place.**

Some tires are very tight and you'll need extra room, so don't hook the first tire lever to the spoke until you get the second lever slid under the tire.

5. **A few inches away, repeat steps 2 and 3 with the second tire lever.**

6. **Repeat steps 2 and 3 with the third lever, but instead of hooking the lever to a spoke, start dragging the lever around the wheel away from the first and second levers (as shown in Figure 6-2).**

You should notice the tire becoming looser until the entire side pops off the rim.

Figure 6-2:
Using tire levers to remove the tire.

7. **Before removing the inner tube from the wheel, pump it up with a little extra air. Later, when you have to look for the puncture, you'll need some air in the tube and it's easier to pump up the tube while it is still on the wheel.**

8. **While the tire is still on the rim, reach under it and pull out the tube.**

9. **When you reach the valve, lift up the tire and pull the valve through the rim, being careful not to damage it.**

Note the position of the tube in relation to the tire so when you find the hole in the tube it will be easier to locate the cause (glass, a nail, a thorn), if it's still embedded in the tire.

Finding the puncture

You'll need to do a little detective work to find the puncture. To track down the source of the problem, follow these steps:

1. **Examine the inner tube by listening for a leak.**

   If it doesn't have air, pump it up to a larger shape than round. With the additional air pressure, the leak may make a hissing sound as the air tries to escape.

2. **If you're having trouble listening for the leak, float your finger above the surface of the inner tube until you feel the flow of air escaping.**

   If you've narrowed the source of the leak to a small area, but you still can't find the actual hole, apply a small amount of saliva to the tube. Bubbles will lead you to the source.

   If you don't want to gross out your riding partners by spitting on your tube, you can sometimes find a very small hole or slow leak by holding the tube near your lips. The lips are very sensitive and should feel the smallest amounts of air leaking out.

3. **If you're still having trouble finding the leak, submerge the tube under water.**

   A stream of bubbles will be clearly evident after submerging the tube. When you remove the tube from the water, wrap it around your finger at the source of the leak or mark it so that you don't lose the location.

In some cases, a hard-to-find leak may be traced to a valve problem. This is one situation in which you may want to employ the saliva technique. Apply a few drops of saliva to the end of the valve to look for signs of air escaping. For a Schrader valve, you can try tightening the valve core. If this doesn't work, you may need to remove the core, put a few drops of oil on the spring, and reinstall the core. This technique requires a valve cap with a built-in valve core tool or a separate valve core tool, something you can buy at bike shop. If the leak is coming from a cracked or cut stem, you'll have to replace the tube. In the case of Presta valves, more likely than a leak is the valve breaking (because valves are fragile).

Valve leaks are hard to find when the tube is outside the tire because the tube usually has very little air pressure and leaks in the valve usually only show up when there is a lot of air pressure (that is, when the tube is sitting inside the tire and the tire is inflated to the proper air pressure).

Patching the tube

After you've identified the source of the leak (see the preceding section), follow these steps to patch the tube:

1. **Lay the tube on a flat surface.**

2. **Using the abrasive paper or metal scraper included in your puncture repair kit, rough up the area around the puncture (as shown in Figure 6-3).**

   The goal is to remove any dirt or debris from the surface and help the patch bond to the tube.

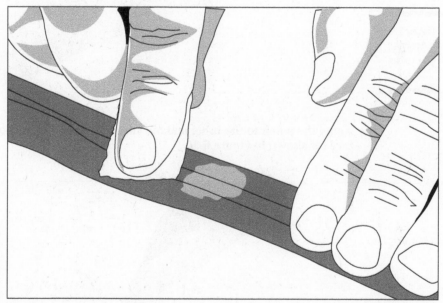

Figure 6-3: Roughing up the tube.

3. **Coat the tube with a thin, even layer of glue from the puncture repair kit in an area centered over the puncture and slightly larger than the size of the patch (as shown in Figure 6-4).**

   Allow the glue to dry completely before proceeding.

4. **Remove the metal backing from the patch (leaving the side covered in cellophane alone).**

   Avoid touching the sticky side of the patch during this process. Doing so can weaken the patch's bonding properties.

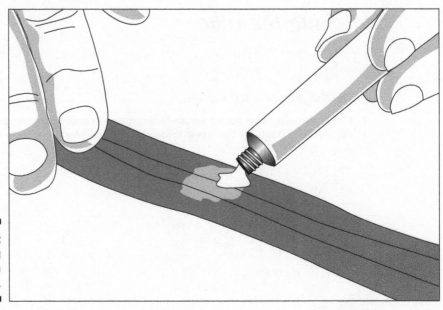

Figure 6-4:
Applying
glue to the
tube.

5. **Apply the patch to the tube, making sure to center it over the puncture (as shown in Figure 6-5).**

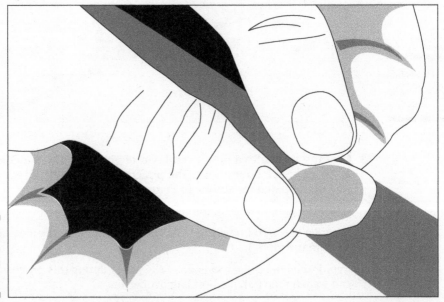

Figure 6-5:
Pressing the
patch onto
the tube.

6. **Press the patch firmly and repeatedly in place and, using a tire lever, smooth it out to remove any trapped air.**

   Leave the cellophane in place — it prevents the glue from sticking to the tire.

If you're using glue-free patches, you'll rough up the tube as in Step 2 and apply the patch directly after removing the backing.

Glue-free patches are designed to provide a quick fix to get you home and are not the long-term solution that the standard glue type patches can be.

Inspecting the tire

After successfully patching or replacing the tube, you'll want to inspect the tire to make sure that there aren't any sharp objects in it which could re-puncture the tube. Here's how:

1. **Drag a rag or a biking glove along the inside of the tire, in both directions, to determine if there is anything lodged in the tire.**

   Always drag the rag of the glove in both directions through the inside of the tire. Sometimes the object is at an angle and won't be detected until it's wiped in the opposite direction.

2. **Visually inspect the inside and outside of the tire, looking for any objects wedged inside the tread or cut into the sidewall.**

When it's more than just a flat

When you inspect the tire after repairing the tube, pay attention to any tears or rips in the tires. Whatever punctured your tube may have caused damage to the structural integrity of the tire.

If the tire has a tear, inflating the newly installed tube or riding on it may cause the tube to explode through the hole in the tire, giving you a startle that packs more punch than a double espresso.

If your tire has any structural damage, you can use a *tire boot* (a temporary patch for tires) to get home. You insert the tire boot between the tube and the tire, and the boot prevents the tube from expanding through the opening in the tire. Some boots can be fastened to the inside of the tire by adhesive backing, and others are designed to be held in place by the pressure of the tube pushing against the inside of the tire wall.

Although a boot will enable you to ride on a damaged tire, it's meant to be temporary, helping you to get home or to a place where you can replace the tire.

To patch a tire with a boot, peel off the backing and adhere the boot to the inside of the tire where the tear or cut is located. If the boot doesn't have adhesive, you have to wrap the boot around the slightly inflated tube at the location of the damage, knowing that, after the tube is fully inflated, the boot will be held in place.

In an emergency, you can use a dollar bill the same way you would a tire boot. Dollar bills are surprisingly strong. Dennis always keeps at lease one in his seat bag.

Ready to Roll!

At this point, you should have a patched or replaced tube, a tire free of debris, and the enthusiasm of knowing that this pit stop is just about over. After you finish the final steps of putting the tire and tube back on the wheel, inflating the tube, and the attaching the wheel to the bike, you're ready to roll! We cover these final steps in this section.

Putting on the tube and tire

To reinstall the tube and the tire on the wheel, follow these steps:

1. **Position the wheel with the valve hole facing upward.**

2. **Pull back the tire and insert the valve of the tube, partially inflated (enough to give it its shape), into the hole.**

3. **Working your way around the tire, tuck the tube up into the tire and on the rim being careful not to twist it.**

4. **Pinch together the sides of the tire in order to lift the other half of the tire bead onto the rim.**

   Try to use your hands to put the tire on the rim. Using the tire levers could re-puncture the tube you just worked so hard to repair or replace.

   When you finish this step half of the tire should be pushed over the rim.

5. **Start with the valve in the bottom, or 6 o'clock position, and begin working your hands away from each other around the wheel and pushing down on the bead with your thumbs or other fingers.**

6. **When your hands get closer together at the top, or the 12 o'clock position, squeeze with as much force as you can muster.**

   You should be able to pop the final portion of the bead into place (as shown in Figure 6-6).

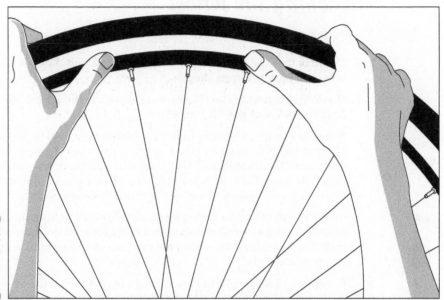

Figure 6-6:
Putting the
tire back on
the rim.

 Sometimes the tire is *very* tight when you get near the top. If this happens, you need to let all the air back out of the tube and start again with your hands at the bottom, or 6 o'clock position, making sure the tire is seated down inside the lip of the rim. Pull the last section of tread with your palms. Rotate the wheel and, from the back, use both hands to pull up repeatedly until the bead snaps in.

 If you must use a tire lever for the last step, be careful not to pinch the tube against the rim, or you could be back to square one. Either way, it's time to put a smile on your face. You're almost finished and everything is downhill from here.

Inspect the tire to make sure that the tube is not sticking out from under it. As a precautionary step, push the valve up into the tire to make sure that the part of the tube surrounding the value is not pinned against the rim and then pull it back down to inflate. If everything looks good, begin to inflate the tube according to the pounds per square inch (PSI) rating, marked on the sidewall of the tire. As you pump it up, examine the tire to make sure the tube is expanding consistently within the tire and isn't bulging in any areas. If the tube isn't expanding consistently or is bulging, the tube may be twisted or pinched by the tire and need to be reinstalled.

Attaching the wheel

To attach the wheel, follow these simple steps:

1. **Confirm that the brakes have been released and there is space for the wheel to pass between them.**

2. ***If you're attaching the front wheel,*** **position the wheel hub within the frame's fork and slide it into place.**

   If you have a quick-release hub, the quick release will be loose in the open position. It starts to get snug when the lever is pointed straight out away from the bicycle, and *very* tight when pivoted into the closed position. You can adjust the tension for the closed position with the hand-turn nut on the opposite end of the quick-release skewer.

   Never use the lever as a wing nut and crank it to tighten the quick release. Doing so won't result in sufficient force to hold the wheel to the fork. The lever must be closed for the cam mechanism to securely clamp down on the fork.

   If you don't have a quick release, begin by tightening the axle nuts on both sides of the hub a little at a time until both are securely in place.

3. ***If you're attaching the rear wheel,*** **make sure the right-hand shifter is placed into the highest gear, the gear that moves the chain farthest away from the bike and onto the smallest cog.**

4. **Maneuver the wheel into place so that the top part of the chain just above the derailleur falls onto the smallest sprocket.**

   To facilitate this step, push the derailleur arm down and pull the cogs in between the loop.

5. **With the chain sitting on the smallest cog (which is the cog it was on when you removed the wheel), slide the wheel into place into the rear dropout part of the frame.**

6. **Use the instructions in Step 2 to fasten the quick release or the axle nuts.**

Congratulations! Your tire and tube should be in good shape and your flat tire a soon-to-be distant memory. After doing this a few times, you'll find that fixing a flat will be little more than a five- to ten-minute pit stop that will barely give your riding partner time to return from a restroom break.

Coming to a screeching halt: When you get another flat right away

For those of us who have had the excruciatingly frustrating experience of getting a flat five minutes after repairing the first one, we know there are many more descriptive and colorful words come to mind than our publisher will let us print in this book.

If a flat tire strikes twice consider the possible causes:

- ✔ More than one puncture is in the tube and you only patched one of them.
- ✔ A shard of glass or some sharp object is hidden in the tire and has re-punctured the tube.
- ✔ When you reinstalled the tube, part of it was pinched between the rim and the tire.

The solution is to take a deep breath and repeat the process, being extra vigilant when finding the puncture, inspecting the tire, and installing the tube.

Of course, there is always the chance that you did everything perfectly the first time and it just so happened that you had the incredibly bad luck of running into a second sharp object on the road. The good thing is that, over time, the odds even out, and the next time you'll be the one taking the bathroom break while your riding partner is on her knees with tube in hand.

A Pound of Cure: Preventing a Flat

The obvious choice of any bike rider is to *avoid* flats. Although this might be impossible for any wheel system that uses tubes, prevention is the next best option. To help prevent flat tires, proper maintenance is key:

- ✔ Keep your tires inflated to the proper pressure as indicated on the side of the tire.
- ✔ Replace tires at the first sign of worn tread or deteriorating sidewalls.
- ✔ Replace tubes that have already been patched more than a dozen times.
- ✔ Inspect tire tread for objects stuck in the tread that may cause a puncture.

If you're willing to spend a little extra money to prevent punctures, consider investing in Kevlar-reinforced tires. The composite fibers that make up Kevlar are strong enough to resist punctures that would normally occur from contact with sharp objects. Kevlar tires typically run about $15 to $20 more than regular tires.

If Kevlar tires aren't in your budget, try tire liners, which are made of strong, lightweight fibers and line the inside of the tire to provide extra protection to the tube. Other options are thorn-resistant tubes and tubes with flat sealant that fills small holes from the inside without the rider even knowing he's had a puncture.

Even if you take all the preventive steps mentioned in this section, you're still likely to get an occasional flat. Once, on a trip from Ireland to Italy with a heavily loaded bike, Dennis went three months without a single flat. A few months later, on a trip in the United States, he was pulling his hair out on the side of the road after five flats in one week. Go figure!

If you keep a patch kit, tire levers, pump, and spare tube with you while you bike and you practice the steps described in this chapter, the chances are good that you'll be able to fix a flat and be back on your bike quicker than your partner can finish off a PowerBar. This will give you the confidence to take long, worry-free bike rides and save you from the embarrassment of having to ask another biker to show you how to change a flat or from walking your bike home.

Chapter 7

Hugging the Curb: The Wheels

....

In This Chapter

▶ Buying the right wheels for your bike

▶ Caring for and inspecting your wheels

▶ Removing and installing wheels

▶ Working on hubs

▶ Truing a wheel and working on spokes

....

You can't think about caring for your bike without making the wheels a big part of the plan. Wheels that spin straight, round, true, and smooth, on properly inflated tires, greatly contribute to the comfort of a bike ride. Wheels that run rough on tires inflated to the wrong level can, at the very least, take the fun out of a ride and, at worst, be downright dangerous.

In this chapter, we fill you in on the basics of maintaining and repairing the wheels of your bike. Here, you find out how to inspect your wheels to make sure they're in good working order. If your wheels aren't working properly, we give you steps to take to repair them, including overhauling the hubs and truing the spokes.

The Spin on Wheels

If wheels are made of quality material, are built with properly tensioned spokes, and use tires inflated to the correct pounds per square inch (PSI), they should last a long time and not need repair or service other than keeping the hubs lubrications and in good working condition.

In this section, we fill you in on how to care for your wheels, keep them in good working order, and handle problems if they arise. We also give you the skinny on shopping for new wheels, in case you need to replace one.

Shopping for new wheels

Wheels are measured according to their diameter and width. If you're shopping for wheels, you might see a number like 700C x 19. The first number is the diameter of the wheel in millimeters; the second is the width.

Sometimes manufacturers uses the English-American standard and list the numbers in inches (for example, 26 x 1.9). In other cases, manufacturers write one number in inches and the other in millimeters (for example, 26 x 19).

Knowing the size of a wheel is important because not all wheels will fit a bike and not all tires will fit a wheel. The diameter determines what wheel will work with your bike. The forks on a bike are designed to use wheels of a certain size. If the diameter is too large, the wheel won't fit on the bike. If the diameter is too small, the brakes won't align properly with the rim.

The width impacts the tires you can use. Wider rims are usually found on mountain bikes, which use thick tires with heavier tread. Narrower rims are found on road bikes, which use thin tires.

Another consideration when buying wheels for your bike is the width of the hubs — the distance as measured between the two locknuts. It should match up with the distance between the dropouts in the forks and the rear frame dropouts.

Many quick-release hubs are thicker than their nutted, solid-axle counterparts. If your bike is designed with traditional hub nuts, be sure to test new wheels if they use a quick-release axle — otherwise, you may find that they don't fit.

Other than size, another consideration when purchasing a wheel is whether it supports a clincher tire or tubular tire:

- **Clincher tires** are what you find on most bikes today. A clincher combines a tire (which is secured on the rim by two *beads,* or outer edges, that tuck or clinch inside the rim) and an inner tube (which is enclosed by the tire). To protect the tube from the spoke holes, rim tape or some sort of material is used to line the inside of the rim next to the tube.

- **Tubular tires** are found mostly on racing bikes. They consist of a tire material that is sewn together and then attached to the rim with adhesive. If you have a flat, changing a tubular tire is more work, but tubular tires are safer than clinchers if your flat occurs when you're riding at a high speed, because they're less likely to come off the rim while you're riding.

Some downhill mountain bikes are starting to use a new style of rim and tire combination that doesn't use tubes. These are more durable and hold up better to the extreme conditions of mountain biking, but they aren't ideal for every rider because they're very expensive and hard to work with.

Caring for your wheels

In order to maintain proper braking, you should keep your wheels clean and grease-free. Regular washings with soap and water will keep grime from building up. If you have trouble removing residue, try using a solvent and a Brillo pad to clean the rims. Use rubbing alcohol to finish the cleaning and remove all solvents and residue off the sides of the rims.

Make sure you keep the solvent away from the tire — solvent will cause the tire to deteriorate.

Another aspect of care for your wheels is keeping the hubs properly lubricated. At least once a year, overhaul the hubs. Most hubs today have rubber seals that keep a lot of contaminants out of the bearings. If your hubs don't have rubber seals or you're riding in dusty, rainy, or muddy conditions, you'll need to overhaul your hubs and replace the grease more often.

You can do a number of things to extend the life of your wheels and keep them in good working order:

✔ **Properly inflate your tires.** Tires act as the primary suspension for a bike. They cushion the wheel from blows and grip the road as you ride. The most important thing you can do to protect your rims is to keep your tires inflated to the psi indicated on the side of the tires. The number-one cause of damaged rims is under-inflated tires. Keep your tires at the right pressure and, when you hit the next pothole or rock in the road, you'll have a good chance of your wheel surviving it intact. Plus, you'll have the added benefit of not having to expend as much energy to pedal when your bicycle has properly inflated tires.

✔ **Make sure your spokes are properly tensioned.** Wheels with spokes that are tensioned too loosely will have a shorter lifespan and could be dangerous. Loose spokes flex more than tense spokes do, so they fatigue more and are more likely to break. If several spokes give out, the wheel could collapse while you're riding. A wheel with loose spokes will also flex and wobble, causing reduced steering control. At the same time, the answer to loose spokes is not to randomly or overtighten them. A wheel with spokes that over-tensioned can be dangerous as well. A wheel has a high risk of bending like a pretzel with under- or over-tensioned spokes.

You want a wheel with spokes that are tight enough that they don't work their way loose while you ride. Frequently pluck the spokes of your wheel. Spokes of the same tension will make a similar sound, allowing you to quickly identify which ones are loose.

✔ **Make sure you have the right wheels.** Just as important as inflating your tires and properly tensioning your spokes is to pair the right wheels and tires with the type of bike and style of riding you engage in. For example, if you're going off-road, you should have mountain-bike wheels and tires, which are designed to absorb the impact of riding on a trail and other rough surfaces. For touring, you'll want wheels with a greater number of spokes in order to support the weight of loaded pannier bags.

Talk to the staff at your local bike shop and let them know what kind of riding you're planning on doing. They can match you up with the right wheels.

Many riders keep an extra pair of wheels in their garage for specific purposes. If they're hitting the trail, they can take off and exchange their road wheels for a mountain-bike pair.

Wheel sets are one of the best ways to upgrade your bike. If you have a racing bike, new lightweight wheels with fewer spokes can greatly improve performance. If you're starting to tour, some road riders convert to 650B wheels in order to use wider, touring-type tires.

✔ **Take care when you ride.** The way you ride can have a significant impact on the life of your tires. Avoid making contact with objects in the road as much as possible. If you need to cross a curb, think about getting off your bike and lifting it over the curb. If you do have to impact something with your tires, lift yourself off the seat, bend your knees and elbows, and, using your legs and arms as shock absorbers, let your bike rise up over the object.

Inspecting the wheels for problems

Wheels are an amazing work of design. They require spokes that are properly calibrated in order to spin straight and smoothly. If any of the spokes are improperly tensioned, your wheel could come out of alignment or become unstable. Before you ride, take a moment to do a few checks to inspect your wheels:

✔ **Give the wheel a spin — it should continue to rotate smoothly for a period of time.** It's normal for the rear wheel to not spin as long as the front because of the drag of the cassette/freewheel. You shouldn't hear any noises other than the rear cassette/freewheel.

✔ **Grab the wheel with one hand and the frame with the other, and try moving the wheel from side to side.** If it moves side to side, the hubs may be loose and in need of adjustment or overhaul. (See the "Overhauling the hubs" and "Adjusting a hub" sections, later in this chapter.)

✔ **Spin the wheel and keep your eye fixated on the brake; watch the rim as it passes by.** If it is not perfectly centered, it may need to be trued. (See the "Truing a wheel" section, later in this chapter.)

✔ **Pluck the spokes of the wheel and listen to the sounds they make.**
They should make a similar sound if they have the same tension. If one
feels loose or makes a unique sound, it may need to be tightened.

✔ **Check the PSI in both tires with an air pressure gauge.** Don't go by the
feel of your tires — take the time to test them with a pressure gauge.

✔ **Inspect the tread depth and condition of the tires sidewalls, looking
for dry rot, deformities, or slices from road debris.**

Often, tire sidewalls start to corrode or oxidize, vastly reducing their integrity
and lifespan. Consider occasionally applying Armor All or similar vinyl/rubber
protection to the sidewalls using a clean rag.

Taking off a wheel

Before you can remove a wheel, you need to loosen the brakes. Brakes are
designed to grip the rims, which are narrower than the tires, so their position
prevents the wheel from being removed.

Most brakes are designed with a mechanism to allow for a quick release of
the cable that holds the brake adjustment in place. The way in which you'll
detach the cable may vary depending on what type of brakes your bike has.
On some brakes, such as cantilevers, you pull the end of the cable out of the
brake arm.

In most cases, you need to pinch the brakes together to create slack in the
cable, enabling you to lift the end of the cable out of the brake arm. After you
remove the cable and release the brakes, the brakes will spring open. Here's
how to do this for the two main types of brakes:

✔ **If you have V brakes,** you'll need to pull back on the rubber boot of an
L-shaped piece to expose the cable. Pull the cable out of the narrow slot
in the cable holder and release it to open the brakes.

✔ **If you have side-pull brakes,** there will be a small lever on the brake
where the cable is attached. Move the lever to the open position and the
brakes will spread apart. In some cases, there may be a button instead of
a lever; if you have a button, push it to release the tension on the brakes.

Some bikes have the quick-release mechanism built into the brake lever. If you
can't find it on the brakes, look here.

If you can't figure out how to release the brakes, you can always let the air
out of the tires. Sometimes this will provide enough clearance between the
brakes to remove the tires.

After you've released the brakes, follow these steps to remove the front wheel (start with the front wheel — it's the easier of the two):

✔ **If your wheel uses hub nuts or bolts,** use a wrench to loosen the axle (as shown in Figure 7-1). Start with one nut, loosen it slightly, and move to the other nut, switching back and forth until you can free the wheel.

Figure 7-1:
Removing a
wheel with
bolts.

Avoid loosening one side all at once because this could lead to problems with the bike's hub bearings. Alternatively, if you have two wrenches, you can undo both nuts at the same time.

✔ **In place of bolts, many bikes these days are manufactured with a quick release which are loosened by opening the lever on the side of the wheel hub. If your wheel has a quick release, open the lever.** When you release the lever the axle may loosen enough to remove the front wheel. If it doesn't, hold the nut opposite the lever with one hand and rotate the lever a few times to loosen it (as shown in Figure 7-2). The quick-release skewer is shown in Figure 7-3.

Modern bikes are designed with a safety retention device built into the dropout which holds the wheel in place even when the quick-release lever is loosened. There are many different designs, so inspect yours and/or refer to your owner's manual. In order to release the wheel, you have to lift and maneuver the wheel off the dropouts of the frame.

Figure 7-2:
Removing
a quick-
release
wheel.

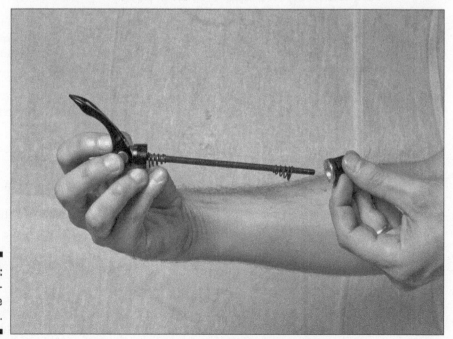

Figure 7-3:
The quick-
release
skewer.

Unlike the front wheel, which drops off as soon as the axle is loosened, the rear wheel requires another step or two to remove it because of the chain and derailleur being attached to it. Here's how to remove the rear wheel:

1. **Shift to the smallest cog on the rear, making the chain more slack.**

2. **Loosen the nuts or the quick release for the rear wheel in the same manner as you did for the front.**

3. **To remove the wheel, you may have to give it a slight blow to knock it loose from the frame.**

4. **When it comes loose, move the wheel away from the derailleur (forward and down) to let the chain fall off.**

Don't be afraid of the rear wheel. The chain and rear derailleur stay on the bicycle and, by removing the rear wheel, you won't effect any of the gear adjustments. In some cases, you may have to use your hand to lift the chain off the cogs or pull back the derailleur from the wheel in order to slack the chain from the cogs.

Repairing dents in the rim

Even if you keep your tires properly inflated and try to avoid obstacles in the road, at some point, if you ride enough miles, you're bound to hit something that will cause a dent in the rim. If this happens to you, don't despair. You don't necessarily have to replace the wheel. Try these steps:

✔ Use an adjustable wrench on the lip of the rim as a lever. Work little by little on the dent, being careful not to bend the rim too much in the other direction.

✔ Put the rim into a vise. Tightening the vise sometimes will squeeze the dent out of the rim.

✔ In the case of a dent on both sides of the rim, try laying the rim on a flat surface like a block of wood. Using a mallet, try flattening out one dent with a sharp blow. Turn the rim over and do the same to the other side.

Installing the front and rear wheels

Installing the front and rear wheels is a fairly simple process but one that should not be taken lightly. The wheels must sit firmly in the frame's front and rear dropouts. If you have anything less than a tight fit, you could be risking the chance of a wheel coming loose, something that would be potentially disastrous if you were biking. Follow these steps and you'll be in good shape:

1. **Make sure that the brakes are open and there is room for the wheel to pass.**

2. **For the front wheel, align the hub with the dropouts in the fork and slide the wheel into place.**

   - *If you have a quick-release hub,* you may need to adjust the nut on the opposite side of the wheel before the quick-release lever can be closed. Be sure not to use the lever to crank the quick release to a tight position. Instead, turn the nut opposite the lever until it's almost tight and then close the quick-release lever.

     When you close the quick-release lever, the lever part should be loose in the open position, start to snug when sticking straight out away from the frame, and tighten fully when closed. It should require enough force that it leaves an indentation on your hand. Any looser and it may not be secure.

   - *For traditional hubs with nuts,* begin by tightening the axle nuts, alternating side to side a little at a time until both are securely in place.

3. **For the rear wheel, start by making sure the right hand shifter is placed into the highest gear.**

   Hold the rear derailleur from the metal tab at the bottom pulley in order to open up the chain into a large loop. Make sure the rear cassette goes into the middle of this loop as you install it.

4. **Maneuver the wheel into place so that the top part of the chain just above the derailleur falls onto the smallest sprocket.**

5. **With the chain sitting on the smallest cog, which is the cog it was on when you removed the wheel sprocket, slide the wheel into place into the rear dropout part of the frame.**

6. **Use the same procedures as you did for the front wheel to fasten the quick release or the axle nuts.**

Hubba-Hubba: Working on the Hubs

Hubs have to hold up under significant pressure and, over time, water, dirt, and grime work their way into the bearings and can cause this pressure to wear them out. The best solution for keeping them in good working order is to perform an overhaul of the hubs at least once a year as part of your annual service — more often if you ride a lot or in wet or muddy conditions.

Hubs are designed to allow the wheel to effortlessly spin around an axle. Bearings inside the hub reduce friction as the axle rotates. If you hear a grinding sound or the wheel doesn't rotate smoothly, it may mean that the hub is too tight and should be adjusted or that an overhaul is in order. If you can wiggle the axle back and forth, this may mean that the hub is too loose.

There are two main styles of hubs:

- **Cup-and-cone (see Figure 7-4):** In the cup-and-cone style, loose ball bearings sit in smooth cup and are held in place by a cone. The cone and cup together create a *race,* in which the bearings can move around the axle in a circle with minimal friction. Washers are used to properly space the cone and cup and a locknut holds everything in place on the axle.

- **Sealed bearing:** The sealed-bearing hub is popular on many midrange to high-end bikes. This style of hub also has a an axle, bearings, race, and cone, but they're assembled as a unit and sealed when they're manufactured to improve their ability to keep water and dirt away from the bearings. Some sealed-bearing hubs can be serviced; others need to be replaced when they give out. The good thing is that they last much longer than cup-and-cone hubs.

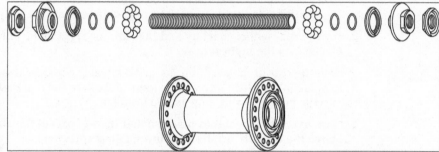

Figure 7-4:
A cup-and-cone hub.

Don't be fooled by the label *sealed mechanism.* These are standard cup-and-cone-style bearings, except they have a rubber seal to help keep contaminates out. They aren't true sealed bearings.

Overhauling the hubs

Well-functioning hubs are critical for smooth spinning wheels and a comfortable ride. To keep your hubs in the best possible shape, plan on overhauling the hubs at least once a year. If you're lucky enough to have sealed-bearing hubs you're off the hook; most of these will last many years without any service. If you have cup and cone hubs, follow these steps:

1. **If you have a quick-release skewer, remove it from the wheel. If there are nuts on the hub remove them with a wrench, alternating side to side as you loosen.**

2. **Using a cone wrench and a second standard wrench, make sure the cone and locknut are tight against each other on one side of the hub.**

3. **On the other side of the hub, using a cone wrench, secure the cone in place while you loosen the locknut in a counterclockwise direction on the same side of the hub (see Figure 7-5).**

   It will usually require some force to initiate movement in the locknut. If you're working on a hub with a freewheel, remove the freewheel (see Chapter 11 for instructions). If you have a cassette hub, work on the side opposite the cassette.

4. **Remove the locknut, washers, and cone from the axle, keeping them in order as you remove them.**

5. **Hold a towel or cup under the hub as you pull out the axle, because some bearings may fall out.**

   Figure 7-6 illustrates the removal of an axle.

   Leave the cone, washers, and locknut in place on the other side of the axle. This will make reassembly easier.

6. **Using a screwdriver, remove the bearings from both sides of the hub (see Figure 7-7).**

   A magnetic screwdriver makes bearing retrieval easier, although a screwdriver tipped with grease will work. Another trick is to push them down through the center of the hub and out the other side.

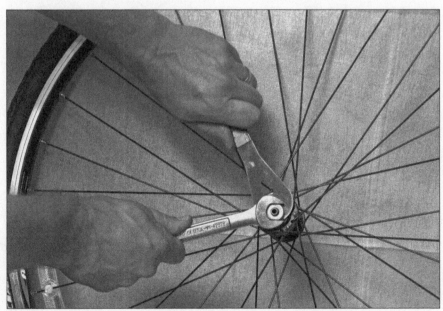

Figure 7-5:
Undoing the
locknut.

Figure 7-6:
Removing
the axle.

Figure 7-7:
Removing
the bear-
ings.

Count the bearings in the hub. Some hubs are designed for ten bearings in the front and nine in the back. Because you'll probably want to replace the bearings with new ones (they're cheap), you'll want to know how many to purchase (and how many to use for reassembly).

7. **After the bearings are removed, wipe the inside of the hub shell with a cloth and then use a degreaser to clean the cups.**

   Examine the cups for wear. If they have dents in the surface, you may need to replace the entire hub.

8. **Clean the axle, nuts, and cones by removing dirt and grime from the threads.**

   Examine them for signs of wear and tear. If you roll the axle across a flat surface and it wobbles, it may be bent and need replacing.

9. **Wipe down the dust seals with a cloth.**

   If they're especially dirty, you can pop them off using a screwdriver for leverage.

10. **After cleaning all parts, allow them to dry thoroughly before reassembly.**

Reassembling the hubs

When you're all done overhauling the hubs, it's time to reassemble them. To reassemble the hubs, follow these steps:

1. **If you removed the dust seals, press them back into place.**

2. **Apply a fresh layer of grease to each of the cups (as shown in Figure 7-8).**

   The general rule is to use enough grease so that a bearing will be covered halfway when placed in the cup.

3. **Using tweezers or pliers, place half the bearings in one cup, spreading them out evenly across the cup (as shown in Figure 7-9).**

   The bearings should be held in place temporarily by the grease. Make sure there is at least a 1mm gap between all the bearings placed in the cup. If the bearings are too tight, remove one, so that each bearing has a few microns of elbow room.

4. **Grease the axle and slide it halfway into the hub to hold the bearings in place while you fill the other cone with bearings.**

   Make sure that no bearings fall out during this procedure.

Figure 7-8:
Filling cups
with new
grease.

Figure 7-9:
Inserting the
bearings.

5. **While you're holding the axle with one hand, place the other half of the bearings into the other cup.**

   After you've finished with all the bearings, slide the axle the rest of the way through.

6. **Thread the cone onto the axle until it begins to press against the bearings in a secure fashion.**

   Twist the axle to ensure that the bearings are snug and in place.

7. **Slide the washers and any spacers on in the axle in the correct order.**

8. **Thread the locknut onto the axle by hand (as shown in Figure 7-10) and, after it tightens, use a wrench to tighten it further while holding the cone in place with a cone wrench.**

   You don't want to tighten the cone, because it could press forcefully against the bearings and damage them.

   When tightening the locknut, leave a slight amount of play in the axle so that it can accept the additional force from the tightening of the quick-release lever.

9. **Adjust the tightness of the hubs by following the procedure in the next section.**

   Figure 7-11 shows an example of tightening the cones in the hub.

Figure 7-10:
Attaching
the locknut.

Figure 7-11:
Tightening
the cones.

Adjusting a hub

The cones on a hub cannot be too loose or too tight — they need to be just right. What does that mean exactly? The tightness should be such that there is little to no play in the hub, but the axle rotates freely. If you have trouble finding the right point between too loose and too tight, err on the side of being slightly loose.

To adjust the tightness of a hub, you need a wrench for the axle locknuts and a cone wrench to fit the cone. To tighten the hub, hold the cone in place with the cone wrench and tighten the locknut with your other wrench. Only the locknut should move; if the cone is moving, it could press against the bearings and damage them. To loosen the hub, loosen the locknut.

If only a small adjustment is needed in the hub, you can adjust the locknut and cone on just one side of the bike.

Whenever you adjust the hubs of a wheel that uses quick releases, leave the cones just a little loose. Tightening the quick release will apply extra pressure to the bearings and take that little wiggle out when clamped in the frame. Be sure to check the adjustment once the wheel is clamped into the bike.

1 Spoke Too Soon: Working on the Spokes

Wheels are an amazing feat of engineering — a handful of thin spokes woven together to provide enough structural integrity to support the weight of a rider going across various types of surfaces. To accomplish this feat, the spokes must be laced to the wheel in just the right pattern and tensioned evenly across the wheel. This aspect makes working on spokes a slightly complicated affair for a beginner. But with some practice, you can master some basic techniques — and that's what this section is about.

Replacing a spoke

Replacing a spoke is manageable and a good place to get started. If you do end up needing to replace a broken spoke, take it with you to your bike store so that you can replace it with another spoke of the same size and width.

 Keep in mind that the spokes on your wheels are probably of different sizes. In many cases, front-wheel spokes are not the same length as rear-wheel spokes. The same is likely true for spokes on the right side of the wheel hub versus the left side.

Here's how to replace a spoke:

1. **Insert the new spoke into the spoke hole from the broken spoke you removed from the hub.**

   You may need to remove the wheel from the bike to perform this procedure (see "Taking off a wheel," earlier in this chapter).

2. **Weave the spoke through the other spokes, following the same pattern, crossing and interweaving the same number of spokes as the others.**

3. **If the old *nipple* (the nut part that the spoke threads into) is undamaged and still in place, thread the end of the new spoke into it.**

   If the nipple is damaged, you'll need to remove the tire, tube, and rim tape to replace the damaged nipple with a new one.

4. **So that you don't lose track of the spoke, mark it with a piece of tape or string.**

5. **Using a spoke wrench, tighten the spoke to the same tension as the other spokes.**

6. **To finish the procedure, true the rest of the wheel (see the following section).**

Truing a wheel

Although wheel truing is an activity that takes time and practice to master, some basic wheel truing is possible for the casual biker. If you have a wheel that's so out of true that it needs to be rebuilt, you probably should leave the job to your local bike shop. But if the wheel just has a slight wobble and needs a little tweaking, you may want to consider doing it yourself.

If the rim is bent, simple truing won't suffice — the rim will have to be repaired.

Here are the steps for truing a wheel when there are only minor imperfections in the wheel:

1. **Remove the tire, tube, and rim strip from the rim.**

   For some truing stands, you can leave the tire, tube, and rim strip on the rim, although we find that we get the best results when working only with the rim.

2. **Secure the wheel in a truing stand (as shown in Figure 7-12) if you have one; otherwise, you can keep the wheel on the bike.**

   If you have to true the wheel while it's attached to the bike, use a bike stand to support the bike. Other options are to hang the bike from the ceiling or to turn the bike upside down on its handlebars.

Figure 7-12:
Using a
truing stand

3. **Before you begin spinning the wheel, check it for loose or damaged spokes (as shown in Figure 7-13).**

4. **Make sure the wheel rim is ¹/₄ inch away from the calipers in the truing stand or the brakes on the bike.**

5. **Give the wheel a gentle spin and keep your eye on the calipers (or brakes).**

   You'll be able to identify wobbles in the rim by where the wheel comes close to or comes in contact with the brakes.

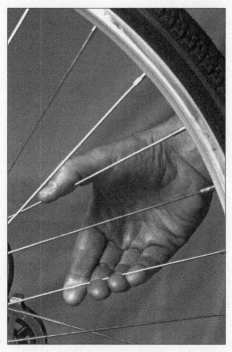

Figure 7-13:
Feeling for
loose areas.

6. **If the rim comes in contact on one side, use a spoke wrench to tighten the nipples of the spokes that come from the opposite hub and loosen those that come from the hub on the same side.**

   Loosen and tighten in small increments, around a quarter of a turn each time. Start in the middle of each wobble and work your way outwards from the center. Decrease the amount for each turn the farther away you move from the center. (Figure 7-14 demonstrates using a spoke wrench.)

   Spoke nipples come in various sizes. Be sure to check the size of your spokes before you buy a spoke wrench.

Figure 7-14:
Using a
spoke
wrench.

To tighten a spoke at the bottom of the wheel, turn the nipple in a counterclockwise direction. When the spoke is at the top of the wheel, the change of position makes it appear as if it's in a clockwise direction.

7. After the wobble has been reduced, you can tighten the calipers to find any smaller wobbles.

As the wobbles become smaller, reduce the amount by which you turn the spoke wrench.

Don't worry about eliminating all the wobble of a rim. It's more important to have evenly tensioned spokes than to have a rim without a wobble.

If you can't get the rim perfectly straight, loosen and adjust your brakes to make them farther away from the rim so they don't rub. If these brakes are no longer satisfactorily strong, however, you may need to replace the rim/wheel.

Chapter 8

Stopping Short: The Brakes

In This Chapter

▶ Identifying the different types of brakes

▶ Removing and installing brakes and brake pads

▶ Adjusting your brakes

▶ Addressing brake issues

*W*hen Dennis was a kid, one of his bikes had a braking system that required him to use his foot to stop the pedals and cranks from rotating forward in order to come to a halt. The advantage of this design was that he could look cool by skidding out when he needed to stop the bike.

Somewhere between then and now, skidding out has lost its appeal, and odds are, you're less concerned with impressing your friends than you are with stopping safely. Fortunately, today's bikes have braking systems that can consistently stop the momentum of the bike and the rider's weight with little more than a firm squeeze of the brake levers.

Although brakes designs have evolved to be highly reliable when it comes to stopping a bike, this doesn't mean that you should take them for granted. Proper maintenance and inspection of your brakes will increase the chances that, if you round that next turn too fast or if someone backs his car out in front of you without looking, you won't have to make one giant skid mark.

We start this chapter with a quick overview of the different types of brakes on the market today. Then we narrow our discussion, focusing on the most popular type of brakes — rim brakes — and the various styles of rim brakes. We tell you how to remove and install brakes and brake pads, make adjustments to your brakes, and address common braking issues.

Types of Brakes

There are three major categories of braking systems on modern bikes:

- ✔ **Rim brakes:** When you squeeze the brake levers of rim brakes, the brake cables pull on one or both brake arms, which causes the rubber brake pads to come in contact with the wheel rims and slow the bike down. The benefits of rim brakes are that they're cheap and relatively easy to maintain, and they have a lot of stopping force. The drawback is that they don't work well in wet or muddy conditions and they can wear out quickly.

  The three popular models of rim brakes are:

  - **Cantilever brakes:** Cantilever brakes (see Figure 8-1) have short, L-shaped brake arms that bolt to the frame and are connected by a straddle cable, which looks like an upside-down Y. They're mounted on two pivots, one on each side of the wheel. The pivots (bosses) are set close to the wheel, which increases their mechanical advantage. Cantilever brakes have very good braking power. They're commonly found on road bikes, mountain bikes, and touring bikes.

  - **V-brakes:** V-brakes (see Figure 8-2) are sometimes referred to as linear-pull or direct-pull brakes. The brake arms are at nearly a 90-degree angle to the brake pads. V-brakes are mounted on two pivots on the frame, one on each side of the wheel. The longer arms give V-brakes improved leverage and greater stopping power. They're commonly found on mountain bikes and hybrid bikes.

  - **Center-mount brakes:** With center-mount brakes (see Figure 8-3), the brake cable attaches to one of the brake arms. The brake arms are together as one unit and mounted to a single pivot, which sits above the wheel. (In the double-pivot variety, there are two pivots — one on each side of the wheel — but still only one center mounting bolt.) The brake pads are at the bottom of the arms. Center-mount brakes don't provide as much power as V-brakes or cantilevers. They're commonly found on road bikes and lower-price bikes.

- ✔ **Disk brakes:** Squeezing the brake levers on disc brakes (see Figure 8-4) causes the brake pads to squeeze against a metal disc that surrounds the hub. There are two main types of disc brakes — mechanical and hydraulic. Mechanical disc brakes utilize a cable to actuate the brake pads, whereas hydraulic brakes use a brake fluid pushed down by a piston through a brake line to generate braking power. Both types work well in both dry and wet conditions, and they're quite responsive, requiring less effort from the hand when breaking. The advantage of disk brakes is they don't heat up the rim on long descents, causing the tire pressure to increase and possibly blow out. Also, they don't wear out the sidewall of a thin and lightweight alloy rim. The disadvantage of disk brakes is that they're usually heavier, cost more, and require a hub that can accept a disk. Disk brakes are commonly found on mountain bikes.

✔ **Hub brakes:** Sometimes called drum brakes, hub brakes are similar to disk brakes except the brake pads are pushed outward against the inside of a cylindrical drum inside the hub. The fact that they're on the inside of the hub means they aren't affected by wet, muddy, or dusty conditions. However, they are the heaviest of all the brakes. They're found on some tandem bikes.

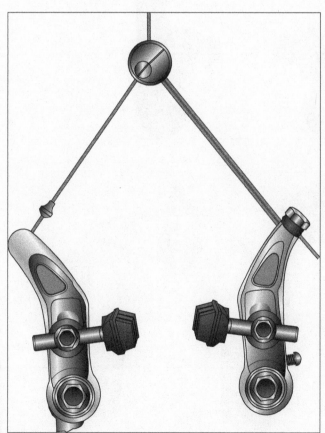

Figure 8-1:
Cantilever
brakes.

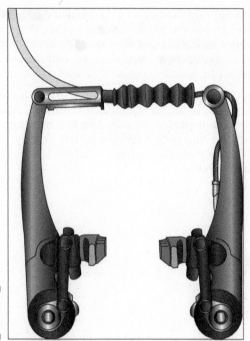

Figure 8-2:
V-brakes.

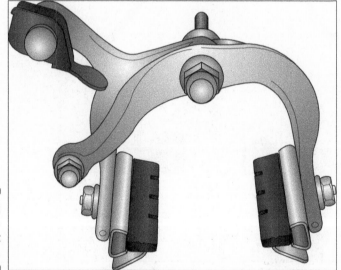

Figure 8-3:
Center-
mount
brakes.

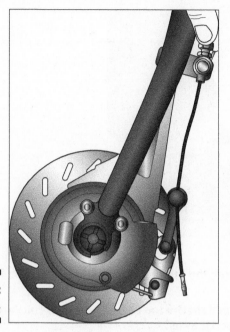

Figure 8-4:
Disk brakes.

Inspecting the Brakes

To ensure that your brakes are in good working order before you set off on your next ride, follow these steps to inspect them:

1. **Examine the brake pads for excessive wear.**

   If they're worn down such that the grooves in the pads are not visible, they should be replaced.

   You may notice uneven wearing of the brake pads, which is usually caused by improperly fitted brake pads that aren't parallel and contact the rim unevenly. When this happens, a curved ridge forms in the brake pad, which sometimes can cause the brake to grab the rim and get stuck.

   The solution for uneven wear on brake pads is to use a utility knife to cut off the ridge and flatten the pad (see Figure 8-5). Another option is to use sandpaper or a file to smooth it out. This is also a good time to adjust the brakes so that they don't continue to wear unevenly (see "Adjusting Brakes," later in this chapter).

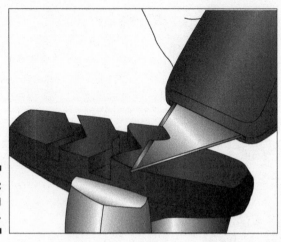

Figure 8-5:
Resurfacing
brake pads.

2. **While you're examining the brake pads, make sure they're about 1mm to 2mm from the rim.**

   They might rub the rim if they're too close or not give you enough braking power if they're too far away.

3. **Squeeze the brake lever and confirm that the brakes grab the rim firmly and parallel to the rim.**

4. **Examine the cable to make sure it's firmly attached to the brakes and is not kinked, frayed, or worn in any spot.**

5. **Check the rims to make sure they aren't dirty.**

   If they are dirty, use a rag and a solvent like rubbing alcohol to clean them.

6. **If you just finished working on the brakes, give them a test drive while biking at a slow speed.**

Removing and Installing Brakes and Brake Pads

If you ride your bike regularly, you'll eventually have to change your brake pads. In this section, we tell you how to change brake pads and how to remove and install brakes (in case you need to overhaul or completely replace them).

Removing brakes and brake pads

The procedures for removing V-brakes and cantilever brakes are the same. Here are the steps to follow:

1. **Pinch the brakes together and lift the end of the cable up and out of the quick release in the brake arm where the cable sits (as shown in Figure 8-6).**

Figure 8-6:
Undoing
the quick-
release.

2. **Undo the bolt that holds the brake onto the pivot (as shown in Figure 8-7).**

   Be careful as you loosen the bolt, because the spring may cause the brake arms to snap back or parts such as washers to shoot off the brake.

3. **Pull the brake off the boss (as shown in Figure 8-8).**

4. **To remove the pad in cartridge-brake shoes, look for a small screw or pin holding the pad in place and remove it as shown in Figure 8-9.**

   Figure 8-10 shows how the pad slides off once the pin is removed. If there isn't one, use a screwdriver to pry the pad off.

Figure 8-7:
Loosening
the brake.

Figure 8-8:
Removing
the brake.

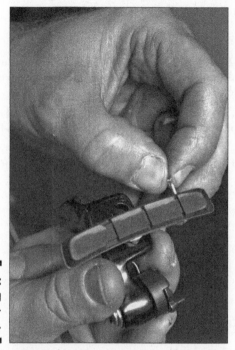

Figure 8-9:
Removing
the brake-
pad pin.

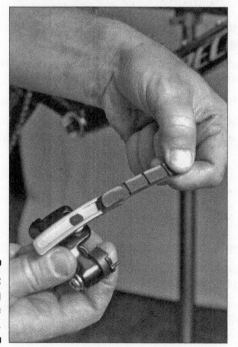

Figure 8-10:
Removing
the brake
pad.

Here's how to remove center-mount brakes:

1. **Loosen the cable anchor bolt and remove the cable.**

2. **Using an Allen wrench or a 10mm open hex wrench, loosen and remove the center bolt mounting nut on the back and remove the complete brake caliper.**

3. **To remove the pad in cartridge brake shoes, look for a small screw or pin holding the pad in place and remove it (refer to Figure 8-9).**

   Refer to Figure 8-10 to see how the pad slides off once the pin is removed. If there isn't one, use a screwdriver to pry the pad off.

Some bikes don't have cartridge brake shoes and have non-replaceable brakes pads. If your bike falls into this category, think about changing to replaceable pads, especially if you ride a lot and will go through pads relatively quickly. With the cartridge pads, you slip a new pad into the brakes and you don't have to readjust the alignment and angle of the brake shoes every time they're replaced.

Installing brakes

After you've reattached the brake pads, you're ready to reinstall the brakes. To install cantilever brakes, follow these steps:

1. **Apply a small amount of grease to the *bosses,* the frame post that the brake arms mount to.**

2. **Slide each brake arm onto a boss, inserting the small pin at the end of the brakes' coiled spring into the middle hole.**

3. **Insert the pivot bolt into the boss and tighten it with an Allen wrench.**

4. **Run the end of the cable through the cable clamp and, while squeezing the brakes against the rim with one hand, tighten the cable clamp bolt with the other.**

   Bike shops often use a fourth-hand tool to help tighten the brake cable (see Figure 8-11).

To install V-brakes, follow these steps:

1. **Apply a small amount of grease to the pivots.**

2. **Slide each brake onto a pivot, inserting the small pin at the end of the brakes' coiled spring into the middle hole.**

   The top hole will give that side of the brake more recoil tension and the lower hole will give that side less recoil tension. These are used if the fine-tuning spring adjustment is not enough (see "Adjusting Brakes," later in this chapter).

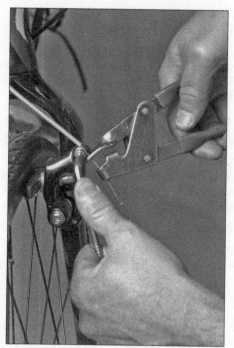

Figure 8-11:
Using a
fourth-hand
tool.

3. **Insert the pivot bolt into the boss and tighten with an Allen wrench.**

4. **Pass the cable wire through the metal curved tube (called the *noodle*) that comes with the brakes.**

5. **Insert the metal tube with cable wire into the slot in the cable holder until the tip is poking out through the other end and is firmly in place.**

6. **Insert the cable wire into the rubber sleeve and slide the sleeve onto the tip of the metal tube.**

7. **Run the end of the cable through the cable clamp and, while holding and squeezing the brakes against the rim with one hand, tighten the cable clamp bolt with the other.**

Bike shops often use a fourth-hand tool, which eliminates the need to hold the brakes together (refer to Figure 8-11).

To install center-mount brakes, follow these steps:

1. **Examine and make note of the spacers and washers on the front and rear center mounting bolts.**

Sometimes they have moon-shaped spacers that need to go next to the front and/or back part of the frame or fork. Other times, they use a recessed mounting nut with the lock washer on the side closest to the brake caliper, or just a standard nut with the lock washer on the back side next to the nut. The front brake will usually have the longer center mounting bolt.

2. **Remove the nut, spacers, and washers that will be on the inside of the frame or fork, and insert the center mounting bolt through the hole either in the fork or the rear brake bridge.**

3. **Install the remaining spacers and washer.**

4. **While holding the brakes so that they're centered over the rim, tighten with the nut.**

5. **Run the end of the cable through the cable housing stop, and then through the cable clamp and, while squeezing the brakes against the rim with one hand, tighten the cable clamp bolt with the other hand.**

6. **Set your pads and make your final adjustments (see "Adjusting Brakes," next).**

7. **Trim the excess cable to about 2 inches, and put a cable end cap on it so it doesn't fray.**

Adjusting Brakes

Adjusting your brakes is important to ensure that you can slow down or come to a stop quickly and effortlessly each time you squeeze the brake levers. In this section, we tell you how to adjust your brakes in order to maximize their effectiveness.

Sometimes brakes are a little temperamental when it comes to adjustments. Just have a little patience and try not to get temperamental *yourself* when it takes several tries to get the position just right. With a little practice, you'll be able to do it in a snap.

Adjusting brake-pad position

In order for your brakes to grab the rim of your bike's wheel firmly, they need to be in the proper position. Follow these steps to adjust your brakes' position:

1. **Hold the brake pad with one hand and undo the nut or bolt holding the brake shoe one or two turns to loosen it just slightly (see Figure 8-12).**

2. **Squeeze one of the brake levers so that the pad is pressed up against the rim.**

3. **While holding the lever with one hand, position the pad so that it lines up parallel with the rim. Also adjust the pad so that the front part of the pad is closer to the rim than the back part.**

   This alignment of the brake pads is called *toe in.*

   Some brakes have concave and convex washers to help with the toe-in adjustments. Sometimes, with center-mount brakes, you need to put an adjustable wrench on the brake arm itself and bend it slightly to make the toe-in adjustment.

4. **Hold the pad in place and release the lever. As you're holding the pad, tighten the bolt to secure the pad in its current position.**

5. **Repeat steps 1 through 4 for the other brake pad.**

   When you're finished, the front part of the brakes should be angled in slightly (toe in) such that that the end of the brake pads closest to the front of the bike is 1mm from the rim and the back part of the brakes pads are 2mm from the rim.

Figure 8-12:
Adjusting
the brake.

Centering and tensioning brakes

To ensure that your brakes operate as they were designed, you may need to make some adjustments to their position. These adjustments include centering the brakes so that the brake pads are aligned evenly with the rim. You may also have to adjust the tension so that the brakes remain within a millimeter or two from the rim and will grab the rim with the slightest grip of the brake lever.

There are a few general rules of thumb you can keep in mind when making adjustments:

- You shouldn't be able to "bottom out" the hand levers against the handlebars while fully clamping down on the brakes.
- Your brakes shouldn't rub the rims.
- You shouldn't be able to push the front or rear wheel and get it to move while the brakes are applied.
- The front and rear brakes should feel relatively even in brake lever tension.

Adjusting brake tension

With properly tensioned brakes, the brake pads should be positioned 1mm to 2mm from the rim and easily grab the rim when the brake lever is squeezed. To adjust the tension, you can do a few things:

- Some brakes have a small screw at the bottom of the brake arm, which allows for small adjustments to be made to the distance between the rim and the pads. Turning the screw clockwise will move the pad away from the rim; turning the screw counterclockwise will move the pad closer (see Figure 8-13).
- Another possibility is to adjust the barrel adjuster at the brake levers or at the brakes. Turn the adjuster one turn, and note the results adjusting for more or less tension.
- You can also try removing both of the brake arms and changing the frame mounting hole in which the spring pin is inserted. Reinstall the brake spring in the top or the highest of the three holes. Readjust the brake and check the results.
- If the fine-tuning of the screw, barrel adjuster, and spring pin is not enough to increase tension on the brakes, you'll have to loosen the cable bolt (which holds the cable in place), pull the cable tighter, and retighten the bolt. Special tools can facilitate this procedure including a third-hand tool (which holds the brakes together) and a fourth-hand tool (which pulls the cable tight). With four hands working for you, you can't go wrong!

Figure 8-13:
Adjusting
brake
tension.

Centering your brakes

In most cases, your brakes should be symmetrical and an equal distance
from the wheel rim. If one of the brake pads touches the rim before the other
or, even worse, rubs on the rim while you're riding, an adjustment to center
the brakes may be needed.

Before you center the brakes, make sure that:

- ✔ Your wheel is centered in the frame or fork.

- ✔ Your wheel is trued.

- ✔ Your wheel is spinning straight.

If your wheel isn't centered, true, and spinning straight, what may appear like
a brake being off-center may be the wheel wobbling toward one of the brakes.
(See Chapter 7 for how to make adjustments to your wheel.)

The procedures for centering brakes may vary slightly depending on what
type of brakes you have, but here are some strategies you may be able to try:

- ✔ If the brakes have a small screw, try adjusting it with a screwdriver or
  Allen wrench and note the result.

✔ In some cases, with center-mount brakes, you may need to rotate the entire brake caliper on the center mounting bolt to get the desired result. Try loosening the mounting bolt, rotating the brake, and then retightening it.

✔ The brakes may have different spring tensions. If so, try removing one of the brake arms and changing the frame mounting hole in which the spring pin is inserted. Reinstall the brake and check the results.

You want to have the adjusting barrels unthreaded (counterclockwise) one or two revolutions when you're finished with your brake adjustments. This allows you to thread them back in (clockwise) if your rim comes out of true on a ride so your brakes aren't rubbing and slowing you down.

To center dual-pivot brakes with a quick-release lever, you can adjust the brake tension using an Allen wrench or screwdriver. First, open the quick-release lever to remove tension on the cable (as shown in Figure 8-14). Then, using the Allen wrench or screwdriver, turn the adjuster clockwise or counterclockwise to make the space between the rim and the brake pads equal on both sides (see Figure 8-15). You can also make smaller, fine-tuning adjustments by turning the barrel adjuster (see Figure 8-16).

Figure 8-14:
Moving the lever on center-mount brakes

Figure 8-15:
Adjusting
center-
mount
brakes.

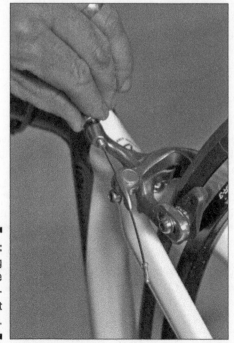

Figure 8-16:
Adjusting
the cable
on center-
mount
brakes.

Silencing those squeaking brakes!

Probably one of the biggest issues with brakes is squeaking. Coming to a stop with a loud screech that makes everyone look up at you is no fun — unless you use the screech in place of a bell or a horn. People will certainly get out of your way!

One of the biggest causes of squeaking is improperly positioned brake pads. If your brakes squeak, try adjusting the pads, as described in the "Adjusting brake-pad position" section, so that the front part is toed inward toward the rims (see Figure 8-17). Many types of brakes have spacers on the pad holder that can be adjusted to move the pad into the proper position. Loosen the mounting bolt and then use your hand to move the spacers and the pad. When you find the toe-in position, tighten the bolt.

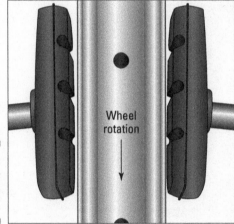

Figure 8-17:
Proper
brake
alignment.

Wheel
rotation

Another possible cause of squeaking is dirty or oily rims. If you haven't cleaned your rims in a while, use some rubbing alcohol and a rag, and wipe them down. To keep them clean going forward, wipe the rims with a damp rag each time you finish a ride.

In some cases, squeaking is caused by brake pads that have hardened over time. If your brakes are more than a few years old try replacing them to eliminate the noise.

Finally, inspect the brake pads for foreign debris. Something wedged into the rubber may be causing the squeal.

Using the brake quick release

Many brakes are designed with a quick-release capability that makes it easy to spread them apart when you need to remove the wheel. This quick release may also be used if you badly bend your wheel rim and the rim is rubbing the brake pads.

Riding with the quick release engaged will greatly reduce the effectiveness of your brakes.

The quick-release mechanism — which may be a button, a lever, or an easy way to detach the cable — differs depending on the type of brake:

- ✔ **For cantilever brakes,** squeeze the brake arms together with one hand to create slack in the cable and, with the other hand, lift the loose end of the cable out of its pocket. Release the breaks and they'll pop open.

- ✔ **For V-brakes,** pinch together the top of the brake arms to loosen the cable. Pull the rubber boot back to expose the cable (see Figure 8-18). Carefully pull the cable out of the narrow slot in the cable holder and release it to open the brakes (see Figure 8-19).

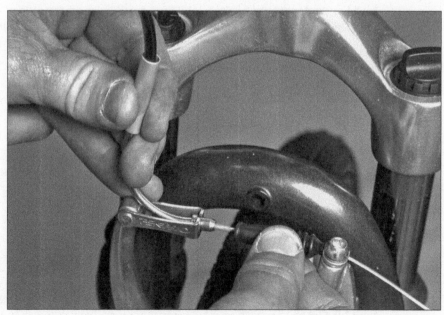

Figure 8-18:
Releasing
V-brakes.

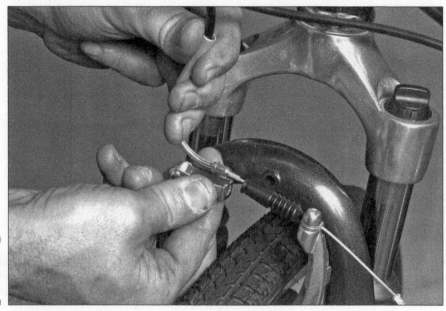

Figure 8-19:
V-brakes
released.

✔ **For center-mount brakes,** look for a small lever on the side of the caliper where the cable is attached (refer to Figure 8-14). Pull it upward and release the brakes just enough to allow the wheel to pass. In some models, you'll need to look for a button on the hand lever and push it to release the tension on the brakes.

If you can't find the release on your brakes, examine the brake levers. On some bikes, there is a quick-release button on the brake lever. Push it to increase the clearance between the brake pads.

If you're trying to remove the tire but you can't figure out how to open the brakes, try letting air out of the tire. This will reduce the width of the tire and may allow it to pass between the brake pads. After you put the wheel back in place, reinflate it.

Replacing brake cables

Brake cables are a critical component of your braking system. You can have new brake pads, but if your brake cables give out, you won't be able to stop your bike when you need to. Each time you give a hard squeeze to your brake levers, the cables must transfer that force to the brake pads. Over time, this force will wear out the cables, causing them to kink, fray, or bend. If you see these signs of wear with your brake cables, do the safe thing and change them immediately. Here's how:

1. **Unfasten the brake cable by loosening the nut or bolt where the cable attaches to the brake arm.**

2. **Squeeze the brake lever so that the nipple at the end of the cable is showing.**

3. **Grab the end of the cable with a pair of pliers and pull the cable slightly out from the brake lever.**

Before you remove the brake cable, take a moment to observe how it is routed around the frame of the bike. Pay attention to the location of the cable housing and where the cable housing meets the cable stops and the cable exits on the other side. You'll need to route the cable and cable housing in the same manner when you reinstall it. You want the housing to be as short as possible. The housing should have gradual curves with out any binding or sharp angles.

4. **Once you grab the cable, use your hands to remove the entire length of the cable (see Figure 8-20).**

5. **Collect any ferrules that were holding the cable housing in place at the anchor points.**

You'll use these when you reinstall the cable.

It's a good practice to change the cable housing when you replace cable wires. Manufacturers often sell cable with the housing included in the package. They normally give you more housing than you need so you'll have to cut it to fit your bike.

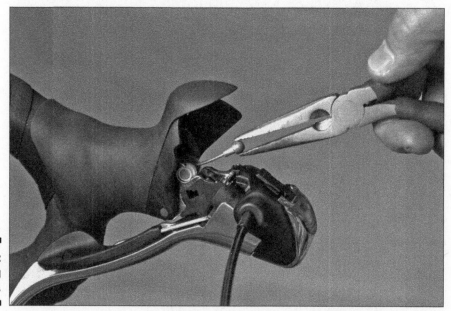

Figure 8-20:
Removing
the cable.

6. **Cut the cable housing with cable cutters (see Figure 8-21).**

   Cable cutters are useful because they cut the housing without compressing the end too much. Assuming the old housing was the proper length, use the older pieces of cable housing as guides for cutting the new pieces.

   Even if you use a cable cutter, you may need to file the end of the cable if it has any sharp edges. You may also need to open the end of the housing up with an awl or other pointed instrument if the end looks like the example on the left in Figure 8-22.

7. **When you're ready to install the new cable, use a rag to apply a light coating of grease to its surface.**

8. **Squeeze the brake lever and insert the cable into the hold from where you originally removed it (as shown in Figure 8-23).**

   You may have to wiggle it around to pass it through the brake lever. Pull the cable out the other side of the brake lever.

   Be cautious with the cable tip to prevent it fraying during the installation.

9. **Attach the ferrules that came with the cable housing to the ends of each piece of housing (as shown in Figure 8-24).**

10. **Insert the cable into the proper cable housing and pull it out the other end.**

Figure 8-21:
Cutting the cable housing.

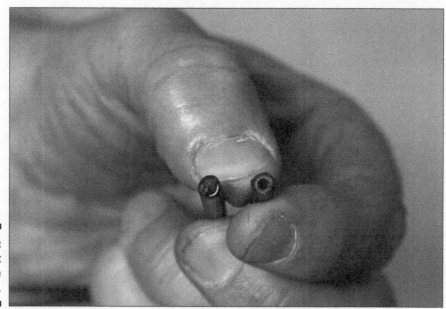

Figure 8-22:
Properly cut
cable
housing.

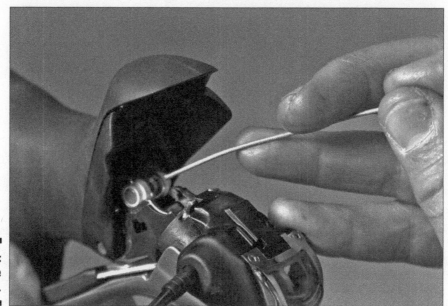

Figure 8-23:
Inserting the
cable.

11. **Route the cable and cable housing around the frame of the bike in the same position as it was previously.**

The ferrules at the end of the cable housing should fit snugly into the cable stops on the frame. In some cases, the ferrule will not fit in, so just remove it — the cable stop acts as built in ferrule at this location.

12. **While holding the brakes against the rim with one hand or a fourth-hand tool, tighten the cable anchor bolt.**

13. **Test the brakes by squeezing the brake lever as hard as you can three or four times.**

    This will stretch the brake cable and seat the ferrules. You may need to readjust the brake cable after this.

Figure 8-24:
A ferrule.

A brake cable may break on you at some point. If this happens, you can continue to ride, although you'll need to use more caution and give yourself greater stopping distance. The front brakes have much more braking power than the rear, so if you're lucky, your rear brakes will go out. This is why you have to replace your front brake pads more often than the rear. Just be careful that you don't apply them too quickly; otherwise, when your front wheel stops, the momentum from your body might send you flying over your handlebars.

If the front brake cable breaks on a long trip, replace it with the rear brake cable.

Chapter 9

Taking Your Seat:
Saddles and Seat Posts

. . . .

In This Chapter

▶ Looking at the different types of saddles

▶ Taking your saddle on and off your bike

▶ Improving your comfort by adjusting your saddle

▶ Using suspension seat posts

. . . .

*T*his chapter is devoted to your butt. In particular, it's devoted to making sure that your butt is not a source of frustration while you ride.

Your body has three points of contact with your bike and your saddle is the part of the bike where the majority of your weight is supported. If you don't have a saddle that suits your anatomy or that's properly adjusted, you can rest assured that your butt is going to be one big *pain* in the butt after your next long ride.

Every butt is unique. There isn't one style of saddle or one formula for adjusting the saddle that works for everyone. Finding a saddle that fits your anatomy and finding the position that's most comfortable both take time.

We start this chapter by covering the various types of saddles available. Then we tell you how to make adjustments to your saddle so you can find an enjoyable riding position.

Even if you find the saddle type and position that's perfect for you, it'll take some time to break in the saddle — and to break in your bum.

Saddle Up! Types of Saddles

No two butts are the same, and there is no such thing as a one-size-fits-all saddle. A wide variety of saddles are on the market — saddles made of different materials, designed for different functions, and tailored for men or women. In this section, we discuss a few of these differences so that you can find the saddle that's best for you.

Material

Bicycle saddles are typically covered with leather, plastic, or vinyl. The most popular saddles on the market today are the ones covered in plastic or vinyl. Underneath the plastic or vinyl covers, they're made of gels and high-density foams. These saddles vary in thickness and weight depending on the type of shell underneath. They don't require much maintenance, they're durable, and they resist water — all of which contributes to their popularity. (See Figure 9-8, later in this chapter, for an example of a vinyl-covered saddle.)

The less-popular leather saddles (such as the one shown in Figure 9-1) are built with a single piece of leather stretched across a steel frame. (Brooks is a well known leather saddle manufacturer.) People usually either love or hate leather saddles. Those who use them usually swear by them and wouldn't consider setting their tushes on anything else.

Figure 9-1:
Leather saddles aren't for everyone, but people who like them swear by them.

Leather saddles are very stiff, but they also provide the maximum support for sit bones without the padding that actually puts more pressure on soft tissue.

But the nice thing about leather is that it's moldable. A leather saddle may feel like a rock when you first buy it, but over time it'll begin to shape to the form of your body. Breaking in a leather saddle takes a little time, but when you're done, you'll have a seat form-fit to your butt.

Leather products such as conditioners, saddle soaps, and other compounds can speed this process. They also help protect and extend the life of your saddle.

When you ride with a leather saddle, take along a plastic bag in case it rains. You can use it protect the saddle from soaking up water and drying out. If the saddle does get wet, allow it to dry naturally.

The base or foundation of the saddle is arguably the important consideration. It doesn't matter how much or what type of padding there is on top, if the base is a piece of sheet metal, hard and stiff, or not the correct shape, you'll have a very uncomfortable ride. Make sure the base or foundation is flexible and the proper fit or style for your butt.

Function

Saddles are built for two main functions: cruising or racing.

Cruising saddles (see Figure 9-2) are wide, extra-cushioned saddles designed for casual riders who sit in the upright position. The extra padding helps support the extra weight on the seat that comes from sitting upright. Sometimes cruising saddles are cushioned with horizontal and/or vertical springs. Most people ride on cruising bikes for leisure, so the wide seat doesn't cause a problem with the restriction of leg movement as it would on a racing-style bicycle.

Racing saddles (see Figure 9-3) are specially designed to allow a full range of motion when pedaling. They're normally lightweight, thin (with little padding), and narrow. They're designed with grooves, channels, and splits in the shell to help reduce pressure on sensitive areas of the pelvic region. These saddles are no longer restricted just to racers — many midrange bikes are now equipped with racing saddles.

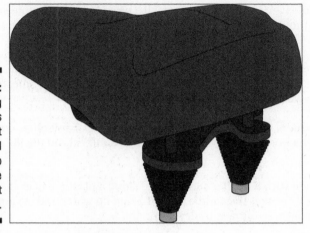

Figure 9-2:
Cruising
saddles
are meant
for casual
riders who
sit in the
upright
position.

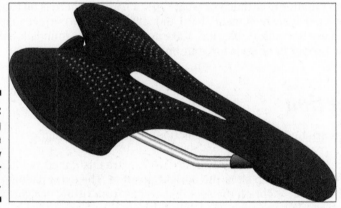

Figure 9-3:
Racing
saddles are
specifically
built for
racers.

Gender

The last factor to consider when choosing a saddle is the gender of the primary rider. Saddles for men and women are designed for the differences in anatomy between the two sexes. Men's saddles are typically longer and narrower in the back, whereas women's saddles are shorter and wider to accommodate women's wider pelvic bones. A women's saddle also frequently has a cut-away behind the nose to provide extra comfort.

Getting comfortable in the saddle

When you first start riding, you may have a literal pain in the butt. But there are some steps you can take to get comfortable in your saddle:

✔ **Try a variety of different saddles.** The only way to tell if you'll like a saddle is to ride on it, so many bike stores will allow you to take a saddle overnight and exchange it for a different one if needed.

✔ **Don't forget to move around.** Instead of sitting in the same position for hours at a time, try shifting your weight and hand position every so often.

✔ **Wear the right clothing.** Biking shorts are designed without seams to help prevent chafing. They also have special fabric to wick away moisture and keep you dry.

✔ **Adjust the height and angle.** Sometimes it takes a little experimenting to find the right combination. Use the advice in this chapter to find the position that's best for you.

✔ **Exercise your butt.** The more you ride, the more your bottom will adjust to sitting on the saddle.

Strange as it sounds, the more you ride, the more you'll like a smaller saddle. Give yourself time to get used to the saddle. A cushy saddle may seem comfortable at first, but it isn't for regular riders.

If a woman were to use a seat designed for a man, the two small bones at the bottom of her pelvic bone would not be supported properly. There are different sit-bone widths, and finding a saddle that corresponds to your sit-bone width, regardless if it's for men or women, is essential.

Removing and Installing a Saddle

There are a number of different ways in which saddles attach to seat posts. On some older or lower-end models, the seat post and the seat clamp are two separate pieces with the bolt horizontal and tightened with a nut (as shown in Figure 9-4). This type of seat clamp only has a limited number of groves and ridges for the seat-angle adjustment — as opposed to the next two clamp styles, which have about twice the number of seat-angle adjustment points, which allows you to find a much more comfortable riding position.

On many bikes, the seat clamp is integrated into the seat post and the saddle is attached with one or two vertical bolts, which are adjusted with an Allen wrench. Figures 9-5 and 9-6 show a saddle with a one-piece clamp.

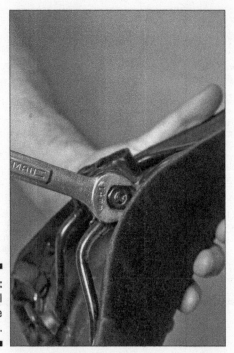

Figure 9-4:
A traditional
saddle
clamp.

Figure 9-5:
One piece
saddle
clamp.

Figure 9-6:
One piece
saddle dis-
assembled.

Another style of clamp is the two-piece clamp. It allows for a lot of flexibility in terms of adjusting the fore and aft of the saddle; however, it is a little trickier to attach. Here's how:

1. **Turn the saddle upside down and remove the seat post.**

2. **Hold the bottom half of the clamp under the seat rails with your fingers.**

3. **While supporting the bottom half of the clamp, slide the square nut under the clamp and hold it in place with your fingers.**

4. **Lay the top half of the clamp on top, making sure that both clamps align with one another.**

   At this point, you should still be supporting the bottom half of the clamp and the square nut with your hand.

5. **Place the seat post on the top clamp, insert the bolt, and tighten (as shown in Figure 9-7).**

Figure 9-7:
Attaching a
two-piece
clamp.

Adjusting the Saddle Fore, Aft, and Height

Adjustments to the saddle can make a big difference in comfort when you ride whether it is a long or even short trip. After all, most of your weight is being supported by the saddle.

In this section, we tell you how to adjust the angle, fore and aft, and height of your saddle. Take the time to adjust your saddle properly, and you'll feel the benefits on your next ride.

Angling for the right angle

If your saddle is tilted slightly downward in the front, your weight is going to be slid forward, putting extra pressure on your arms and shoulders. On the other hand, if the saddle is sloped upward in the front, you may feel extra pressure on the groin area. In general, the recommendation is to keep the saddle flat.

Place a level on top of your saddle to help you set it flat.

To adjust the angle of your saddle, follow these steps:

1. **Loosen the saddle clamp bolt a few turns.**

2. **Work the saddle up and down with your hand, jimmying the saddle into the position you want.**

3. **Retighten the clamp bolt.**

Fore and aft, to and fro

If your seat is too far forward, you won't be using your leg muscles efficiently and your knees can get sore. If your seat is too far to the rear, you'll be stretching to reach the handlebars, which will put strain on your back and knees.

In Chapter 18, we tell you how to use a weighted string to find the fore-and-aft position that's right for you. After you have the position, follow these steps to adjust the saddle backward or forward:

1. **Unloosen the saddle clamp bolt one turn (as shown in Figure 9-8).**

2. **Tap the saddle with your hand to move it forward or backward.**

3. **Retighten the clamp bolt.**

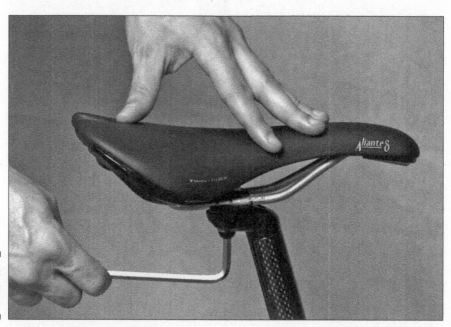

Figure 9-8:
Adjusting
the saddle

Height matters

The proper saddle height is as important as, if not more important than, the angle and fore and aft of the saddle. When your saddle is at the right height for your body, you can efficiently transfer force to the pedals. If you set the height too low, you risk injury by putting undue stress on your knees. Set the height too high, and you'll be bouncing around on the seat, giving the nerves in your butt a Swedish massage.

Follow the instructions in Chapter 18 to find the proper height for your saddle. Then follow these steps to set the height:

1. **Loosen the seat-post bolt or the quick-release binder that's holding the seat post in place.**

   If you don't have a quick release on the seat post, you'll probably have a bolt that can be loosened with an Allen wrench (as shown in Figure 9-9).

Figure 9-9:
If you don't have a quick-release on your seat post, you'll need to loosen the clamp bolt.

After loosening the seat post, you should be able to slide the seat post up and down. If the post is difficult to move, try rotating the seat back and forth while pulling up on the seat. This is usually enough to pry it free.

If the post still won't move for you, you can try dripping some oil or penetrating lubricant on the seat post and letting it work its way down between the frame and the seat post. Another last-ditch trick is to use a screwdriver and pry apart the clamp or lug pinching the post together.

2. **If you used oil or penetrating lubricant to loosen the post, use a degreaser afterwards to clean it off.**

   You'll want it clean so that, when you apply grease to prevent corrosion, the grease will adhere to the post.

   Before installing the post, apply grease to its shaft to prevent corrosion.

   Don't use grease if you have a carbon frame or seat post. Grease can cause a chemical reaction that can attack the carbon frame and/or carbon seat post.

3. **Set the saddle and seat post to the proper height while tightening the bolt or quick-release clamp.**

   Make sure the saddle is aligned straight.

4. **Give the bike a test drive to confirm that the saddle is at the right height.**

   When you're comfortable with the height, use a file or other tool with a sharp edge to mark the correct height of the post. If you have an expensive or stylish seat post that you don't want to mar, you can also use a piece of electrical tape to mark the seat post. This marking will allow you to reset the height if the post loosens for some reason.

Suspension seat posts

When most people think about suspension on bikes, they think of rear and front suspension on mountain bikes. What doesn't get a lot of attention is suspension in the seat post (see the figure). If you're looking for a more comfortable ride, you might want to consider this option.

When you're installing a suspension seat post, read the owner's manual to understand how to preload it for your weight. Heavier riders need a stiffer suspension than lighter riders do.

Suspension posts should be set a little higher than normal because your weight will cause it drop slightly. Riding a bicycle with a suspension seat post takes a little getting used to because it's a couple inches higher when you first get on, and then it compresses with your weight to the proper height for riding. Take your Allen wrench along when you ride and you can adjust it when needed.

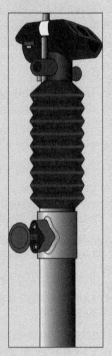

Chapter 10

Hitting the Links: The Chain

In This Chapter

▶ Identifying the different types of chains

▶ Dealing with common problems with chains

▶ Replacing your chain

▶ Caring for your chain

*A*lthough it doesn't garner much attention, the chain is an especially important part of the bike. If one of your cables breaks or a derailleur gives out, you can still ride your bike. But if the chain snaps or malfunctions, you can't do much except walk your bike home. The chain is also important because it comes in contact with other parts of your bike. If the chain is dirty or needs to be replaced, it will cause cogs, chainrings, and derailleurs to wear out more quickly.

To look at a chain, you might think that it doesn't require much care. After all, a *chain* is supposed to be something durable and unbreakable, right? Unfortunately, this isn't the case with a bike chain, where any one link can be the "weak link."

In order to ensure that your chain has the long life that the manufacturer intended and doesn't wear out other components prematurely, invest time in cleaning and lubricating the chain on a regular basis. In this chapter, we tell you how to clean and lube your chain properly and describe the kind of lubrications available to keep it functioning in peak form. We also show you how to replace a chain, which you'll need to do when the chain begins to stretch or wear out.

A Chain Is Not a Chain Is Not a Chain: Types of Chains

To the untrained eye, most bike chains look the same. But pull two bikes off the road and compare the chains and you'll likely find that they have different chains, designed specifically to work with the bikes' particular components.

For example, a $\frac{1}{8}$-inch-wide chain is designed to work with kids' single-speed, fixed-gear, and three-speed bikes (basically most bicycles without a rear derailleur). The majority of bikes use a $\frac{3}{32}$-inch-wide chain. However, knowing the width is not enough. You need to purchase a chain that is designed to work with the number of cogs on your bike. If you tell someone in your local bike store how many cogs are on your bike, they can help you find the right chain.

Here are the two major types of chains you're likely to find:

- ✔ **SRAM PowerLink–type chains:** SRAM PowerLink and other similar types of chains resemble the old master-link chains found on single-speed bikes. You may remember these from when you were a kid (if you were a kid in the '60s or '70s). Figure 10-1 shows an example of an SRAM PowerLink chain, and Figure 10-2 shows an old-school master-link chain.

  By the way, SRAM is a manufacturer of bike components. You can find out more at www.sram.com.

- ✔ **Shimano- and Campagnolo-type chains:** Most bikes have chains that fall into this category. Shimano- and Campagnolo-type chains use a special replacement pin for installation (see Figure 10-3).

  Shimano and Campagnolo are manufacturers of bike components. You can find out more at www.shimano.com and www.campagnolo.com.

- ✔ **Chains with reusable rivets:** This type of chain uses reusable rivets, which are partially pressed out of the chain during separation and then pressed back in with a chain tool. This saves you from having to keep special replacement pins handy.

Figure 10-1:
An SRAM
PowerLink
chain.

Figure 10-2:
A masterlink
chain —
straight out
of the past.

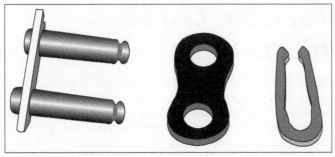

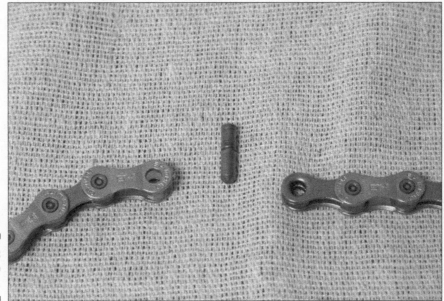

Figure 10-3:
A Shimano
chain.

If you're replacing a chain, make sure you choose one that matches the number of cogs on your cassette. If you choose the wrong size chain, you may have shifting troubles. It's also important to identify whether you have a drivetrain that requires a specially designed chain. For example, Shimano makes a Hyperglide line of products that include specially shaped cogs that facilitate shifting. When in doubt, take your bike into your local bike shop so that they can quickly tell you which kind of chain you need. To read more about cogs and cassettes and the drivetrain, refer to Chapters 11 and 13, respectively.

Recognizing What Can Go Wrong with the Chain

The chain is completely exposed at the bottom of your bike, so it easily picks up dirt and grime, twigs and leaves can get caught in it, and it can be impacted with foreign objects (especially if you're riding off-road) — all of which can undermine the chain's integrity and lead to a break at the most inopportune time.

There are a number of telltale signs that you have an issue with your chain:

✔ You have to exaggerate the movement of your shifter to force the chain to jump to another cog on the rear wheel.

✔ The pedal jerks forward when you're applying pressure, because the chain skipped a tooth on a cog.

✔ Pedaling is not as smooth as it once was.

✔ The chain makes a lot of noise while you pedal but not while you coast.

Issues with your chain can be caused by a number of factors. The most common of them are dirt, stiff links, and normal wear and tear.

Getting down and dirty

The chain is one of the parts of your bike that's completely exposed to the elements. This, combined with the fact that it has to be covered in lubrication to work properly, makes the chain a magnet for dirt and grime.

The abrasive qualities of dirt begin to wear down the chain and the other parts that the chain comes in contact with, such as the cogs, chainrings, and rear derailleur pulley wheels. When dirt works its way into the chain links, they become stiff, which hampers your bike's shifting ability (see the following section).

Stuck in a rut: Stiff links

If you find that your chain is skipping or making a consistent, repetitive noise when you're pedaling, you may have a stiff link. To find a stiff link, follow these steps:

1. **Shift the chain onto the smallest cog.**

This puts the most bend in the chain and causes the stiff link to be more apparent.

2. **Slowly rotate the pedals backward, keeping your eye on the chain and the rear derailleur.**

   If the chain has difficulty moving through the pulley wheels at one point, you've likely got a stiff link.

Stiff links are sometimes caused by a lack of lubrication. The other possibility is that, when the chain was connected, the chain plates in the link were compressed tightly together, making it difficult for the link to pivot.

To take care of a stiff link, first try lubricating the rollers that sit inside the offending link. Give the lubrication a little time to work its way down into the joint and then, while holding each side of the link (use a rag if you don't want to be covered in grease), pivot the link up and down to try to loosen it.

If lubrication doesn't solve the problem, try flexing the chain back and forth by pushing inward with your thumbs and twisting outward with your hands to work it free, as shown in Figure 10-4. Reverse the position by pushing inward with your thumbs on the other side of the chain a few times. This should be enough to restore flexibility to the chain.

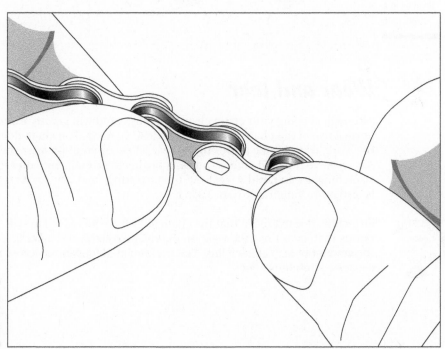

Figure 10-4:
Loosening a stiff chain.

Sometimes with a stiff chain, you'll notice that a rivet is sticking out to one side more than the other rivets are. In this case, you'll need to use a chain tool to push it back in. Put the chain in the chain tool and turn the handle just a small amount, maybe one-eighth of a turn. If the link is still tight, try repeating the procedure from the other side, rotating until it loosens up.

Some chain tools have two slots, or *cradles,* where you can rest the chain (see Figure 10-5). The slot farthest away from the handle is the primary cradle and is used for breaking and connecting chains. The other cradle is specifically designed for tight links, so make sure you use this one.

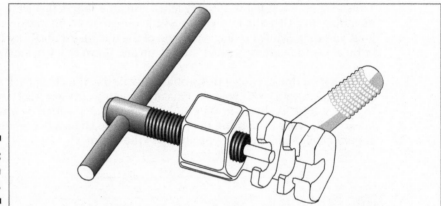

Figure 10-5: Cradles in a chain tool.

Wear and tear

Although keeping your chain clean and lubricated will greatly extend its life, normal use of the chain will eventually lead to wear. The chain does most of the work, transferring power to the rear wheel, revolution after revolution. After you've traveled enough miles, it begins to stretch, and after it starts stretching, it can rapidly wear out the chainrings and cogs. A stretched chain is also more vulnerable to breaking.

Stretching doesn't mean that the chain links have increased in size. It just means that, over time, the wear on the rivets, rollers, and inner links increases the amount of play at each link. The accumulated looseness across many links causes a stretching effect.

The best strategy is to be proactive and frequently inspect the chain for wear, at least during your monthly maintenance check.

The simplest way to check for chain wear is to measure the chain. To measure the chain, use a ruler and measure from pin center to pin center as is shown in Figure 10-6. Twelve paired links of a chain should measure 12 inches from pin center to pin center. A slightly longer length means that the chain has stretched.

Some companies offer chain measuring tools (see Figure 10-7) that are easy to use. If both ends of the tools set down inside the chain, the chain is the appropriate length.

Chains wear out at a faster rate than chainrings and cogs. If you determine early enough that your chain has started to wear or stretch, you can replace only the chain, which will save you a lot of money. If you're really on top of things, you may go through two or three chains before you have to replace the more expensive chainrings and cogs.

If your chain is skipping when you apply force when pedaling, it may be due to worn teeth on the freewheel, cassette cogs, or chainring. Examine both and replace them as needed. (See Chapter 11 for more information on caring for cogs and Chapter 13 for chainrings.)

Figure 10-6:
Measuring
a chain
the old-
fashioned
way, with
a ruler.

Figure 10-7:
A chain
measuring
tool makes
measuring a
chain easy.

If you determine that the chain needs replacing, inspect the chainrings and cogs for wear. If the teeth on a cog or chainring are no longer symmetrical and look like an ocean wave or as though they've been filed down on one side (as shown in Figure 10-8), it's time to replace the part. Another sign of tooth wear is the chain skipping when you pedal with a lot of force.

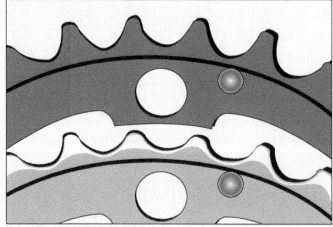

Figure 10-8:
Worn teeth
on a cog or
chainring
should be
replaced.

Sometimes only one cog will wear out. This is usually the cog that corresponds with the gear you use most when riding. If this is the case, you can replace just the cog and not the entire cassette, although sometimes it's cheaper to buy a cassette than a set of replacement cogs. More often, you'll end up replacing a single chainring and an entire cassette.

Caring for Your Chain

A bike's chain is one of the most important parts of the bike to keep clean. It attracts dirt and grime because it is exposed on the bottom of your bike where it is close to the ground. Because it comes into contact with other parts of the bike, such as the derailleurs, it can spread dirt around your bike causing parts to wear out prematurely. Our best advice is to give the chain a simple cleaning each time you ride and then, once a month, give it a deeper cleaning.

Every time you ride, you should give your chain a simple cleaning and lubrication. And at least once a month, you should give it a deeper cleaning. In the following sections, we cover both types of cleaning.

It is best to clean the chain while it is on the bike unless it is extremely dirty or it has been a long time since you have cleaned it.

Put the chain on the smallest sprocket before cleaning. This will expand it slightly and expose the pivoting points of the chain to allow degreaser and lubrication to work its way inside the links.

If the chain has a lot of mud or dirt caked on, rinse it off with water before beginning.

Clean the pulley wheels of the derailleur, chainrings, and cogs if they are dirty. You don't want to undo all your hard work by running a newly cleaned chain across any other filthy components.

Keeping it simple: Cleaning and lubricating your chain

If you only have a few minutes and your chain is not overly dirty, all you need to clean your chain is a rag and a bottle of lube. (See the nearby sidebar, "Bike lubricants out the wazoo," for more on different types of lubrication.)

Bike lubricants out the wazoo

When you're shopping for lubricants, the first step is to make sure you get one formulated for bikes (as opposed to something that's all-purpose, or meant for motorcycle chains, chainsaws, or car engines).

After you've narrowed down the possibilities to the lubes meant for bikes, your next choice will likely be *dry* (meaning, they pick up less dirt) or *wet* (meaning, they're harder to wash away in wet conditions). Unless you're going to be riding in wet conditions or crossing streams, we recommend sticking to a dry lubricant.

You may also see wax-based lubes — these are dry lubes that attract the least amount of dirt and grime and will keep your chain looking clean. But they need frequent application because they don't last long, especially in wet conditions. Also, they work best when they're applied or bonded to a chain that has been completely degreased. Unless you're willing to commit to frequent applications of lubrication, we recommend against wax-based lubes.

Lubricants are sold in aerosol spray cans and squeeze bottles. Many riders prefer squeeze bottles because they can control the flow, applying lubrication drop by drop. With a spray can, it's too easy to get lubrication where you don't need it (such as on the outside of the chain) or where you definitely don't want it (such as on wheel rims).

Some manufacturers recommend that when you start with a lubricant you stick with it, and not change horses midstream. Regular cleaning and lubrication of your chain is probably more important than whether you mix lubricants, but if you're finicky about your bike, sticking with one lubricant doesn't hurt.

Remember: New chains are lubricated by the manufacturer before they're shipped. The quality of this straight-from-the-manufacturer lubrication is better than what you can achieve with a store-bought lube. Under normal riding conditions, you should be able to get several hundred miles with a new chain before you need to apply lubrication.

Here's how to give your chain a simple cleaning and lubrication:

1. **With a clean rag, grab the chain on the bottom, between the lower derailleur jockey wheel and the bottom of the chainring.**

2. **Rotate the pedals in reverse to move the chain through the rag.**

3. **After you've wiped down the chain, apply lubrication to the top of the lower rung of the chain, where it exits from the rear derailleur, using a spray can or squeeze bottle.**

4. **Rotate the pedals in reverse to move the chain as you lube it, completing ten revolutions of the chain to make sure you haven't missed any links.**

   You don't need to douse the entire chain in lubricant. The goal is for the lubrication to work its way into the rollers inside the chain. There's no need for the outer links to be covered in lubricant.

5. **Wipe off any excess lubrication using a clean rag, as shown in Figure 10-9.**

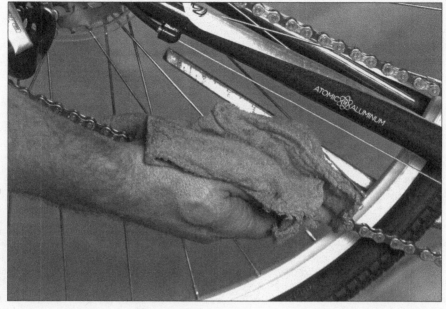

Figure 10-9:
Wiping excess lubrication off the chain.

6. **With a clean rag, grab the chain on the bottom, between the lower derailleur jockey wheel and the bottom of the chainring.**

7. **Rotate the pedals in reverse to move the chain through the rag, and do this for several full revolutions.**

Going deeper: Giving your chain a heavy-duty cleaning

You should give your chain a deeper cleaning at least once a month — more often depending on the conditions you ride in. With a deeper cleaning, you still leave the chain on the bike (see the preceding section) — the difference is, you first use a degreaser to remove any remaining, broken-down lubrication. You also give the chain a more rigorous cleaning by using a brush or a special chain scrubbing tool.

Most bike shops sell a chain cleaning tool (see Figure 10-10) that has a plastic housing that immerses a chain in degreaser while internal brushes scrub the chain links. This tool gives the chain a much deeper cleaning than you can accomplish with a rag or even a handheld brush.

To give your chain a deep cleaning by hand, follow these steps:

1. **With a clean rag, grab the chain on the bottom, between the lower derailleur jockey wheel and the bottom of the chainring.**

Figure 10-10:
A chain cleaning tool takes your cleaning to the next level.

2. **Rotate the pedals in reverse to move the chain through the rag.**

3. **Drench a rag in degreaser, lightly grab the chain with the rag, and rotate the pedals in reverse to apply the degreaser to the chain.**

4. **Drag the chain along the surface of a toothbrush while you rotate the chain.**

   Every few revolutions, rinse the brush off with degreaser.

5. **With a clean rag, grab the chain on the bottom, between the lower derailleur jockey wheel and the bottom of the chainring. Rotate the pedals in reverse to move the chain through the rag to remove the degreaser.**

6. **After you've wiped down the chain, apply lubrication to the top of the lower rung of the chain, where it exits from the rear derailleur using a spray can or squeeze bottle.**

   Be sure all the degreaser is removed before applying new lubrication.

7. **Rotate the pedals in reverse to move the chain as you lube it, completing ten revolutions of the chain to make sure you haven't missed any links.**

   You don't need to douse the entire chain in lubricant.

8. **Wipe off any excess lubrication using a clean rag (refer to Figure 10-9).**

If you have a chain cleaning tool, follow these steps:

1. With a clean rag, grab the chain on the bottom, between the lower derailleur jockey wheel and the bottom of the chainring.

2. Rotate the pedals in reverse to move the chain through the rag.

3. Fill the chain cleaning tool with degreaser to the mark.

4. In front of the rear derailleur where the chain exits, enclose the tool around the chain and rotate the pedals in reverse.

5. With a clean rag, grab the chain on the bottom, between the lower derailleur jockey wheel and the bottom of the chainring. Rotate the pedals in reverse to move the chain through the rag to remove the degreaser.

6. Apply lubrication to the top of the lower rung of the chain, where it exits from the rear derailleur using a spray can or squeeze bottle.

   Be sure all the degreaser is removed before applying new lubrication.

7. Rotate the pedals in reverse to move the chain as you lube it, completing ten revolutions of the chain to make sure you haven't missed any links.

   You don't need to douse the entire chain in lubricant.

8. Wipe off any excess lubrication using a clean rag (refer to Figure 10-9).

Replacing a Chain

Despite your best efforts at keeping the chain clean, eventually all your pedaling is going to wear it out. The chain is under constant force and tension and, as it's shifted back and forth across the different gears, it begins to stretch. You can still ride on a stretched chain, but it'll cause your cogs and chainrings to wear out faster. Because replacing the chain is much cheaper than replacing the cogs and chainrings, we recommend replacing your chain at the first sign of wear. In this section, we talk about how to remove a chain and then how to measure it and reconnect it when you're ready to reinstall it.

Before you try to remove or install a chain, you need to know what type of chain you have (see "A Chain Is Not a Chain Is Not a Chain: Types of Chains," earlier in this chapter). Each type of chain requires a different procedure for removing it and installing it.

Unchain me! Removing the chain

Before attempting to remove or cut the chain while it's on a bike, shift it to the smallest cog in the rear and onto the frame and to the side of the small chainring in the front. If you don't do this, the chain will be under tension and, as soon as it's separated, it may be thrown back at you.

SRAM PowerLink–type chains have a single master link that can be separated and reconnected with common hand tools (pliers and/or a screwdriver), making chain removal and installation a simple task. To remove a PowerLink-type chain:

1. **Find the master link.**

2. **Pinch the outer plates together and, at the same time, slide one plate forward and the other plate backward.**

   This will unlock the connecting plates and allow you to separate the chain.

If you have the most common type of chain, the Shimano- or Campagnolo-type chain, you'll need to use a special chain tool to push out one of the current pins and push another pin in its place when it's time to connect it. In order to cut the chain, follow these steps:

1. **Position the chain into the cradle of the chain tool that is farthest away from the handle (as shown in Figure 10-11).**

2. **Turn the handle clockwise until the chain tool pin comes in contact with the chain rivet, and then stop.**

   There may be one or more black rivets in the chain from where it was last connected. Select an original silver rivet.

3. **Examine the chain tool pin to make sure it's lined up with the center of the chain rivet.**

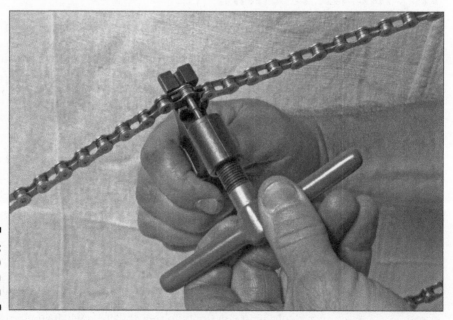

Figure 10-11:
Preparing to
separate a
chain

4. **Begin turning the handle to push out the pin.**

   You may notice that it's difficult to turn at first.

5. **Continue turning the handle until the pin falls out.**

If you have a chain with reusable rivets, follow the same procedure as for the Shimano and Campagnolo chains, but **be *very* careful not to push the pin completely out of the link** — you'll use the same pin to reconnect the chain. The end of the pin has an expanded surface and you won't be able to reinstall it into the link if you push it completely out.

If you have any questions about your chain, consult your owner's manual or visit your local bike shop.

Measuring your new chain

If you buy a new chain, you'll find that it's probably much too long for your bike — manufacturers sell chains longer than necessary so that they can fit a variety of different types of bikes. You need to make sure you're using the proper length chain for your particular bike. If you use a chain that's too short, you won't be able to shift it into some gears. If you use a chain that's too long, shifting will become sluggish or the chain will start to fall off.

To measure a chain, follow these steps:

1. **Wind one end of the chain around the smallest cog and through the rear derailleur.**

   Make sure the derailleur is shifted to the smallest cog or the position farthest to the outside.

2. **Wind the other part of the chain through the front derailleur and around the largest chainring.**

   Make sure the front derailleur is shifted to the smallest chainring or the farthest gear away from the bike.

3. **Using a little bit of force, bring both ends of the chain together (as shown in Figure 10-12).**

   This will pull the pulleys of the rear derailleur forward.

4. **Shorten the chain by hand, one link at a time, until you get the correct length.**

   You know you're at the right length when there's approximately ¹/₂ inch to 1 inch of space between the top pulley and the chain.

5. **On the end of the chain with extra links, pinch the link with your thumb and forefinger where you need to cut the chain.**

   This will help you remember where to break it.

Figure 10-12:
Measuring
the chain

Reassembling your chain

After you've repaired and measured your chain, it's time to reattach it to your bike. If you have an SRAM PowerLink-type chain, here's how:

1. **After having measured the chain (see the preceding section), remove any extra links using the chain tool.**

2. **Grab both connecting pieces that make up the master link.**

3. **Making sure to use inner links only, connect one piece from the inside of the chain and another piece from the outside of the chain.**

4. **Press the pins on both pieces through the rollers in the links, and snap the master link together (as shown in Figure 10-13).**

5. **Pull the chain to lock the pieces in place.**

6. **Visually examine the master link to make sure it's securely in place.**

If you have a Shimano- or Campagnolo-type chain or a chain with reusable rivets, follow these steps:

1. **After having measured the chain (see the preceding section), remove any extra links using the chain tool.**

2. **Making sure to use inner links only, connect one piece from the inside of the chain and another piece from the outside of the chain.**

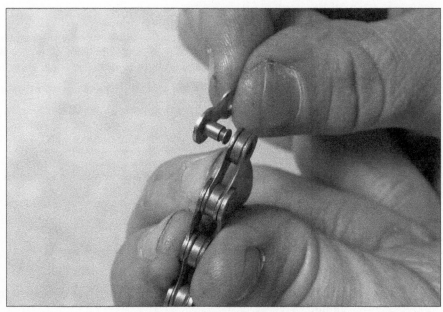

Figure 10-13:
Connecting
an SRAM
PowerLink-
type chain.

3. **Where the two ends of the chain come together, insert the replacement pin into the links just far enough to hold the chain together
while you place it into the chain tool (as shown in Figure 10-14).**

Figure 10-14:
Inserting
the pin.

If you have a chain with a reusable rivet, the rivet will already be in place.

The pin has a tapered head that looks like a rocket ship. Make sure you insert the pin with the tapered head first. The head of the pin is designed to guide the pin into the chain and not to hold the chain together.

4. **Rotate the handle of the chain tool to press the rivet into the chain.**

    Be careful not to push the rivet too far into the chain. You want to push the tapered head of the rivet all the way through and out the other side to have the non-tapered head protruding only as far as the neighboring rivets protrude.

5. **Using pliers, snap the tapered head off the pin (as shown in Figure 10-15).**

If you have a chain that uses reusable rivets, here's how to reinstall it:

1. **Grab both connecting pieces where the chain was broken.**

2. **Join the links together and place into the chain tool.**

3. **Turn the handle of the chain tool until the rivet is pressed into the chain.**

    An equal amount of rivet should be showing on each side of the chain

4. **Remove the chain tool from the chain.**

Figure 10-15:
Snapping
off the
replacement
pin's head.

Chapter 11

Gearing Up: Freewheels and Cassettes

In This Chapter

▶ Getting clear on cassettes and freewheels

▶ Inspecting, cleaning, and lubricating cassettes and freewheels

▶ Removing and installing cassettes and freewheels

*O*ne of the most enjoyable experiences when riding is the exhilaration that comes after having reached the top of a tall peak, when the downhill begins almost immediately and you're rewarded with a long descent. The satisfaction of having conquered the ascent, the relief of being able to rest your legs for a moment, and the rush of coasting at high speed with the wind in your face are what keeps people coming back for the climb.

What makes the coasting part possible is the topic of this chapter. Freewheels and cassettes are like the clutch on your car — disengage it and the car is rolls free in neutral. In a bike's case, stopping pedaling does the trick. In this chapter, we fill you in on some of the basics of how the freewheel and cassette work and how coasting is possible, as well as everything you need to know about their maintenance, including inspecting, removing, and reinstalling them.

The Dirt on Freewheels and Cassettes

Think about a kid's fixed-gear bike: Every time the rear wheel spins, the pedals and cranks rotate with it or the front wheel. For young children, this isn't a big deal — they usually don't ride very fast, and they have more energy than they know what to do with. However, if your bike worked the same way and you were riding down a hill at a high rate of speed, your legs would have to keep up with the pedals and cranks, which would be spinning at a furious rate. Talk about dangerous.

Fortunately, modern bikes have a clutch system that allows you to coast when you stop pedaling, and move forward again by pedaling when you slow down. This system is made up of either a freewheel or a cassette, the subject of this section.

To determine whether you have a freewheel or cassette, examine the smallest cog. If there is a screw-on lock ring with the word *lock* on it, which rotates with the cogs when you spin the freewheel, you probably have a cassette. If in doubt, take your bike to your local bike shop and ask the people there.

What's so free about a freewheel?

The *freewheel* (shown in Figure 11-1) is a part of a clutch-like system that was a significant advance in the design of bicycles. Older bikes are designed with freewheels that consist of individual *cogs* (toothed disks surrounding the hub on your rear wheel that combine to form the freewheel of your bike), bearings, pawls, pawl springs, and gears that are screwed directly on to the hub.

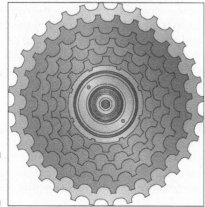

Figure 11-1:
A freewheel

One disadvantage to freewheels is that the force from pedaling can tighten them, making removal difficult. Another problem with freewheels is that, because of the spacing requirements, the bearings on each side of the hub are located closer together toward the center of the hub, while the axle is extended outward from the bearings to support the freewheel. As a result, the axle receives less support and can break or bend under the right amount of force.

If you have a traditional freewheel, when your cogs wear out you may want to think about converting to a cassette system (see the following section). If you do opt for a cassette system, your best bet is to replace the hub with a free hub. The alternative is to buy a freewheel hub and rebuild your wheel.

The best things come in packages: The cassette

Cassette systems (see Figure 11-2), which are found on most modern bikes, improved many of the deficiencies with freewheels (see the preceding section). One of the biggest changes with cassettes is that the ratcheting system is built into the hub itself. Cassettes use a *free hub,* which looks like a traditional hub but with a thick extension on one side with grooves or splines built into it. This design allows the bearings to be spaced farther apart, providing greater support for the axle.

Figure 11-2: Cassettes improved upon freewheels.

Another advantage of the cassette system is removal: Cassettes have cogs that are normally held together as a unit and that slide on and off the hub. After the *lock ring* (which holds the cogs in place) is removed, the cogs slide off together as one. Freewheels, on the other hand, are a group of cogs held together as a unit but must be threaded onto the hub.

Cassettes come with a variety of different gearing options. The gears are defined by the number of teeth on each cog and, depending on your biking needs, you may need a specific range of gears. For example, if you're planning on touring, you'll want high enough gears to help you ascend inclines while your bike is weighed down with packed pannier bags.

Some cogs are manufactured with the number of teeth marked on the side. These markings will save you from having to count the teeth in order to determine the gear.

If you're shopping for a cassette, be sure you buy one that's compatible with your hub. Manufacturers like Shimano and Campagnolo have designed cassettes that work only with their hubs. If you aren't sure about which cassette will work with your hub, check with the folks at your local bike shop.

Inspecting Your Freewheel or Cassette

Just like other parts of a bike, a freewheel or cassette will eventually wear out and have to be replaced. You can identify a worn freewheel the same way you identify a worn chainring (see Chapter 10) — by the teeth. Here are some clues for identifying worn teeth on a freewheel or cassette:

- ✔ They no longer have sharp edges.
- ✔ They look like they've been filed down.
- ✔ They lack symmetry.
- ✔ They have the shape of an ocean wave.

If your chain is skipping when you apply force when pedaling, it may be due to worn teeth on either the freewheel or cassette cogs or the chainring. Examine both and replace them as needed.

Sometimes only one cog will wear out — if this happens, it's usually the cog that corresponds with the gear you use most when riding. (For many bikers, this'll be cogs with 15 to 18 teeth.) If you have just one cog that needs to be replaced, you may be able to buy just that one cog — although often buying the entire cassette or a freewheel is cheaper.

Cleaning the Freewheel or Cassette

Caring for a freewheel or cassette is pretty straightforward. Unlike other components of the bike, where you're concerned about the *internal* parts, with freewheels your goal is to keep the *outside* of the cogs clean. Dirt and grime quickly work their way onto the surface of the cogs and in between them. This buildup can muck up the chain, spread dirt around your bike, and cause premature wear for all the parts.

You don't have to remove the freewheel or cassette to clean it.

To clean the freewheel or cassette , follow these steps:

1. **Remove the rear wheel from the bike by following the directions in Chapter 7.**

   Removing the rear wheel gives you better access to the cogs.

2. ***If the freewheel or cassette is very dirty,* wash it with soap and water.**

   Avoid spraying water directly. Use a brush on the freewheel as you wash the wheel.

3. ***If the freewheel or cassette is not overly dirty,* clean it with a rag.**

   Drop an edge of the rag between each freewheel cog and, while holding each corner of the rag with your hands, clean between the cogs in a back-and-forth motion.

   Dip the cloth or brush in degreaser before using it. But try to keep the degreaser from getting on the tire.

4. **To remove dirt that's trapped between the cogs, use a narrow brush or a screwdriver to scrape it out.**

   Some manufacturers make a tool with a brush specially designed for this purpose.

If the freewheel or cassette is *really* dirty, try removing and soaking it in a degreaser.

Lubricating the Freewheel or Cassette

Although you won't be overhauling a freewheel or cassette the way you would with a bottom bracket or headset, you can do some simple lubrication of the bearings using a lightweight oil.

Follow these steps to lubricate the freewheel or cassette while it's on the wheel:

1. **After you've cleaned the freewheel or cassette (see the preceding section), wipe off any excess degreaser and let it dry.**

2. **Lay down the wheel with the freewheel on its side, with the freewheel facing up.**

3. **Using a light to medium oil, drip or spray the oil into the gap between the freewheel and the center, fixed part of the hub axle, while you're spinning the free hub in a counterclockwise direction.**

   When you see oil coming through the other side, there is sufficient oil to lube the pawls and bearings. (In general, the higher the quality of the freewheel, the tighter the tolerances and the longer this takes.)

4. **Use a rag to wipe off any excess lubrication between the cogs.**

Removing a Freewheel or Cassette

You'll have to remove a freewheel or cassette in the following situations:

- If you're replacing the freewheel or cassette
- If you're replacing a spoke and need to insert it into the *flange* (the part that flares out at the ends of the hubs)
- If you're overhauling the hubs
- If you're replacing the hubs

In the following sections, we walk you through removing a freewheel and removing a cassette, as well as removing individual cogs and removing the free hub.

Removing a freewheel

If your bike has a freewheel, follow these steps to remove it. (If you're not sure whether your bike has a freewheel or cassette, turn to "The Dirt on Freewheels and Cassettes," earlier in this chapter.)

1. **Remove the rear wheel from the bike (see Chapter 7).**

2. **Remove the quick-release skewer or axle nut.**

3. **Stand the wheel up on the floor.**

4. **Attach the freewheel remover tool to the center of the freewheel.**

   Be sure to use the correct type of freewheel remover tool. Check with your local bike shop or read your bike owner's manual to find out which model is appropriate for your freewheel.

   To hold the freewheel removal tool in place, use the axle nut or insert the quick-release skewer through the center of the tool and tighten the nut to hold it in place.

5. **Using an adjustable wrench, turn the freewheel remover in a counter-clockwise direction.**

6. **When the freewheel remover loosens, remove the quick-release skewer or axle nut.**

7. **Continue to unscrew the freewheel remover either by hand or with the wrench, until the freewheel is unthreaded from the hub.**

Removing a freewheel, which tightens at every pedal stroke, can often be extremely difficult. If you can't remove it with a full-size crescent wrench, more leverage is needed. You may be able to use an extension pipe or, more effectively, a heavy-duty vice (maybe borrowed from your local bike shop). Being unable to remove a freewheel is a very common frustration of home mechanics.

Removing a cassette

Most modern cassettes are designed to slide onto the free-hub body with splines and then be held in place by a cassette lockring. On some older cassettes, the cassette is secured to the hub by the first cog.

To determine which type of cassette you have, look at the first cog. If it has grooves or splines cut into the center of it, you have the lockring style. If not, you have the older cassette style. (When in doubt, check with the people at your local bike shop.)

On many lockrings, you can sometimes find the word *lock* with an arrow pointing in the direction for locking.

In order to remove a splined cassette, you need a freewheel removal tool, a chain whip, and an adjustable crescent wrench. If you have a traditional cassette, you'll need two chain whips.

Different types of cassettes require freewheel removers that are specially designed to work with the number of splines in the hub. Make sure you purchase one that's compatible with your cassette.

Splined cassettes

To remove a modern-style, splined cassette, follow these steps:

1. **Remove the rear wheel from the bike (see Chapter 7).**

2. **Remove the quick-release skewer or axle nut.**

3. **Stand the wheel up on the floor.**

4. **Insert the freewheel remover to the center of the cassette (as shown in Figure 11-3).**

   To hold the lockring in place, insert the quick-release skewer through the center of the tool and lightly tighten the nut to hold it in place. You can do the same thing with the axle nut if you have axle nuts instead of a quick release.

5. **Wrap the chain of the chain-whip tool around one of the larger cogs.**

6. **Secure an adjustable wrench to the flat edges of the freewheel tool.**

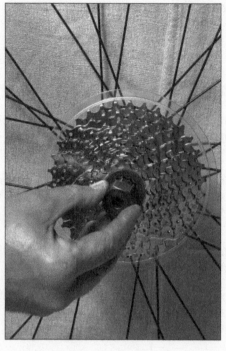

Figure 11-3:
Inserting the
freewheel
remover
tool into
the center
of the
cassette.

7. **Holding the chain-whip tool in one hand and the adjustable wrench in the other (as shown in Figure 11-4), push down on the adjustable wrench.**

   You'll hear a clicking sound as the lockring loosens.

   You may be able to get greater leverage by standing behind the wheel and leaning over the top as you push down on the wrench.

8. **After the lockring loosens, remove the nut or quick-release skewer.**

9. **Unscrew the lockring by hand until you can remove it.**

10. **Slide the cassette off the freehub.**

    Some of the first few cogs may not be attached to the cassette body (as shown in Figure 11-5). Keep track of any spacers that exist in between the cogs — these should be returned to their proper position when you reinstall the cassette.

Figure 11-6 shows the free hub after the cassette is removed. Notice the splines cut into the extended part of the hub.

Figure 11-4:
Using a
chain whip
to loosen
the lockring.

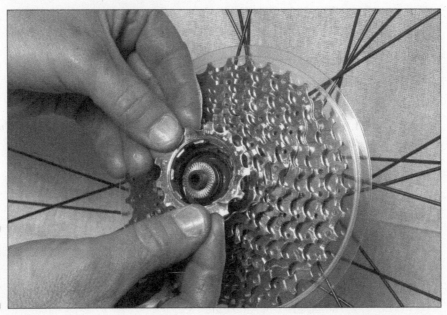

Figure 11-5:
Removing
the cogs on
a cassette

Figure 11-6:
Free-hub
splines.

Traditional cassettes

To remove a traditional cassette, follow these steps:

1. **Remove the rear wheel from the bike (see Chapter 7).**

2. **Remove the quick-release skewer or axle nut.**

3. **Stand the wheel up on the floor.**

4. **Facing the cassette, attach the chain of one chain whip to the largest cog and hold the handle of the chain whip with your right hand at the two or three o'clock position.**

5. **Attach the chain of the other chain whip to the smallest cog and support the tool with your left hand in the nine or ten o'clock position.**

6. **Push down on the chain attached to the smallest cog while holding the other chain whip in place.**

   You may be able to get greater leverage by standing behind the wheel and leaning over the top as you push down on the chain whip.

7. **Remove the smallest cog after it's loose.**

   The others will slide off.

Removing individual the cogs on a freewheel or cassette

Occasionally, you may decide to replace an individual cog because of wear or because you want to change its size. After you've removed your freewheel or cassette, you can follow these steps to remove individuals cogs:

1. **Secure the freewheel or cassette in a vise (as shown in Figure 11-7).**

2. **Wrap the chain of a chain whip around the smallest cog.**

3. **Turn the chain whip in a counterclockwise direction to remove the cog (as shown in Figure 11-8).**

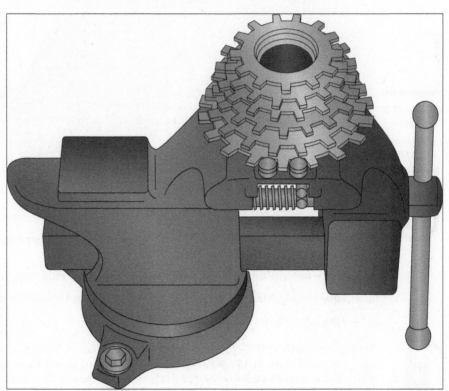

Figure 11-7:
Preparing
to remove
individual
freewheels.

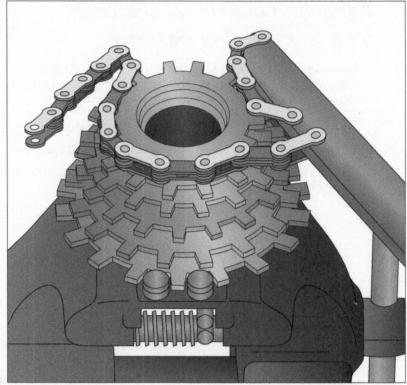

Figure 11-8:
Removing a
cog from a
freewheel.

TIP

If you don't have a vise, you can use two chain whips together:

1. **Wrap the chains of the chain whip around two adjacent cogs such that the handles of the tools cross.**

   You'll have more leverage if you keep the handles close together.

2. **Squeeze together the two chain whips until you loosen the cogs.**

   This procedure is shown in Figure 11-9.

REMEMBER

Whichever method you choose, as you remove the cogs keep track of any spacers (see Figure 11-10) between them. You'll want to put these back in place in the proper order when your reinstall the freewheel.

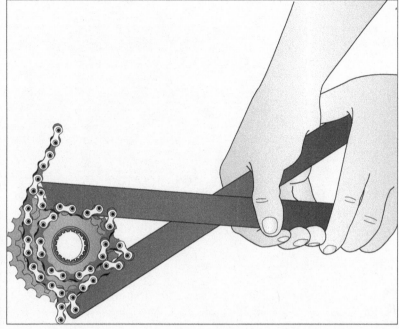

Figure 11-9:
Using a pair
of chain
whips to
loosen the
cogs.

Removing the free-hub body

If the free-hub body's ratcheting mechanism gives out or if it's making noise, you may have to replace it or remove it for lubrication if you have a model that allows for this.

To remove the freehub body, follow these steps:

1. **Remove the rear wheel from the bike (see Chapter 7).**

2. **Remove the cassette from the free hub (see "Removing a cassette," earlier in this chapter).**

3. **Remove the lock nut and cone from the other side of wheel and pull the axle through.**

4. **Remove the hub bearings.**

   Replace them if necessary.

5. **Use the proper size Allen wrench to unscrew the bolt in the center of the free-hub body and remove the free-hub body.**

6. **Clean the body with a degreaser, apply oil, wipe off any excess lubrication, and reassemble using the reverse of this procedure.**

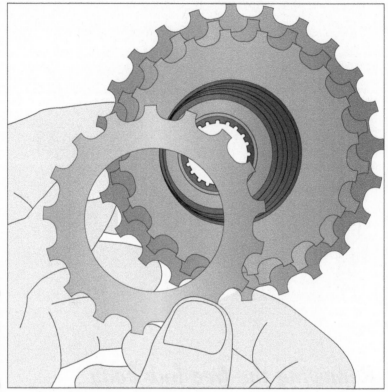

Figure 11-10:
Keep track
of spacers
between
the cogs.

Installing a Freewheel or Cassette

To install a freewheel, follow these steps:

1. **Apply grease to the threads on the inside of the freewheel and to those on the hub.**

2. **Thread the freewheel in a clockwise direction, being careful to make sure that the threads align properly.**

3. **Thread the freewheel by hand until it begins to tighten.**

   You can use a chain whip to tighten the freewheel further, although this usually isn't necessary because riding the bike will tighten it.

To install a cassette, following these steps:

1. **Slide the cassette onto the body of the free hub.**

   Find the one spline on the freehub that is wider than the others, and align it with the same wide spline on the inside of the cassette.

2. **Slide any smaller individual cogs onto the hub.**

   If there are spacers be sure to include them in the proper position.

3. **Grease the threads of the lockring and screw it into place on the hub.**

4. **Attach the freewheel remover to the center of the cassette.**

5. **Insert the quick-release skewer into the center of the hub, and tighten the nut to hold it in place.**

6. **Using an adjustable wrench, turn the freewheel remover in a clockwise direction to tighten.**

   After you hand-tighten the lockring, you only need to tighten the lockring about five to ten clicks with the tool. *Do not overtighten.*

Part III

Shifting into a Higher Gear: Advanced Bike Repairs

The 5th Wave   By Rich Tennant

"There's a slight crack in your frame, but it's hard to tell what caused it—stress, proximity to water, or a combination of both."

In this part . . .

If you're planning on overhauling your bike, replacing some of its components, or performing major repairs, this part is for you. Here we focus on several "systems," including the frame and suspension, the drivetrain, the steering system, and the shifting system. Although these procedures are more advanced than those in Part II, with this book by your side, you can do these yourself as long as you have the right tools — and patience. After you tackle the repairs in these chapters, you'll be chatting up your local bike-shop mechanic, watching the Tour de France with a new appreciation, and impressing your friends with your mastery of bike repair and maintenance.

Chapter 12

Holding It All Together:
The Frame and Suspension

· ·

In This Chapter

▶ Understanding how your frame is built

▶ Knowing what to look for in a frame

▶ Inspecting a frame for problems

▶ Identifying the different types of suspension

▶ Adjusting and maintaining your suspension

· ·

For all the focus given to other parts of the bike when it comes to improving comfort and bike handling, the frame is given surprisingly little attention, especially considering how important it is to your bike. The frame dramatically impacts the personality of your bike — its stability, how it handles corners, whether it can carry loads, and how aerodynamic it is. It also determines your position on the bike in relation to the pedals, the seat, and the handlebars. Slight changes in this position can greatly impact the way a bike rides.

In this chapter, we take a closer look at the frame and how it impacts the biking experience. We discuss how frames are designed and constructed and what qualities you should look for when shopping for a new frame. We also provide advice for inspecting and maintaining your frame.

We also discuss bike suspension in this chapter. The suspension acts as an extension of the frame by being an intermediary between the road and the bike to absorb the bumps and jars so your frame and body won't have to. Suspension is found on more and more bikes these days, so understanding how suspension works and the steps to adjust and care for it is a good idea — if your current bike doesn't have suspension, your next one just might.

I've Been Framed: Your Bike's Frame

Although there are a number of different frame designs, some more strange than others, the diamond shape is most popular. In this design, there is a main triangle that includes the following:

- **Head tube:** The head tube is where the fork connects with the frame and where the headset sits to enable steering.

- **Top tube:** The top tube connects the seat tube with the head tube and can be horizontal or angled up or down, depending on the style of the bike. Cables are frequently run along the top tube.

- **Down tube:** The down tube connects the head tube with the bottom bracket. This is where your water-bottle cage usually goes. On older bikes, this was the location for the friction shifters.

- **Seat tube:** The seat tube is what supports your butt by holding the seat post and saddle in place. It's often used for attaching water-bottle cages and bike pumps.

- **Bottom-bracket shell:** This is a short, fat tube that holds the bottom bracket. It runs sideways across the bottom of the bike and is usually threaded.

There also is a rear triangle, which consists of the seat tube, along with the following:

- **Chain stays:** Chain stays run parallel to the bike chain and connect the bottom bracket to the rear dropouts. On some bikes, cables are routed along the chain stays.

- **Seat stays:** The seat stays connect the seat tube with the rear dropouts. They're often used for mounting brakes, fenders, or bike racks.

The final section of the frame is the fork and steerer tube. The fork is how the front wheel connects to the bike. It consists of two legs with a dropout each for the wheel and a steerer tube, which inserts into the head tube.

A number of factors in the geometry of a frame affect how the bike handles:

- **Seat-tube angle:** The seat-tube angle is based on the angle of the seat tube in relation to the ground. This angle determines how your weight is distributed between the saddle and the handlebars. A steeper seat tube creates a more aerodynamic position with more of your weight shifted forward to the handlebars. With a shallower seat tube, the saddle is positioned farther behind the bottom bracket and your weight is directed toward the back of the bike.

The angle of the seat tube also impacts how you pedal, because it changes your position in relation to the bottom bracket, where all the pedaling takes place. A steeper seat-tube position provides a more direct transfer of power from your legs and is better for higher-cadence pedaling. A shallower seat tube is better for slower pedaling, such as climbing while seated.

✔ **Head-tube angle:** The head-tube angle impacts your bike's handling. A steeper head tube will provide more responsive steering, whereas a more shallow tube will give you more relaxed steering. If you use your bike on mountain trails and need quick, responsive turning to avoid hitting objects, a steeper head tube is for you. On the other hand, if your riding consists of taking two-week tours where you're on long stretches of road for hours at a time, a more shallow seat tube is probably the way to go.

✔ **Chain-stay length:** Chain-stay length also impacts a bike's handling. A shorter chain stay brings the wheel closer to the bottom bracket and makes the bike's handling more responsive. For racing and performance, a shorter chain stay won't allow the frame to flex as much, so more of your pedaling energy is transferred to the rear wheel. In addition, because more of your body is above the rear wheel, traction is improved, which is useful on mountain bikes.

A longer chain stay flexes more and provides a larger wheel base, which improves stability and comfort. Longer chain stays are found on many touring bike frames, where stability for a loaded bike is important. Having the wheel farther back also helps keep your foot from hitting the pannier bags.

✔ **Bottom-bracket drop:** The *bottom-bracket drop* is how far the bottom bracket sits below an imaginary horizontal line drawn between the front and rear dropouts. Most mountain bikes have less of a bottom-bracket drop because they need the extra clearance to avoid the obstacles found on trails. Racing bikes also are designed with less of a bottom-bracket drop to prevent the pedals from hitting the road in tight corners. An increased bottom-bracket drop extends the wheelbase and lowers the bike's center of gravity, both of which improve stability. As you may expect, a lower bottom-bracket drop is found on touring bikes where stability is valued.

So how do all these frame options come together to form the bike that's perfect for you? For the average rider, bike frames designed with comfort and stability in mind are probably going to be the best choice. Frames with slightly longer chain stays, lower bottom-bracket drops, and more relaxed seat-tube and head-tube angles provide this. For mountain bikes and more expensive road bikes, the tendency will be for more responsive and stiffer rides with frames that have shorter chain stays, higher bottom-bracket drops, and steeper seat-tube and head-tube angles.

Figure 12-1 illustrates a mountain bike frame and Figure 12-2 shows a road-bike frame. See if you can notice some of the differences between the two frames: The mountain bike has a shorter chain stay, a higher bottom bracket, and steeper seat tube and head tubes than the road bike.

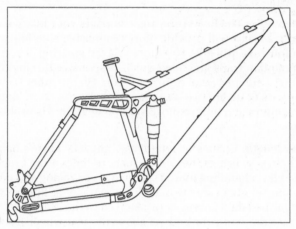

Figure 12-1:
A mountain-bike frame.

Figure 12-2:
A road-bike frame.

What to look for in a frame

Frame materials are often compared based on the qualities of strength, stiffness, and weight:

✔ **Strength:** *Strength* refers to the durability of the frame. If you crashed, a stronger frame would be more likely to survive the crash intact. For a mountain bike that's going to be put through some challenging trail rides, strength is important.

✔ **Stiffness:** Stiffness describes how much the frame material flexes under a force. For example, when you pedal, you're applying a force to the frame; around the bottom bracket, it'll flex slightly depending on the frame material.

✔ **Weight:** Weight is an important factor with frame materials. In an ideal world, you'd have the lightest frame possible so on your next climb it wouldn't feel like you were hauling a sack of potatoes with you. Of course, lighter frames require more expensive materials, which makes them cost prohibitive for some riders.

Types of frame materials

The most common frame materials are

✔ **Steel:** Steel frames have been around for a long time, and the best of them can still compete with some of today's frames fashioned from fancier materials. The higher-end steels or steel/alloy blends (such as chrome-moly) are very strong, offer significant stiffness, and are long lasting, all for decent prices. Cheaper, mild steels or high-tensile steel are found on lower-end bikes where the frames are thick and heavy.

The downside to steel, other than the weight, is that it can rust. Also, high-tensile or mild steel is very uncomfortable — all the road vibrations are transferred through the frame to your butt. The better-quality chrome-moly frames with butted tubing are much more comfortable than the mild steel.

✔ **Aluminum:** Aluminum has become the most popular choice for manufacturers of bike frames. It's lighter than steel, has better stiffness, and, unlike steel, it doesn't rust. The other benefit of aluminum is that it can be easily formed into different shapes to improve the performance and aerodynamics of the frame. The downside of aluminum is that it's not as strong as steel, so a big-time crash could leave your frame mangled beyond repair. The other factor with aluminum is that it fatigues over time, increasing the chances that the frame could break. Aluminum also transmits road vibration far more severely then steel or carbon fiber.

✔ **Carbon fiber:** Carbon-fiber frames are made by gluing, with an epoxy resin, individual carbon-fiber sheets together in patterns that enhance its strength. Manufacturers use this technique to customize frame strength by adding layers of fibers to the parts of the frame that require greater strength, and removing layers of fibers from the parts of the frame that doesn't need as much strength.

The fact that carbon is strong and light makes it a desirable material for frames. However, carbon fiber is expensive. Carbon-fiber frames offer the most comfortable ride with the most efficient use of energy. The other nice thing about carbon fiber is that the frame can be made in almost any shape or size. Manufacturers aren't limited to the standard tube sizes or the typical rounded shape of a frame tube.

✔ **Titanium:** Titanium, like carbon, is on every serious biker's wish list when it comes to frame materials. Titanium is light, it doesn't rust, and it's as strong as most steels. It's less stiff than steel and flexes to give a comfortable ride. Unfortunately, titanium is very expensive and out of reach for most bikers.

Inspecting your frame

Even though the frame may appear to be one solid, immovable object, it's not unheard of for them to go out of alignment occasionally. Any kind of impact — whether it's an accident, your bike falling over, or jumping your bike over a curb — could impact the alignment.

To inspect your frame for issues, follow these steps:

1. **Stand in front of your bike and peer down the center of the frame (as shown in Figure 12-3).**

   You should see the head tube line up with the seat tube.

2. **Facing forward, straddle your bike with both legs and look down at the frame (as shown in Figure 12-4).**

   You should see the top tube line up with the down tube. The front forks should also be equidistant apart from each side of the wheel.

3. **Stand behind the bike and check that the seat tube lines up with the head tube (see Figure 12-5). Look down at the seat stays and make sure they are parallel.**

Figure 12-3:
Checking
the frame
from the
front.

Figure 12-4:
Checking
the frame
from the
top.

Figure 12-5:
Checking
the frame
from the
back.

4. **Visually inspect the frame for defects (as shown in Figure 12-6).**

   Pay particular attention to where the frame is welded together. For hard-to-see places, close your eyes and run your fingers along the side of the tube. (Closing your eyes allows you to actually feel and not have your eyes trick your brain.) If you see or feel bubbles, ripples, or cracks in the paint, it could be a sign that your frame has issues. Take it to your local bike shop for further inspection.

5. **Tie a string to the rear dropout on one side, and run it toward the front of the bicycle head tube and then back to the dropout on the other side and tie it.**

   Measure the distance from the string to the seat tube on each side. If the measurement's are not exactly the same, your frame is bent and out of alignment.

If you think your bike is out of alignment, take it to your local bike shop. Many shops have tools that can check the alignment and straighten the frame as needed. If your frame is made of steel, repairing it is usually much easier than if you have an aluminum, carbon, or titanium frame. If your frame is not made of steel, your best bet might be to turn to your bike's warranty.

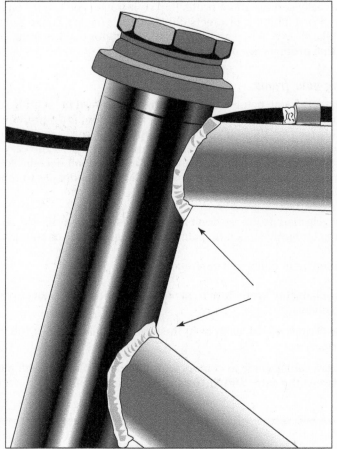

Figure 12-6:
Checking
the frame
for defects.

Maintaining your frame

In general, the frame is one of the lowest-maintenance parts of your bike. Nevertheless, you shouldn't ignore it when you care for your bike — there are a number of things you can do to make sure it lasts as long as the manufacturer intended. We cover these basic maintenance tasks in this section.

Preventing rust

For steel frames, rust is the number-one enemy. Water from rain, sweat, or muddy conditions can work itself into the frame and start corroding it. To minimize the chances of this happening, spray an anti-rust product, such as WD-40, into the frame every opportunity you have.

If you're really serious about protecting your frame, you can try one of a number of rust-inhibitor products (such as J. P. Weigle's Frame Saver, available at bike shops). When you spray a rust inhibitor inside a frame, it forms a barrier that protects against rust.

Painting your frame

Keeping your frame painted can go a long way toward preventing rust. Small chips in the frame's paint may allow rust to take root in your frame and spread. If you have time on your hands during the winter months, give your bike a fresh coat of paint as part of its annual overhaul. At the very least, touch up any small chips in the paint so that they don't become sources of rust. If rust has already appeared, use a fine-grain sandpaper to remove the rust before painting.

Most bicycle manufacturers don't make touch-up paint available, so use a similar color automotive touch-up paint from an auto dealer or auto parts store.

Try to keep paint chips to a minimum:

- Use chainstay protectors to protect your chainstay against impact from the chain.

- Use O-rings on cables to keep them from rubbing against the frame's surface.

- Where cables come in contact with the frame, place a small piece of tape between the cable and the frame, to protect the frame's surface.

Butt out! Frame butting

When it comes to crafting bike frames, manufacturers have more tricks up their sleeves than just changing the frame material. Engineers have come up with a variety of ways to manipulate strength and rigidity of frames, including changing the tube width, the thickness of tube walls, and the tube shape.

Butting is one such technique. It's the process of making one part of a tube thicker than another part of the same tube. This is usually done on the inside walls of the tube, so the outside — the part that you see — is all the same. The thicker part of the tube provides strength where it's needed more, and the thinner part of the tube helps reduce weight. Single-butted tubes have one side of the tube that's thicker than the other. They're often found on seat tubes where the thicker part of the tube is attached to the bottom bracket to provide support against the force of pedaling. Double-butted tubing is thin in the middle, where less strength is needed, and thicker on both ends, where the tube connects to other tubes. On some frames, manufacturers may even use triple- or quadruple-butted tubes.

Waxing your frame

Waxing is not only a great way to keep your bike looking shiny and new, it's effective at keeping rust at bay. Give your bike a thorough waxing as a part of your annual overhaul, when the frame will be more accessible. If you ride a lot, think about waxing the frame every few months.

Although there are a number of waxes designed for bikes, any all-purpose car wax should do the trick.

Suspended in Disbelief: The Suspension

In the continuing trend toward bikes offering a more comfortable ride, suspension has played a leading role. Riding a bike without suspension on a rough road makes you feel like *you're* the shock absorber. Every road or trail shock that hits a stiff rigid bike is transferred directly into your arms, legs, and the rest of your body. Not only that, but if you hit something on the road or trail with enough force, the bike may stop suddenly and send you flying like Superman.

On a bike with suspension, when you hit a pothole or run over a rock, the shock absorber dissipates the force before it's absorbed by your bike and body. It improves safety, comfort, and riding efficiency (because you won't have to hover over your seat to act as your own personal shock absorber). Bicycles with suspension are safer because they give you more control of the bicycle — the wheels stay in contact with the ground more and you don't get bounced around on the trail as much.

The main idea behind suspension is that the coiling of a spring keeps you floating or suspended when you ride. This provides the bounciness or springiness of the suspension. The second idea is that the bounciness of the spring is better suited for a bike if it can be controlled or dampened. A spring with too much bounce will make you feel as though your bike is attached to a pogo stick.

Suspension is generally found on four places on a bike:

- ✔ Fork
- ✔ Stem
- ✔ Seat post
- ✔ Rear axle

Types of suspension

Most suspension systems use some type of spring to absorb impacts from the road. Generally, three types of springs are used:

- **Coil:** Coil springs are made from steel of different gauges and are the most popular type of spring.
- **Air:** Air maintained inside a sealed chamber acts as another kind of spring.
- **Elastomer:** Elastomers are made of urethane and aren't as common these days as they were in the past.

Suspension works best when a spring is paired with some kind of damping system. *Damping* is the ability to slow the rebound of the suspension. *Rebound* is the speed at which the suspension returns to its original position after it has been compressed. And *compression* is the amount of time it takes for the suspension to absorb your weight. If your suspension has unchecked rebound, you'll feel like you're riding a bouncing ball. If your suspension has the bouncing-ball feeling, adjusting the damping can reduce the speed at which the suspension compresses and rebounds.

Air and oil are two types of damping systems. In an air-based damping system, air pressure is adjusted to change the amount of damping. In oil-based damping systems, a piston flows through a volume of oil. Adjusting the size of the hole in the piston changes the amount of damping.

Many suspension systems have adjusters that allow you to change the amount of damping and *preload* (the amount of compression applied to suspension before it supports any weight). By preloading the suspension, it will sag less and give you a stiffer ride. Reducing the preload will cause the suspension to sag more. On many suspension forks, the preload adjuster is found on the top of the fork and the damping adjustment at the bottom of the fork.

Tuning the suspension

Although there are a number of ways to tune suspension, we'll focus on one of the most basic adjustments — controlling the amount of *sag* (the amount of movement in the suspension when you're sitting on your saddle). The amount of recommended sag for most bikes is normally around 25 percent.

You can adjust the suspension much easier if you have a friend around to assist you.

To adjust the rear suspension sag, follow these steps:

1. **For a coiled-spring-covered shock, determine the amount of** *travel* **(the total range that the suspension can move) by measuring the length of the coil when it's fully extended, without any weight on the bike.**

   Suspension on the front forks usually has a greater travel than the rear suspension. Too much travel is not a good thing — it can damage your suspension by causing it to bottom out.

2. **Sit on you bike while it's stationary and don't touch the ground with your feet.**

   Have your friend support you if needed.

3. **Measure the length of the coil to determine the amount of sag.**

4. **Divide the measurement from Step 3 by the measurement from Step 1, to determine the percentage of sag.**

   For example, if the amount of travel was 4 inches and your sag was 1 inch, the percentage of sag is 1 ÷ 4 = 0.25, or 25 percent.

   If your sag is less than 25 percent, the suspension is too stiff. Proceed to Step 5.

   If your sag is more than 30 percent, the suspension is too soft. Proceed to Step 6.

5. **Adjust the spring tension in front by rotating the spring seat (as shown in Figure 12-7). To reduce tension and increase sag, turn the knob counterclockwise one turn.**

   Repeat steps 2 through 4 until the sag is between 25 percent and 30 percent.

6. **Adjust the spring tension in front by rotating the spring seat (refer to Figure 12-7). To increase tension and reduce sag, turn the spring seat clockwise one turn.**

   Repeat steps 2 through 4 until the sag is between 25 percent and 30 percent.

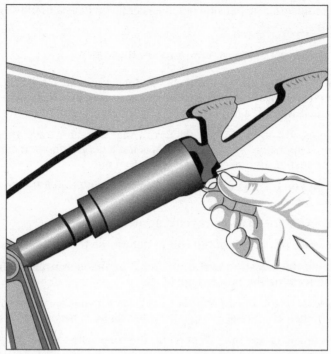

Figure 12-7:
Adjusting
rear sus-
pension.

To adjust the front suspension sag, follow these steps:

1. **Determine the total amount of travel by measuring from the top part of your forks to the seal of the forks or the lowest part of the shock that moves relative to the rest of the bike.**

2. **Sit on you bike while it's stationary and don't touch the ground with your feet.**

   Have your friend support you if needed.

3. **Measure the distance between the two points again to determine the amount of sag.**

4. **Divide the measurement from Step 3 by the measurement from Step 1, to determine the percentage of sag.**

   For example, if the amount of travel was 4 inches and your sag was 1 inch, the percentage of sag is 1 ÷ 4 = 0.25, or 25 percent.

   If the sag was less than 25 percent, the forks are too stiff. Proceed to Step 5.

   If the sage was more than 30 percent, the forks are too soft. Proceed to Step 6.

5. **Adjust the spring tension in front by rotating your screw knob on the top of your fork (as shown in Figure 12-8). To reduce tension and increase sag, turn the knob counterclockwise one turn.**

   Repeat steps 2 through 4 until the sag is between 25 percent and 30 percent.

6. **Adjust the spring tension in front by rotating your screw knob on the top of your fork (refer to Figure 12-8). To increase tension and reduce sag, turn the knob clockwise one turn.**

   Repeat steps 2 through 4 until the sag is between 25 percent and 30 percent.

If your friends have deserted you for the day, do the same process except use a zip tie around the fork instead of just eyeballing or measuring by hand. Use it to get the total travel and then reset it to get the sag. This gives you a more accurate measurement and is easier to perform.

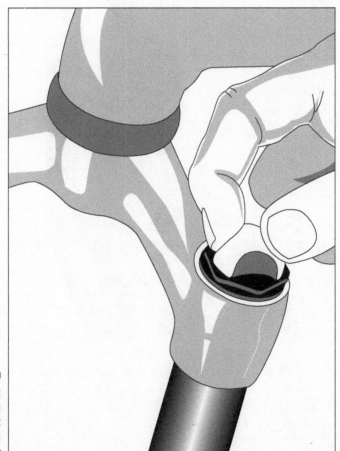

Figure 12-8:
Adjusting
the front
suspension

Maintaining the suspension

How to maintain a bike's suspension varies depending on the type of suspension. Suspension systems that use oil need more attention and maintenance than those that used coil-based springs. Follow your bike's owner's manual for how to maintain the suspension properly.

One of the most important things you can do for your suspension is to keep it clean. Disassemble your forks regularly and according to the recommended timeframe in the owner's manual. (Figure 12-9 shows a disassembled suspension fork.) As a part of your annual overhaul, you'll want to disassemble the forks and replace seals, wipers, and bushings.

Also, regularly inspect your bike's suspension for signs of oil leaks. If you notice a leak, you should replace the seals as soon as possible.

Figure 12-9:
A dis-
assembled
suspension
fork.

Chapter 13

Putting the Pedal to the Metal: The Drivetrain

In This Chapter

▶ Working on pedals

▶ Removing and installing crank arms

▶ Dealing with chainrings

▶ Handling the bottom bracket

*T*he drivetrain is sort of like your bike's transmission. It converts energy from your legs into mechanical force to power you forward. The drivetrain starts with pedals attached to the bike's crank arms, which are mounted to the frame by the bottom bracket. Moving the pedals begins a process that drives your energy through the chain to the back wheel, moving the bicycle forward down the trail. In this chapter, we explain how to remove, install, and overhaul each of the components that make up the drivetrain.

Working on the drivetrain is not overly complicated, but it does require some special tools, including special wrenches, bottom bracket tools, crank-arm extractors, and so on. If you're committed to a long-term relationship with your bike and want to do your own repair and maintenance, purchasing these tools will be a good investment. Otherwise, when it comes time to overhaul these parts, you can always take your bike to your local bike shop and let the experts there handle the job.

Putting the Pedal to the Metal

The pedals are an important link in the transfer of power from your legs to your bike. However, if you were buying a new bike, you wouldn't get that impression because manufacturers sometimes install the cheapest, most low-end pedals possible.

Dennis recently bought a new road bike for his wife. To look at it was to admire a work of art . . . except for the ugly, thick, rubber pedals attached to the cranks, which looked as if they were taken from a child's bike.

Manufacturers use cheap pedals because many bicyclists develop personal preferences for certain types of pedals and, when they buy a new bicycle, they have their old pedals mounted on their new bikes — or buy a new set of pedals.

In this section, we show you what to look for in new pedals and tell you how to keep your pedals working well.

Shopping for new pedals

There are many different pedal styles on the market. The traditional style pedals are flat. Other styles have binding systems that allow you to strap your foot to the pedal with a toe clip and strap or lock your shoe into the pedal with a clipless pedal.

Many casual riders think that having their feet attached to the pedal would be uncomfortable or worry that disengaging their feet would be difficult. On the contrary, toe clips or clipless pedals are easy to manage, and they offer significant gains in performance.

On most pedals, you can attach a toe clip and strap, which helps prevent your foot from slipping off the pedal and keeps the ball of your foot centered over the pedal, which improves the efficiency of your pedaling. Toe clips include a buckle that allows you to adjust the strap so that it can fit a variety of shoe types and sizes. Because you can wear any type of shoe with them, these are especially nice if you're a casual rider and like to get off your bike occasionally and sightsee or just walk around.

Another option is to go with clipless pedals, which are similar to ski bindings. They're designed to grab a cleat built into the bottom of specially designed biking shoes. These pedals hold your foot in place while you pedal, greatly increasing your pedaling efficiency. Snapping your shoe into the pedal is a breeze, and unlocking the cleat and removing your shoe from the pedal is a quick, natural movement with an outward twist of your heel.

There are a number of different clipless systems on the market each with a slightly different method for locking the cleat into the pedal. If you're buying biking shoes, make sure you check them for their compatibility with your pedals, and vice versa.

If you're worried about whether you'll be able to unlock the cleat from the pedal quickly enough in an emergency, don't be. We can pull our shoes off the pedals faster with clipless pedals than we can with toe clips. Plus, clipless pedals are usually designed with a tension adjustment — usually a small bolt that's turned clockwise to increase tension and counterclockwise to reduce tension. If you find that the cleat in your shoe is a little difficult to remove, try adjusting the tension. Practice getting in and out of your clipless pedals a few times before you ride so that you don't come to your first stop and fall over with your shoes locked into your pedals.

If you opt for clipless pedals, you'll want to adjust them to the pedaling position that is most natural for you. Many shoes allow you to move the position of the cleat. In addition, some pedal systems provide for some movement or float after the cleat locks into the pedal — this gives your feet some ability to move on the pedal, which reduces tension and stress on the knees and keeps you from staying in one position during your ride.

Talk to the staff in your local bike shop to find the right adjustment for your pedaling system. This will help ensure that you don't end up locking your shoes into pedals in a position that's unnatural for your body and puts strain on your legs when you bike.

Identifying worn-out pedals

Pedals are often subject to a lot of abuse. Not only do they absorb energy from your body, but they're low to the ground and away from the center of the bike, which means they're often exposed to harsher conditions than the rest of the bike.

If you're hearing creaking or grating sounds or noticing any general looseness when you rotate the pedals, they may need to be replaced. Be sure to isolate the sounds or looseness to the pedals and not the bottom bracket before you start spending money replacing parts.

Removing pedals

Pedals can sometimes be difficult to remove. They're usually torqued pretty well because the pedaling motion gradually tightens the screws. If your pedals haven't been removed for a while, or if not much grease was applied the last time they were installed, this may make it harder for you to remove them.

Keep in mind that the threads for the left pedal (the left side as you're sitting on the bicycle — usually the non-chainring side) is reversed. Both pedals loosen by moving the wrench toward the back of the bike, and both pedals tighten by moving toward the front of the bike. In other words, forward pedal motion tightens, and reverse pedal motion loosens.

Pedals are designed this way so that when you pedal, the thread doesn't come loose.

The best way to remove a pedal is to use a pedal wrench, which allows you to get a firm fit on the wrench flats, as shown in Figure 13-1.

Follow these steps to remove your pedals:

1. **Spray some penetrating oil into the pedal where the threads are screwed into the cranks.**

   Allow the oil to work itself into the threads for a few minutes.

2. **Rotate the crank arms into a three o'clock and nine o'clock position.**

3. **Using a pedal wrench, hold the crank arm steady, and unscrew the right pedal from the crank in a counterclockwise direction.**

4. **Repeat Step 3, except unscrew the left pedal in a clockwise direction.**

If you have trouble loosening the pedals, here are some tips to try:

✔ Slide a piece of pipe over the end of the wrench (as shown in Figure 13-2), effectively extending the length of the wrench, which will give you more leverage and increase the amount of force you can apply.

Figure 13-1: Using a pedal wrench to remove a pedal.

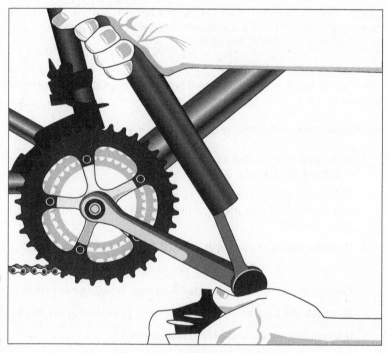

Figure 13-2:
Using a pipe
for leverage.

✔ Remove the crank arm and then secure it with a vise. In this manner,
you won't have to worry about the crank arms moving while you try to
loosen the pedal. Place a soft cloth around the crank arm so you don't
damage or scratch it.

Be careful when trying to free a tight pedal. It's very easy for the wrench, the
crankarm, or your hand to slip while you're applying force, which could cause
you to smack your hand or arm against your bike. Wear a pair of work gloves
to save your knuckles from being scuffed up on the chainrings.

Overhauling the pedals

Pedals depend on internal bearings to spin smoothly. Over time, the bearings
wear out causing the pedals to spin less smoothly, which reduces performance. This section describes some steps you can take to overhaul the

pedals. For cheaper pedals, overhauling isn't an option, because they're made too cheaply to be serviceable. For higher-quality pedals, an overhaul is a good way to extend their life.

As you take apart the pedal, place each component on a clean flat surface in the order it was removed. This will help you reinstall the components in the correct order.

Here's how to overhaul your pedals:

1. **If the pedal has a flat medal cage, remove it before beginning to overhaul the pedals.**

   This will make working with the pedal easier. There should be several screws holding it in place, which can be removed with a screwdriver or Allen wrench.

2. **Remove the dust cap with a small flathead screwdriver.**

   Be careful not to damage the dust cap.

3. **Loosen the locknut under the dust cap, holding everything in place.**

   To reach the locknut, you may be need to use a socket wrench.

4. **If there is a washer in place, remove it.**

   If the washer is difficult to lift out, use a flathead screwdriver or needle-nose pliers.

5. **Remove the cone that is holding the bearings in place.**

   The cone may lift out or need to be unthreaded with a screwdriver or needle-nose pliers.

   Make sure you're supporting the axle. If the axle drops out, the bearings will fall out and you'll be searching for them on the floor for hours.

6. **Scoop out all the bearings and inspect their surfaces.**

   If they're dull and have dents, they need to be replaced.

7. **Clean all the parts, and then install them in reverse order from how you disassembled them.**

   Be sure to apply a liberal coat of grease inside each side of the pedal. This will help hold the bearings in place until you thread the cone, washer, and locknut back on.

8. **Finish the reassembly by refitting the dust cap.**

   This is important to keep dirt and water out of bearings and ensure that your overhaul lasts.

Installing new pedals

Many pedals are marked with an *L* or an *R* to help you figure out which pedal should go on which side. You want to make sure you have the correct pedal, because the left pedal unscrews in a clockwise direction and the right pedal unscrews counterclockwise. If you try to screw in the wrong pedal, you'll damage the threads.

To install new pedals, follow these steps:

1. **Apply grease to the threads of each pedal (as shown in Figure 13-3).**

2. **Start with the right pedal, and remember that you'll be turning the pedal in a clockwise direction.**

3. **To ensure that you don't damage any threads, screw the pedal in by hand using care (as is shown in Figure 13-4).**

Figure 13-3: Lubricating the pedal.

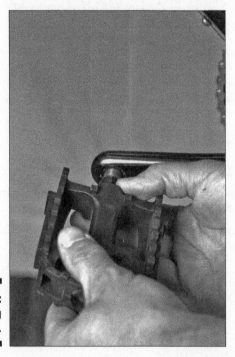

Figure 13-4:
Reattaching
the pedal.

4. **When the threads engage, use the wrench to tighten the pedal.**

   One way to tighten the pedal is to use one hand to keep the wrench on the pedal's wrench flats and then, with the other hand, rotate the opposite crank arm to tighten.

   Tighten until the pedals are secure, but don't overtighten. Carefully check the crank arm for any metal shavings at the base of the pedal and, if necessary, remove them with a file.

5. **Repeat steps 1 through 4 for the left pedal, except screwing it in a counterclockwise direction to tighten.**

Crank It Up! Working on the Crankset and Bottom Bracket

The two major components of the drivetrain are the crankset and the bottom bracket (see Figure 13-5). In this section, we explain how to service different types of crank arms and the two major types of bottom brackets — cartridges and adjustable bottom brackets.

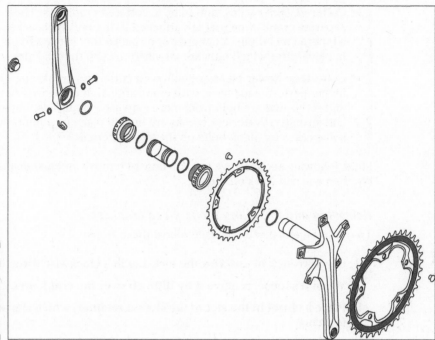

Figure 13-5:
The crank-
set and
bottom
bracket.

The crankset

The crankset plays the leading role in moving you forward when you bike. Consisting of the cranks, the chainrings, and the bottom bracket assembly, the crankset's job is to transfer power with the chain from your legs and the pedals to the chain and back to the rear wheel.

On the crankset, the crank and chainrings play important roles. The cranks are what connect the pedals to the bike, and the chainrings guide the chain as it receives the force from the turning cranks.

Of the different cranksets on the market, there are three main categories:

✔ **One-piece:** Children's bikes and some low-end adult bikes have one-piece cranksets, where the crank arms are one, long, S-shaped piece and the bottom bracket has two large bearing retainers that are serviceable and adjustable. One-piece crankset are made to be fairly durable to hold up to the kind of abuse a kid can dish out on bike, but as you might expect for a low-end product, they're heavy and not designed for performance.

✔ **Cottered:** Older bikes tend to have cottered cranksets. These consist of separate crank arms that are attached to the bottom bracket axle using a tapered metal pin. A hammer or a special tool is used to put these pins in place, after which nuts are attached to keep them secure.

✔ **Cotterless:** Newer bikes are built with cotterless cranksets. These are higher-performance parts with crank arms that come in a variety of sizes and styles and are built from more expensive materials that are lighter and stronger. Cotterless cranks are held in place by a nut or a bolt or in some cases by pinch bolts on the left-side crank.

In the following sections, we tell you how to remove and install all three types so you can work on them.

Removing and installing a one-piece crankset

To remove a one-piece crankset, follow these steps:

1. **Use a wrench to unscrew the lockring in a clockwise direction.**

2. **When it's loose, remove it by lifting it over the crank arm.**

3. **Place a chisel in the slot of the slotted retainer, which sits under the lockring.**

4. **Tap the chisel lightly with a hammer in a clockwise direction.**

5. **When it's loose, remove it by lifting it over the crank arm.**

6. **Pull the entire crank assembly out of the bottom bracket shell.**

7. **Use the chisel and hammer to lightly knock out the bearing cups that sit within the bottom-bracket shell.**

To install the one piece crankset, follow these procedures in reverse.

Removing and installing a cottered crankset

On some older bikes, cranksets are attached using a cotter pin, which has to be removed and installed with a blow of a hammer (as shown in Figure 13-6). Remove the nut and washer from the pin using a wrench. Drive the pin out by hitting it with a standard (not rubber) hammer.

If you have trouble moving the pin, use some penetrating oil and then try using a *punch* (a chisel-like tool with a pointed end). Many times, whether you're using a hammer or another tool like a punch, the pin will have to be replaced because the removal process will likely damage it.

To install a cotterless crankset with a socket bolt, follow these steps:

1. **If the pin was not damaged during removal you can reuse it. Otherwise, take the old one to your local bike shop to buy a replacement.**

Figure 13-6:
Removing
the cotter
pin.

2. **Slide the crank arm onto the crankset and insert the pin.**

3. **Hammer the pin until it is firmly set in the crank and exposed on the other side.**

4. **Put the washer and bolt on the end of the pin and tighten with a wrench.**

Removing and installing a cotterless crankset

Cotterless cranksets are held in place in one of three ways: with a socket bolt, by a nut and bolt, or by pinch bolts. The method for removing the crankset varies depending on how the crankset is held in place. We cover all three in the following sections.

With a socket bolt

Most bikes these days have cotterless cranksets that are attached with socket bolts. (These cranksets are sometimes called *one-key release*.) This type of crankset is easy to remove because it has a crank extractor built in (see the next section for more on extractors). There is usually not a dust cap, but if there is one, you can use a screwdriver to remove it.

Using an extra-long 7mm or 8mm Allen wrench, turn the bolts in a counter-clockwise direction, holding the cranks from moving with your free hand (as shown in Figure 13-7).

Figure 13-7:
Loosening
a cotter-
less crank
with a Allen
wrench.

To install a cotterless crankset with a socket bolt, follow these steps:

1. **Apply grease to the threads of the nut or bolt.**

2. **Insert the right crankarm into the right bottom bracket.**

3. **Insert the left crankarm onto the end of the axle of the right crankarm, and screw in the bolt, being careful to align the threads.**

4. **Tighten the bolt to secure the crankarm.**

This type of crankset usually doesn't have a dust cap, but if there is a dust cap, grease the threads and install it.

With nuts and bolts

To remove a cotterless crankset that's held in place with nuts and bolts, you need a crank-arm extractor (see Figure 13-8) that fits your bike. One side of the crank extractor is used to remove the bolt holding the crankarm on the axle. The other side of the extractor allows you to remove the crankarm.

Here are the steps to take:

1. **Use a screwdriver and remove the dust cap that covers the threads inside the crank arm.**

   Be careful not to damage the dust cap.

2. **Fit the extractor onto the nut or bolt inside the crank arm.**

3. **Using a wrench, turn the extractor in a counterclockwise direction.**

4. **When the nut or bolt is loose, use your fingers to remove the nut or bolt.**

   If there is a washer with the nut or bolt, make sure to remove that as well.

5. **Thread the other side of the extractor into the threads of the crank arm.**

   Be careful to make sure that the threads are aligned and that the extractor is not being screwed in at an angle.

6. **When it becomes too difficult to turn the extractor, use a wrench and continue to snugly screw the extractor into the crankarm until it gently pushes against the axle.**

7. **Turn the handle of the extractor to push the center core of the extractor against the axle.**

   It will eventually push the crank off the axle.

The extractor is actually two tools: a 14mm or 15mm socket wrench and, separately, a threaded center pushing extractor tool. Sometimes these tools are integrated as one tool with two sides.

Figure 13-8:
Using the
crank-arm
extractor.

To install a cotterless crankset with nuts and bolts, follow these steps:

1. **Apply grease to the threads of the nut or bolt.**

2. **Insert the right crankarm into the right bottom bracket.**

3. **Insert the left crankarm onto the end of the axle of the right crankarm and screw in the nut or bolt, being careful to align the threads.**

4. **Tighten the nut or bolt to secure the crank arm.**

5. **If there is a dust cap, grease the threads and install.**

With pinch bolts

Some manufacturers including Shimano make cranks that are held in place by pinch bolts on the left crank arm. These types of cranks do not require a crank arm extractor for removal.

Here are the steps for removing a cotterless crank held in place with pinch bolts:

1. **Loosen the pinch bolts on the left crank arm.**

2. **Remove the cap on the left crank arm.**

   To remove the cap, you may need a special tool. In some cases, caps are designed to be removed with an Allen wrench.

3. **Pull off the left crank arm.**

4. **Pull off the right crank arm.**

   If it's tight, give the end of its axle a light tap with a rubber hammer or mallet. Be careful not to mar your crank arm during this procedure.

To reinstall cotterless crankarms with pinch bolts, follow these steps:

1. **Insert the right-side crankarm with the chainrings into the bottom bracket, with the crank arm pointing downward at the six o'clock position.**

2. **Insert the left crankarm into the bottom bracket, with the crankarm pointing upward to the 12 o'clock position.**

3. **On the end of the axle of the right crank unit, there will be threads with one groove larger than the other. Align this larger groove with the groove on the inside of the left crank arm.**

   This assures that both arms are exactly 180 degrees apart.

4. **Apply grease to the ends of the cap and insert it into the center of the left crankarm.**

5. **Apply grease to the threads of the two pinch bolts and insert them into the left crank arm.**

As you tighten, switch between the bolts every few turns to make sure they tighten evenly.

For Shimano cranks of this type, make sure to tighten the threaded dust cap that actually helps bind the crank. Provided with your cranks is a small tool used to hand-tighten this piece before you tighten the pinch bolts.

Working on chainrings

Over time, the chainrings will wear down, making shifting more difficult. If you have an old, stretched chain on your bike that you haven't replaced in a while, this will cause the teeth on your chainrings to wear out. Likewise, worn teeth on chainrings will cause accelerated wear and stretching of the chain. Normally a chain will wear out faster than the chainrings. If you regularly check your chain for wear and replace it at the first signs of wear, you'll be able to get two to three chain lives before you need to replace your chainrings.

Chainrings that need to be replaced have teeth that are thinner and look like waves from the ocean as opposed to cleanly cut teeth (the way they look when they're first manufactured). To remove chainrings, find a clean, flat surface, and follow these steps:

1. **Use an Allen wrench to remove the bolts holding the chainrings in place (as shown in Figure 13-9).**

Figure 13-9:
Removing
chainrings.

2. Use a flathead screwdriver or a special slotted wrench (as shown in Figure 13-10) to hold the nuts in place while you use the Allen wrench.

3. After you remove one chainring, there may be another set of bolts holding the other chainring(s) in place. If so, remove these as well.

Be careful to hold onto any spacers when you remove the chainrings. You'll need to put these back in place if you're replacing or remounting any of the chainrings.

If you end up in an accident or run the side of your bike into something, you could bend the teeth on a chainring. If this causes a tooth to break or leads to serious damage to the overall chainring, you'll probably want to replace it. However, if just one tooth or a few teeth are slightly bent, causing shifting and chain problems, you may be able to bend them back in place. Bike shops have a special chainring tooth alignment tool that is designed for this procedure. In some cases, you may be able to do the job with an adjustable wrench, although this is a little riskier.

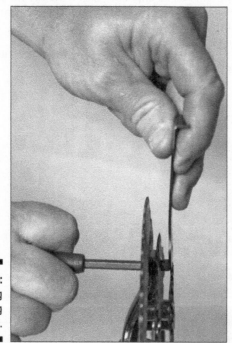

Figure 13-10:
Undoing chainring bolts.

To straighten chainring teeth, follow these steps:

1. **Spin the chainring without the chain to identify which tooth or teeth are bent.**

   If the bent tooth or teeth are on the large chainring, sometimes you can straighten it or them without removing the chainring from the bicycle. If not, you'll need to remove the chainring.

2. **If you removed the chainring, secure it in a vise as close to the bend and with as much of the chainring being supported or clamped in the vise as possible.**

   Cover the chainring with a soft cloth so you don't scratch or damage it with the vise.

3. **Using the chainring tooth tool or an adjustable wrench, grab the tooth, being sure not to grab the chainring itself.**

   If you use an adjustable wrench, tighten it onto the tooth as snugly as possible.

5. **Bend the tooth slightly in the other direction to straighten it.**

   Only try to bend or straighten one tooth at a time.

6. **Place the chainring on a flat hard surface and examine your efforts.**

Reinstall the chainring by inserting the bolts that hold it in place and reversing the steps you used to remove it. If nuts are used to hold the bolts in place, insert these and tighten. Once you're finished, test the chainring to make sure the chain shifts and runs smoothly around the chainring.

The bottom bracket

Crucial to the crankset is the bottom bracket. Of all the bearings on a bike, the bottom bracket is the one that has to bear the heaviest load. Not only does the bottom bracket have to spin while you pedal, but it takes the force of all the twisting and turning that occurs during pedaling.

There are two main types of bottom brackets:

✔ **Adjustable:** If you have an older or lower-end bike, you may have an adjustable bottom bracket. This type of bottom bracket has a cup that holds bearings and an axle that spins within the bottom bracket. An adjustable bottom bracket is much more susceptible to wear and tear than a cartridge-type (see the next bullet), because water and dirt can enter the cup where the bearings are held. Plus, an adjustable bottom bracket needs to be adjusted perfectly, or the bearings will prematurely wear out.

If you have this style of bottom bracket you may want to think of upgrading to a cartridge bottom bracket. At the very least, you'll want to overhaul the bottom bracket at least once a year — more often if you do a lot of biking in wet or muddy conditions.

✔ **Cartridge:** Most newer bikes have a sealed-cartridge style of bottom bracket. A cartridge has a longer life than an ordinary bottom bracket — because they're sealed, water and dirt are kept away from the bearings. They're also easier to install and maintain because they don't need to be adjusted the way standard bottom brackets with cups and cones do.

The other advantage to cartridges is that installing them is easier and quicker. When they do finally wear out, you replace the entire cartridge. But don't worry — you'll ride several thousand miles before you need to go shopping for a new bottom-bracket cartridge.

If the bottom bracket is squeaking or if the cranks don't rotate smoothly by hand with the chain off, it's time to overhaul. If you hear any squeaking or grinding, if the bottom bracket is slightly loose, or if you feel a vibration when you pull on the cranks, you should also prepare for an overhaul.

Adjustable bottom brackets should be overhauled as part of your annual maintenance. Cartridge bottom brackets are replaced rather than overhauled — and replacement isn't usually necessary until you've ridden a few thousand miles.

Removing and installing a cartridge bottom bracket

To remove a cartridge bottom bracket, follow these steps:

1. **Remove the cranks following the procedure described earlier for the type of crankset you have (one-piece, cottered, or cotterless).**

2. **Attach the appropriate bottom bracket tool to the left side of the bike (as shown in Figure 13-11).**

There are many different types of tools designed to fit many specific types of bottom brackets. The different tools usually have a different number of notches or splines, which match the number of notches or splines in the cup that secures the cartridge in place. Check with your local bike shop to determine which tool is appropriate for your bike.

3. **Use an adjustable wrench to turn the bottom bracket tool in a counter-clockwise direction (as shown in Figure 13-12).**

The one common problem in removing cartridges is that the tools slip while under torque, stripping the splines. Because removing the bottom bracket can take a tremendous amount of force, the pressure needs to be applied on the tool in the direction of the bike to avoid stripping the splines or the tool.

Figure 13-11:
Attaching
a bottom
bracket tool.

Figure 13-12:
Using the
bottom
bracket tool.

4. **Perform the same procedure on the right side except turn the tool clockwise.**

5. **When the lock ring is loose, use your hand to unscrew it the rest of the way.**

   It's attached to the bottom bracket, which will come out when you're finished unscrewing it (as shown in Figure 13-13).

To reinstall a cartridge bottom bracket, read the manufacturer's instructions and follow these steps:

1. **Coat the threads of the bottom bracket with grease.**

   Some bike shops prefer to use an anti-seize agent or plumber's thread tape, which hardens and expands once it dries, helping to keep the bottom bracket secure and protecting the threads.

2. **Examine the cartridge for an *R* and an *L*, signifying the right and left side.**

3. **Insert the *L* side into the right side through to the left side of the bottom bracket shell of the frame and carefully align the threads of the cartridge with the threads of the frame. Screw in the cartridge in a counterclockwise direction.**

Figure 13-13:
Removing
the
cartridge

4. **When it becomes more difficult to turn the cartridge, attach the bottom bracket tool.**

5. **Using an adjustable wrench, fully tighten the cartridge.**

   Most manufacturers recommend a significant amount of torque for the bottom bracket, which means you need to apply a lot of force to tighten the bottom bracket.

6. **Attach the cup to the other side and, using a wrench, tighten it in a clockwise direction.**

Removing and installing an adjustable bottom bracket

To remove an adjustable bottom bracket, follow these steps:

1. **Remove the cranks following the procedure described earlier for the type of crankset you have (one-piece, cottered, or cotterless).**

2. **On the left side of the bike, you'll see a lock ring with grooves cut into it. Unloosen the lock ring in a counterclockwise direction by using a specialized tool called a C-wrench (shown in Figure 13-14) or lock-ring wrench.**

   If you don't have a C-wrench, use a chisel or — as a last resort — a flathead screwdriver to tap against the grooves or the lock ring to break it free. Be careful, because this may damage your screwdriver!

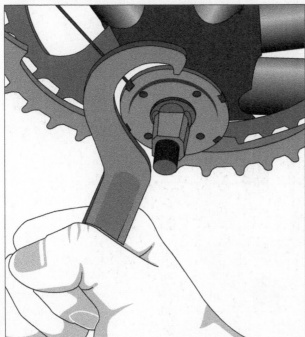

Figure 13-14:
Using a
C-wrench.

3. **After removing the lock ring, you'll see an adjustable cup that holds the bearings. Remove this cap.**

   Some adjustable cups have pin holes which require a special tool. Figure 13-15 is an example of using a pin spanner to remove the adjustable cup. Unscrew the adjustable cup being careful to catch any loose bearings that may exist. The axle will slide out at this point.

4. **On the right side of the bike, remove the fixed cup, which is screwed into the bottom bracket shell of the frame.**

   You may not be able to remove the fixed cup, so consider taking the bike to your local bike shop where they'll have a fixed-cup removal tool.

   You'll need a large enough crescent or adjustable wrench to fit around the fixed cup. This time, turn in a clockwise direction. This side may be very tight.

To install an adjustable bottom bracket, follow these steps:

1. **Clean all the parts with degreaser.**

2. **Inspect the ball bearings, cups, and axle.**

   If they look dull or the bearing surfaces are not smooth, replace them.

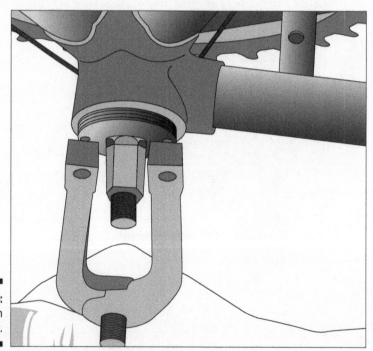

Figure 13-15:
Using a pin
spanner.

3. **Fill both cups with a layer of grease.**

4. **Place the same number of ball bearings in that were originally each cup.**

    If you aren't sure of the number, use as many as necessary to fit securely with a small gap to allow each bearing "elbow room."

5. **Use a screwdriver or other tool to push the bearings into the grease.**

6. **Cover the bearings with another layer of grease.**

    Figure 13-16 has an example of bearings packed in grease.

Figure 13-16:
Repacking
the bearings
in grease.

7. **On the right side, screw on the fixed cup by hand until it tightens. Then very firmly tighten this side with a wrench.**

8. **On the left side of the bike, insert the longer end of the axle into the bottom bracket shell and into the fixed cup.**

9. **Screw on the adjustable cup until tight. Try rotating the axle. If it's tight, slightly loosen the cup.**

10. **Place the lock ring on the bottom bracket and tighten, checking to ensure that the axle rotates smoothly and not too tightly.**

    It may take a few tries to get an adjustment that is not too tight and not too loose.

Shopping for a new crankset and bottom bracket

If you have an older bike and you'd like to upgrade the crankset and bottom bracket, there are a few things to think about:

✔ **Buy a cartridge bottom bracket.** This is the most popular style of bottom bracket on the market and shouldn't be a problem unless your bike requires a special bottom bracket. When the cartridge bottom bracket is in place, you'll be able to relax knowing that most likely you won't have to touch it for a number of years.

✔ If you're moving from a cottered crankset to a cotterless one, you'll to need replace both the cranks and the bottom bracket. You can't mix a cottered crank with a cotterless bottom bracket.

✔ **Make sure that the axle style and the threads match.** There are different types of bottom bracket threading. The threads need to match your frame and the axle style needs to match the crankset.

Consult with your local bike shop to confirm which bottom brackets will fit the threads on your bike.

✔ **Make sure you have the right size bottom bracket.** There are many different widths for bottom brackets. You need to know the width of the bottom bracket shell on the frame and the overall length needed for the specific crankset you're using. Sometimes mountain bikes have wider bottom brackets than road bikes. In addition, cranks with three chainrings need wider bottom brackets than two-chainring cranks.

Again, talk with the folks at your local bike shop to make sure you're getting the right size for your bike.

✔ **Pay attention to crank-arm length.** Crank arms change the circumference in which the pedals rotate, so with larger crank arms you'll be pedaling in a wider circumference and getting more leverage as you pedal. Having longer cranks and more power is beneficial if you're doing a lot of climbing. The downside of a larger crank is that, because of the wider circumference, it takes more effort to spin quickly — so if speed is a consideration, a smaller crank may be in order.

The most common crank-arm lengths are 172.5mm or 175mm. If you're a short person, you'll want to try using a shorter crank. At the same time, if you're tall, a longer crank will work with your leg muscles better. A few manufacturers sell cranks of 185mm or more. The best advice is to work with your local bike store to find the crank the best suits you.

With longer crank arms, it's important to make sure the bottom bracket has enough clearance or else the crank arms could hit the ground when you' re cornering or climbing over logs.

Chapter 14

Dropping It into Gear: The Shifting System

. . . .

In This Chapter

▶ Understanding how derailleurs work

▶ Removing, installing, and adjusting the rear and front derailleurs

▶ Changing derailleur cables

▶ Removing and installing the shifters

. . . .

*T*his chapter covers inspection, removal, installation, and adjustment of the shifting system, including the cable system, shifters, and derailleurs. Whew!

Demystifying Derailleurs

Derailleurs are the mechanisms for "de-railing" or moving the chain from cog to cog and chainring to chain ring, allowing you to shift and change gears when you ride. The derailleurs don't so much move the chain as they guide it from one side to the other, which is only possible if you're pedaling forward and the chain is moving.

Both the front and rear derailleurs work through the use of an internal spring, which pulls the derailleur toward the bike or pushes the derailleur away from the bike, while the cable attached to the bike's shifter opposes the force of the spring. When the shifter pulls the cable, the cable overcomes the spring and moves the chain toward or away from the bike. When the shifter releases the cable, the derailleur moves back to its normal position.

The fact that springs and cables are pushing and pulling on the derailleurs would be a problem if there were nothing stopping the derailleurs from moving the chain too far in one direction or the other. Fortunately, derailleurs are designed with a pair of stop-limit screws, which limit the movement of the derailleurs in both directions. These screws are usually marked with an *H* and an *L*, for high and low. The high-limit screw controls the distance that the derailleur can move *away* from the bike (toward the higher gears), and the low-limit screw controls the distance the derailleur can move *toward* the bike (toward the lower gears).

Limit screws physically limit movement as they're screwed deeper into the derailleur. Turning the screws clockwise drives them in deeper and restricts the range of movement; turning the screws counterclockwise loosens them and increases the range of movement. If you were to tighten both limit screws to their maximum depth, you would limit the derailleur to a single position. This is good to know if you break a derailleur or chain and need to set the bike up for just one gear to get home.

Both derailleurs have difficult jobs when it comes to keeping up with the demands of a biker who is shifting to higher and lower gears. Moving the chain toward the frame puts the bike in a lower gear, whereas moving the chain away from the bike puts the bike in a higher gear. Just as with a car, lower gears are useful when you're going slow (for example, climbing a steep hill), whereas higher gears serve you on the descent, when you're riding at a faster speed.

The front derailleur has the unenviable task of moving the chain sideways as it's under force. This part of the chain transmits power to the rear wheel, which is why when you're applying a lot of power and moving slowly (such as climbing a hill) it's hard for the front derailleur to shift.

Rear derailleurs have the job of swinging their arm or cage back and forth under the freewheel, guiding the chain from one cog to the next. The rear derailleur cage has the familiar S shape, with two jockey wheels. The top jockey wheel guides the chain onto the cog and the bottom jockey wheel is designed to keep tension on the chain and take up slack.

The rear derailleur

Rear derailleurs (shown in Figure 14-1) have been known to give even experienced bike mechanics headaches at times. They do double-duty: keeping the chain under tension and guiding it back and forth between the cogs as the rider shifts. Slight changes in tension of the cable to which the derailleur is attached can cause shifting to become out of whack. Just as with the front derailleur, you can improve its functioning and longevity if you keep it clean, lubricated, and adjusted as needed.

The following sections describe how to remove and reinstall the derailleur.

Figure 14-1:
A rear
derailleur.

Removing the rear derailleur

To remove your rear derailleur, follow these instructions:

1. **Shift the rear derailleur to the smallest cog.**

2. **Using an Allen wrench or box wrench, loosen the bolt that's holding the cable in place.**

   Note that if you don't shift the rear derailleur to the smallest cog, it could spring back at you because it's under tension from the cable.

3. **Use an Allen wrench or box wrench (as shown in Figure 14-2) to remove the bolt that is holding bottom jockey wheel in place.**

   Spray some lubricant on the jockey wheel if the bolt will not budge.

4. **After the bolt is removed, lift out the jockey wheel.**

5. **Use an Allen wrench or box wrench (as shown in Figure 14-3) and reach around the derailleur to loosen the bolt that holds the top jockey wheel in place.**

Figure 14-2:
Loosening
the
bottom
jockey
wheel.

Figure 14-3:
Loosening
the top
jockey
wheel.

6. **After the bolt is loose, you should be able to separate the cage (as shown in Figure 14-4).**

7. **With the cage separated, lift the chain off the top jockey wheel and away from the derailleur.**

   Rest the chain on one of the cogs, letting the slack hang down.

8. **Use an Allen wrench to remove the pivot bolt (see Figure 14-5), which will allow you to remove the derailleur.**

Figure 14-4: Separating the cage.

Figure 14-5: Undoing the pivot bolt.

Installing the rear derailleur

To install the rear derailleur, follow the steps in this section.

1. **Position the derailleur so that the chain wraps around the right half of the top jockey wheel (as you're facing the right side of the bike).**

2. **Align the mounting bolt with the gear hanger on the frame.**

3. **Insert the mounting bolt and tighten with an Allen wrench.**

4. **Pull the chain through the cage and, while holding the cage and chain with one hand, insert the bottom jockey wheel so that the chain wraps around the left side of the wheel.**

5. **Close the cage so that the holes align with the hole in the bottom jockey.**

6. **Insert the bolt and tighten both jockey wheel mounting bolts securely.**

7. **Adjust the H limit screw (see Figure 14-6) and the L limit screw (see Figure 14-7) so that they limit the derailleur from throwing the chain off the bike or, even worse, into your spokes.**

   Tighten both screws in a clockwise direction two turns. This will restrict the movement further than it was before.

Figure 14-6:
Adjusting
the H screw.

Figure 14-7:
Adjusting
the L screw.

8. **To stimulate shifting with the cable, practice turning the pedals with your right hand while pushing inward and upward on the derailleur with your left thumb. Wrap your index finger around the cage and push on the cage with your thumb.**

   Note: These steps are for the most common type of rear derailleur. If you have a rapid-rise rear derailleur, the spring is opposite and pulls the derailleur toward the low gear. Therefore, you'll need to reverse the process when moving the derailleur with your hand.

9. **Using the method in Step 8, try to shift the chain to the largest cog. (It won't succeed on the first attempt because you tightened the L limit screw as a safety precaution.) Loosen the L limit screw by a slight amount, about one-quarter to one-half a revolution, and then begin turning the pedals again.**

   Do this in incremental steps until you're able to shift the chain onto the largest cog. The chain should spin smoothly on the largest cog and not make any grinding sounds.

10. **Perform Step 9 in the opposite direction making incremental adjustments to the H limit screw until the chain arrives on the smallest cog.**

   You won't need to move the derailleur with your hand because the spring in the derailleur will pull it down and outward. Now you're ready to attach the cable and make finer adjustments to the shifting.

11. **Run the cable through the cable-adjusting barrel hole and through the cable anchor bolt clamp.**

    There should be a notch in the cable anchor bolt clamp where the cable is designed to sit when the clamp is tightened.

12. **Tighten the clamp with an Allen wrench or box wrench (as shown in Figure 14-8).**

13. **To make the cable taut, use a pair of pliers or a fourth-hand tool, and pull the cable as you tighten the cable clamp bolt.**

14. **Test the shifting of the derailleur down onto the highest gear.**

    Sometimes when you're tightening the cable, you can pull the derailleur over just a little and then it'll not drop down onto the highest gear.

15. **Attach a cable cap (see Figure 14-9) to the end of the cable and use a pair of pliers to crimp it into place.**

    This will prevent the cable from fraying.

    Always leave about 2 inches of cable on the outside or past the cable anchor bolt. This will make future adjustment to the cable and/or derailleur much easier.

Figure 14-8:
Attaching
the cable.

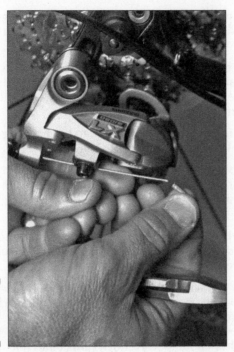

Figure 14-9:
The cable
cap.

Many rear derailleurs have a third screw called a B-angle screw. This is used to adjust the space between the upper jockey wheel and the cogs. Normally, you won't need to adjust this unless you're installing a new derailleur. If you do install a new one, adjust this screw until the upper jockey wheel is close but still has enough space to allow the chain to pass freely without making contact with the cogs.

Adjusting the rear derailleur

If you find that your chain is jumping back and forth between gears or getting stuck on a cog and needs an extra click or two to shift, you need to make an adjustment to your rear derailleur.

The easiest way to recognize that your derailleur needs adjustment is a rattling or clanking noise from the chain when you're pedaling.

Here's how to adjust the rear derailleur:

1. **Use a bike stand or other mechanism to support the bike with the back wheel off the ground.**

   You'll need to pedal the bike with one hand and shift with the other, so having the bike up off the ground is essential

2. **Start by examining how well the derailleur shifts to lower gears or to the larger cogs: Shift the derailleur until it moves the chain onto the largest cog.**

   If it struggles to reach the largest cog, loosen the L-limit screw (refer to Figure 14-7) by a quarter- or half-turn until the chain easily reaches the largest cog. If the chain goes over the cog, tighten the L-limit screw to restrict the movement of the derailleur.

3. **Shift the derailleur in the opposite direction to the higher gears, focusing on how well the chain shifts onto the smallest cog.**

   If it hesitates to drop down, loosen the H-limit screw (refer to Figure 14-8) by a quarter- or half-turn until the chain sits easily on the smallest cog. If the chain is thrown off the freewheel to the outside, tighten the H-limit screw.

4. **After the limits for the derailleur have been set, shift through all the gears, making sure that the chain moves to another cog with each click of the shift lever.**

   If the chain hesitates or makes a lot of noise, you'll need to use the barrel adjuster to do some fine-tuning (see Figure 14-10): Start with the chain on the smallest cog and, while pedaling, shift one click. The derailleur should move the chain instantly to the next cog. If it doesn't, turn the barrel adjuster about a quarter of a turn counterclockwise. If the opposite problem is true and the chain shifted two places, turn the barrel clockwise. Repeat this procedure for each of the cogs on the freewheel until the chain is shifting smoothly for each click of the shifter.

Figure 14-10:
The barrel
adjuster.

If the derailleur is shifting well going up to the larger cogs and slow or hesitating coming down to the smaller cogs there may be a kink or problem with the cable not moving smoothly through the housing. Remove the cable, inspect it, and replace it if it is kinked, frayed, or damaged.

The rear derailleur is a very exposed part of the bike and is prone to being bent or damaged if the bike falls over on top of it. If this happens, all you may need to do is bend the derailleur back into shape. Here's how:

1. **Use one hand to insert an Allen wrench into the mounting bolt.**

2. **With the other hand wrapped around the body of the derailleur, leverage the derailleur back into place so it's suspended in a straight line under one of the cogs.**

If you have problems aligning your derailleur, make a visit to your local bike shop. Most shops have a specialty tool called a derailleur hanger alignment tool, which is made to perform this task and measure the positioning.

Cleaning the rear derailleur

Because the rear derailleur is so close to the ground and so exposed, it accumulates a lot of dirt and grit over time. If you do a lot of riding, especially any off-road riding, you may want to think about adding a rear derailleur cleaning to your monthly maintenance activities (see Chapter 17).

You can clean the rear derailleur on the bike by using a solvent and a brush to scrub it down. But for a more thorough cleaning, consider removing it and then soaking it in a strong degreaser solvent. After it's soaked for bit, use a brush to remove any dirt and grit trapped in its inside parts. Use a rag and clean the jockey wheels — dirt and grime will normally be caked onto their surfaces. Rinse with warm water and then blow-dry with compressed air. Let the derailleur dry completely before reinstalling, and then lubricate the pivots in the derailleur and the inside and outside center of the jockey wheels.

A cassette cleaning brush is very useful for regularly clearing dirt and muck from the jockey wheels.

Most jockey wheels are made of plastic, so regularly inspect them for wear. When the teeth start to get pointed and sharp and they're no longer nice, squared-off tops, replace them.

The front derailleur

Your front derailleur probably won't give you as many headaches as the rear derailleur will over the life of your bike, but it will need occasional care and service. If you have a front derailleur that's acting up, it probably needs a new cable or just a thorough cleaning and lubrication, which will be more effective if you perform it while the derailleur is off the bike. The following sections describe how to remove and then reinstall the front derailleur, as well as how to adjust it.

Removing a front derailleur

To remove a front derailleur, follow these steps:

1. **Shift the derailleur to the smallest chain ring to remove tension on the cable.**

2. **Using an Allen wrench or a box wrench, detach the cable by loosening the anchor bolt that holds it in place (see Figure 14-11).**

3. **Use an Allen wrench or box wrench and undo the pivot bolt that holds the derailleur to the seat tube (see Figure 14-12).**

4. **To remove the chain from the derailleur cage, remove the nut and bolt holding the cage together, and pull apart the cage so that the chain will slide through (see Figure 14-13).**

   Some front derailleurs have a rivet holding the cage together, which requires you to first remove the chain from the bicycle and then proceed.

Figure 14-11: Removing the cable.

Figure 14-12:
Removing
the pivot
bolt.

Figure 14-13:
Pulling the
cage apart.

5. **Spread apart the derailleur mounting clamp and remove the derailleur from the seat tube.**

Installing a front derailleur

Follow these steps to install a front derailleur:

1. **Open the cage of the front derailleur and wrap it around the chain.**

2. **Replace the nut and bolt that holds together the cage.**

3. **Wrap the derailleur mounting clamp around the seat post, and thread the clamp bolt enough so that it isn't tight but allows the derailleur to be moved by hand.**

4. **Align the derailleur so that its outside cage edge runs parallel with the chainrings.**

   Visually inspect the position by standing overhead and looking down on the derailleur.

5. **Position the derailleur at a height that places it about 2mm above the teeth of the largest chainring.**

6. **After aligning and positioning, firmly tighten the mounting clamp bolt.**

   In order to limit the movement of the derailleur so that it doesn't throw the chain off the chainrings, you need to set the H- and L-limit screws.

7. **Set the L-limit screw so that the side of the cage closest to the bike is about 2mm inward of the smallest chainring.**

8. **Pull the derailleur away from the bike and over the large chainring.**

9. **Set the H-limit screw so that when you move the derailleur as far as it will go, it reaches to a position 2mm outward of the largest chainring.**

10. **After you've found the correct position for the derailleur, pass the cable through to the anchor bolt and, while holding the cable taut with a pair of pliers or a fourth-hand tool, tighten the anchor bolt.**

    Make sure you follow the correct route for the front derailleur cable. Some bikes are designed with the cable coming up from the bottom bracket, and others drop down the length of the seat tube.

11. **For a new cable, shift the levers a few times to stretch and seat the cable. Then loosen the cable anchor bolt, pull the cable taut, and retighten if necessary.**

12. **If you have installed a new cable, cut off any extra and then attach a cable cap to the end. Crimp the end cap in place with pliers.**

    Always leave about 2 inches of cable on the outside or past the cable anchor bolt. This will make future adjustment to the cable and/or derailleur much easier.

Adjusting the front derailleur

One of the first things you need to do to adjust the front derailleur is to set limit screws so that the derailleur doesn't move too far and push or pull the chain off the chain rings. There is nothing worse than hitting a steep hill, shifting to your smallest chainring, and having the chain fly off the chainring and become stuck in between the chainring and chainstay. A properly adjusted limit screw will ensure that the chain doesn't go past the smallest chainring when shifting.

1. **Shift the derailleur to move the chain onto the smallest chainring.**

2. **Set the L-limit screw so that the side of the cage closest to the bike is about 2mm outside the smallest chainring (see Figure 14-14).**

3. **Shift the derailleur to the largest chainring.**

4. **Set the H-limit screw so that the cage plate farthest from the bike is about 2mm outside the largest chainring.**

5. **Try shifting between the two or three chainrings on your bike.**

   If the chain doesn't not move easily to the appropriate chainring or it rubs on the side of the derailleur cage, you may need to make some fine-tuning adjustments (see the following steps).

Figure 14-14:
Adjusting
the L-limit
screw.

6. **To fine-tune the front derailleur, try increasing the tension using the cable adjuster.**

   On front derailleurs, this is usually located where the cable enters the left shift lever. Make quarter- to half-turns of the adjuster and recheck.

   You can also make small adjustments to the H- and L-limit screws to improve shifting or prevent the chain from rubbing on the cage.

The derailleur cable

If the cable is frayed, kinked, or worn, it probably needs replacing. When you go to buy a new cable, make sure you buy cable and *housing* (the rubber coated sheath) that is made specifically for derailleurs — it's normally a little thinner than brake cable, which has to be able to handle greater force.

You'll be able to tell that it's derailleur housing because the inner core wires run linearly with the length of the housing, which makes for a much more rigid housing and doesn't allow any compression, resulting in a more precise shift. Brake cable housing has the inner core wires wound around like a coil, which allows more flexibility in the housing and a more controlled brake-lever feel.

Before you remove the shifter cable, take a moment to observe how it's routed around the frame of the bike. Pay attention to the location of the cable housing, where the cable housing meets the cable stops, and the how the cable exits on the other side. You'll need to route the cable and cable housing in the same manner when you reinstall it. You want the housing to be as short as possible. The housing should have gradual curves without any binding or sharp angles.

Follow these steps for removing the derailleur cable:

1. **Shift the chain onto the small cog for the rear of the bike or the small chainring for the front.**

   This will put the index ratcheting system in the relaxed position and allow you to remove the cable.

   Very few bicycles have reverse springs in either the front or rear derailleur; if yours does, you'll need to shift into the large cog or the large chainring to put the derailleur in the relaxed position.

2. **Unfasten the derailleur cable by loosening the cable anchor bolt where the cable attaches to the rear or front derailleur.**

3. **To remove the cable, you need to push it through the other side of the shifter.**

   To do this, look for where the cable enters the shift lever and pull back on the cable housing to expose the cable

4. **For STI shifters, squeeze the brake lever and press the shifter inward at the same time.**

   This will open up the center core of the shifter where the barrel at the end of the cable is seated. You should be able to see the barrel.

5. **Push the cable into the shifter so that the barrel is forced through and out the other side.**

   Handlebar shifters have different ways of concealing the barrel end of the cable. On some, there may be a screw-in plug or rubber cap that hides the cables. On the popular Shimano STI–style shifter, where the shift lever is integrated into the brake level, the cable runs sideways through the shifter. When the chain is on the smallest gear and you pull back on the brake lever and shift lever at the same time, you can see the barrel on the end of the cable.

   Use pliers to grab the barrel and pull the cable the rest of the way out of the lever.

6. **Collect any ferrules that were holding the cable housing in place at the anchor points or cable stops.**

   You'll use them when you reinstall the cable.

It's a good practice to change the cable housing when you replace cable wires. Manufacturers often sell cable with the housing included in the package. They normally give you more housing than you need, so you'll have to cut it to fit your bike.

Follow these steps to install the derailleur cable:

1. **To install new cable and housing, you first need to prepare the cable housing.**

   Assuming that the old housing was the proper length, use the older pieces of cable housing as guides for cutting the new pieces. Use a cable cutter for this procedure — they cut the housing without compressing the end too much.

   Even if you use cable cutter, you may need to file the end if it has any sharp edges. You may also need to open up the end of the housing with an awl or another pointed instrument if the end is closed up after cutting.

2. **When you're ready to install the new cable, use a rag to apply a light coating of grease to its surface.**

3. **For STI-style shifters, squeeze the brake lever, push the shifter to the inside to expose the hole for the cable, and insert the cable.**

   You may have to wiggle it around to pass it through the shifter.

4. **Pull the cable out the other side of the shifter.**

    Some trigger shifters and most grip shifters will require you to open the shifter body to load the cable. This may be challenging, especially on grip shifters.

5. **Attach the ferrules that came with the cable housing to the ends of each piece of housing where needed.**

6. **Insert the cable into the proper cable housing and pull it out the other end.**

7. **Route the cable and cable housing around the frame of the bike in the same position as it was before.**

    The ferrules at the ends of the cable housing should fit snugly into the cable stops on the frame.

8. **Run the cable through the cable anchor bolt on whichever derailleur is correct for that cable and tighten the cable anchor bolt.**

    If you're installing cables for the first time, they're likely to stretch a little after you've used them. It's a good idea to shift them though the full range of gears a few times after connecting them. Then pull the cable taut and reconnect the cable anchor bolt if necessary.

Gear Shifters

There are a variety of different shifters available today but they all do pretty much the same thing: pulling a cable to move a derailleur in one direction and then releasing the cable to allow the derailleur spring to move it in the other direction.

Most bikes these days use index shifters that are mounted on the handlebars. Index shifters make a click each time a gear change is made, which prevents riders from missing a shift. They're much easier to use than the traditional friction-type shifters, seen mostly on older bikes. Friction shifters are usually mounted on the down tube as two levers that the rider moves up or down to move the derailleurs. For someone not used to friction shifters, it can be a little unnerving to take your hand off the handlebars to make a shift.

Most shifters today, such as the one shown in Figure 14-15, do not require much maintenance and are not designed to be dissembled. In some cases, worn levers can be replaced, but if the internal mechanism of the shifter starts to wear out and the clicks become less distinct, it's probably time to replace the levers.

The one thing you can do with shifters is give an occasional spray of a light lubrication into their internal parts. Operate the shifter a few times after the application, and wipe off any excess grease.

To adjust the position, loosen the clamp bolt if there is one, and move the shifters to a more comfortable position (as shown in Figure 14-16). If the shifters are on a road bike and are wrapped with tape, instead of removing the tape, you can loosen the clamp holding the handlebars and rotate the handlebars forward or backward slightly.

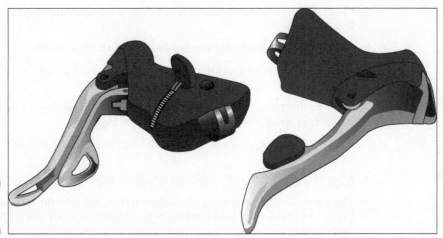

Figure 14-15:
Gear shifter.

Figure 14-16:
Adjusting
the position
of the gear
shifters.

Removing shifters

In this section, we tell you how to remove shifters on road bikes, with a focus on STI-style shifters, where the shifter is integrated into the brake lever. To remove the shifters follow these steps:

1. **Unscrew or remove the handlebar end plugs and then remove the handlebar tape.**

2. **Locate the bolt that holds the shifter onto the handlebars.**

   The position varies on different types of shifters although in many cases you need to roll back the rubber hood to find it.

3. **After pulling back the rubber hood and finding the bolt, use an Allen wrench to loosen the bolt without removing it.**

   This will loosen the bracket and allow you to slide the shifter off the handlebars.

4. **Repeat steps 1 through 3 for the other shifter.**

5. **The final step in removing the shifters is to remove the brake (see Chapter 8) and shift lever cables (see "The derailleur cable," earlier in this chapter).**

Installing shifters

To install shifters, follow these steps:

1. **Slide the bracket that holds the shifter onto the end of the handlebar and move the shifter toward the top of the handlebar.**

2. **Place a ruler against the bottom of the shifter lever and align it with the curved part of the handlebars.**

   This is a good starting point. From here, you can raise them slightly higher for a more casual and comfortable riding position.

3. **Repeat steps 1 and 2 for other shifter.**

4. **To make sure the shifters are level, set the ruler across the top of both and adjust their position as needed.**

5. **When you've found the proper position for the shifters, tighten the mounting bolts.**

6. **With the shifters in place, thread both the derailleur and brake cables through the shifters and continue the cable installation according to the instructions in this chapter for derailleur cables and Chapter 8 for brake cables.**

7. **Tape the handlebars according to the instructions in Chapter 15.**

Chapter 15

Turning on a Dime:
The Steering System

. . . .

In This Chapter

▶ Looking at the different types of handlebars

▶ Taping your handlebars

▶ Inspecting your headset

▶ Adjusting and overhauling your headset

. . . .

*I*n this chapter, we take a look at your bike's steering system and this system's most important component, the headset. The steering system includes the handlebars, which are held in place by a stem. The stem connects to the top of the fork, which sits inside the head tube. On the inside of the top and bottom of the head tube are the bearings. When these parts are in good working order, they provide you with a steering experience that is smooth and effortless.

At the center of the steering system is the headset, the group of parts (including the bearings) that are connected to the head tube and allow the handlebars, stem, and fork to turn. Although you may think that the headset plays a small role in the biking experience, it has to work hard to give you smooth, responsive turning, especially because the bearings it contains can take a serious beating when you ride. The constant bumps, jarring, and impacts are absorbed by the front wheel and transferred up the fork and into the bearings — and that's what causes them to wear out over time. When your bearings start to wear out, what at one point felt like automatic steering on a luxury vehicle will start acting like rack-and-pinion steering on an old beater. So do yourself a favor and inspect your headset on a regular basis and overhaul it as a part of your annual maintenance — we tell you how in this chapter.

We also give you information on handlebars including the different types available for most bikes. Finally, we give you information on wrapping your handlebars with new tape, which can not only add a touch of color and a fresh look to your bike, but increase your comfort — for little cost and effort.

Gimme a Hand: Types of Handlebars

Without the handlebars, you wouldn't be able to steer your bike. The handlebars are one of the three points where your body comes in contact with the bike, so you need to find handlebars that fit you well. The best fit handlebars can give you a great ride and even make up for a frame that doesn't fit you perfectly. Poorly chosen handlebars can force you into an awkward position when you ride, making you uncomfortable, giving you numb hands and a stiff back, or worse.

If you're shopping for handlebars, we recommend that you find ones that are designed to fit the type of bike you have, match the style of riding you plan on doing, and work well with the proportions of your body.

Here are the three main types of handlebars (see Figure 15-1):

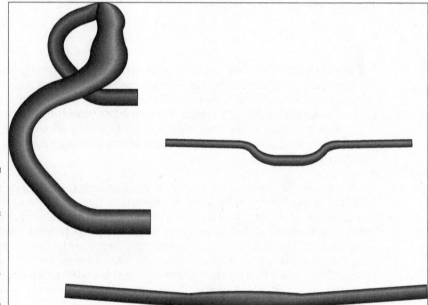

Figure 15-1:
The three types of handlebars: drop bars, flat bars, and riser bars.

✔ **Drop bars:** Drop bars are popular on road bikes. Because of their design, they offer more hand positions, which is a luxury on long rides. They also provide a more aerodynamic position when you put your hands on the *drops,* or the curved part of the bars, which is helpful if you're facing a headwind and want to get as low as possible.

One drawback of drop bars is that, if you rest your hands close together on the tops (the flat part on either side of the clamp), your hands won't be close to the brakes if you need to brake suddenly — although they do make a second set of brake levers that are accessible for your hands on the flat part of the bars.

There are many different styles, shapes, and sizes of drop bars. Some have a flattened area in the curve of the drop section for greater support of your hands. Others have an expanded flat platform section on the upper flat part for more surface contact area for your palms.

✔ **Flat bars:** Flat bars are popular on mountain and hybrid bikes. Their design provides more control and leverage in low-speed maneuvering, which is helpful if you're maneuvering around obstacles on an off-road trail. Flat bars are nice for the recreational rider, because you're sitting more upright and able to look around and enjoy the scenery.

The downside of flat bars is that they offer fewer positions in which to rest your hands. However, this isn't usually a problem, because most riders are seated in a more upright position with less pressure on the arms and hands in the first place.

If you feel numbness in your hands, which can happen with any type of handlebar, check to make sure that you aren't leaning too far over the handlebars. If you are, you may need to adjust your saddle forward, install a shorter stem, or consider buying a *riser bar* (on which both ends of the handlebar rise up slightly). Another option is to buy cycling gloves, which help reduce the impact and vibration of the ride.

✔ **Riser bars:** On mountain bikes you sometimes need *lift* (the ability to raise your front wheel over obstacles). For road bikes, this isn't an issue because your center of gravity is normally low and you're riding on flat surfaces.

Handlebars designed with a rise improve the lift of a bike. *Rise* is the amount that the ends of the bars are higher than the clamp. With greater rise, the rider can move her weight back over the rear tire and increase lift, which is important for downhill biking competitions. This also allows the bars to be rolled or moved closer or farther away from you for your comfort and control.

Delving Deeper: Handlebar Options

There are a number of options when it comes to handlebars, and which ones you need to pay attention to depend on the kind of riding you'll be doing and what style matches the physical proportions of your body. Here are the main options to consider:

✔ **Width:** One measure for handlebars is their size from end to end. Narrow handlebars give you less turning power but more precise steering, sensitivity to slight movements. Wider handlebars give you leverage; they may not be as responsive to steering, but they give you a more stable, controlled ride, especially on rough terrain.

You normally want handlebars that are as wide as your shoulder bones. Handlebars that are narrower than your shoulders will constrict your breathing, because your arms are holding your chest inward. If your arms spread out too much wider than your shoulders, you actually begin to lose leverage.

✔ **Material:** Most handlebars are made of either steel, *chromoly* (a steel alloy), aluminum, or carbon fiber. Aluminum and carbon are lighter and more comfortable than steel and chromoly. You'll save weight with carbon, but you'll end up paying more for it.

On flat bars made of steel, aluminum, or chromoly, you can shorten the width by cutting the ends.

✔ **Sweep:** Handlebars may also have a certain amount of *sweep* (the angle that the handlebars bend either forward or backward from the stem clamp). The benefit of greater sweep is that it allows your wrists to be in a more natural and comfortable bent position. It also brings the bars back closer to you for easier control.

✔ **Taper:** Some handlebars are narrower toward the ends. This saves weight and keeps the handlebars strong where they need to be.

✔ **Flare:** On flared handlebars, the handlebar ends flare out rather than dropping straight down. They're used in off-road racing.

✔ **Butting:** Butting takes material out of the center section of the tube, while leaving the ends of the tube thicker where it's needed for joint strength. Butting is used to increase the strength of the handlebars without adding weight. Butting is most often found toward the center of the handlebars. This design is used on specialized handlebars particularly risers used for downhill mountain-bike racing.

✔ **Bar ends:** Bar ends are extensions added to the end of flat handlebars. They give you an increased number of positions for your hands and provide leverage when you're climbing, by helping you move your weight back and lower your center of gravity.

If you're shopping for new handlebars, make sure you check the clamp size for your stem. The most popular clamp size with road and mountain bikes is 25.4mm. In recent years, an oversize 31.8mm clamp size has been becoming popular on some mountain and road bikes. If you're unsure of what size you have on your bike, check the owner's manual or visit your local bike shop.

Taping Your Handlebars

Nothing makes a bike look more worn than ragged and tattered tape on the handlebars. Replacing old tape is a relatively simple and cheap procedure, and it's a great way to add a little color and a fresh look to your bike while improving your comfort and grip.

To begin, you'll need to remove the plugs from the end of the handlebars using a screwdriver to unscrew them or pry them off. If your brake levers have rubber or gum hoods, roll the back away from the handlebars — you don't need to remove these hoods. Also, peel off the old tape, cleaning any sticky residue from the bars.

Here are some tips you should keep in mind when wrapping your handlebars with tape:

- **Some tape comes with gel patches for added comfort.** If you're using this kind of tape, place it on the handlebars in the positions described in the packaging instructions.

- **The tape will stay in place longer if you start at the bottom and work your way to the center of the bars.**

- **When you start wrapping, leave about an inch of tape off the end of the handlebars.** You'll tuck these ends in with the plugs when you're finished and they'll help keep the bar end plugs in place.

- **Most tapes come with two small pieces that are used to cover the back of the clamps which hold the brakes in place.** You don't have to use these, but it gives you a much cleaner and finished look.

- **Overlap the tape by about a quarter to a half of the previous wrap.** Pull it tightly but not so tightly that it'll break.

- **When you reach the center of the handlebars, you should be out of tape.** If you have additional length, you can continue wrapping in the opposite direction or cut off the excess.

- **When you're finished, use electrical tape to secure the edge of the wrapping to the center of the handlebars.** Wrap the electrical tape around the bars three to four times, pulling snugly until the last time around. Cut the electrical tape with scissors and then secure the electrical tape without stretching it. If you pull and stretch the electrical tape, because of the elasticity of the tape, it'll pull back halfway through your first ride.

To tape your handlebars, follow these steps:

1. **Begin by wrapping the tape from the end of the handlebar, overlapping at least a quarter of the tape with each wrap (see Figure 15-2).**

2. **Continue wrapping the tape until you come to the bottom of the shifters.**

   When you purchase handlebar tape, it should come with a small piece that covers the part of the handlebar where the shifter is connected. Make sure you attach this piece (as shown in Figure 15-3).

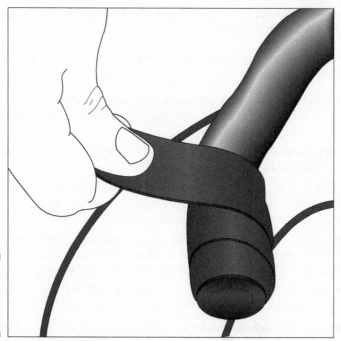

Figure 15-2:
Start at the end of the handlebar.

3. **Pull the tape up and under the handlebar in preparation to pull the tape back down and around the shifters (see Figure 15-4).**

4. **Pull the tape upward so that there is no slack (see Figure 15-5).**

5. **Pull the tape downward and away from the shifters (see Figure 15-6).**

6. **Pull the tape downward, around the handlebar, and toward the shifters (see Figure 15-7).**

7. **Wrap the tape around the handlebar, away from the shifters and overlapping with some of the tape from a previous wrap (see Figure 15-8).**

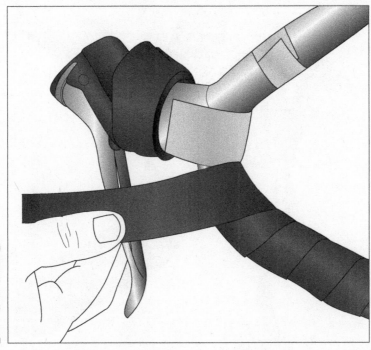

Figure 15-3:
Continue
until the
bottom of
the shifters.

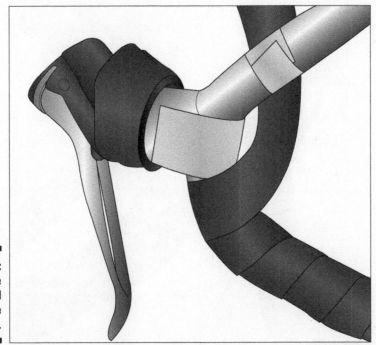

Figure 15-4:
Wrap the
tape up and
under the
handlebar.

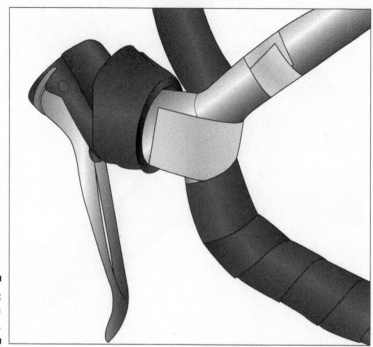

Figure 15-5:
Pull the tape upward.

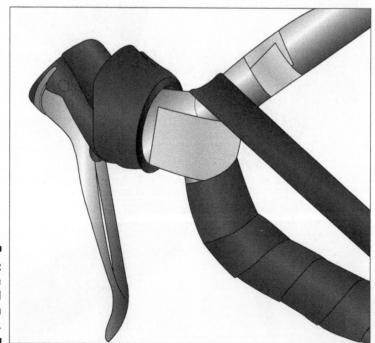

Figure 15-6:
Pull the tape down and away from the shifters.

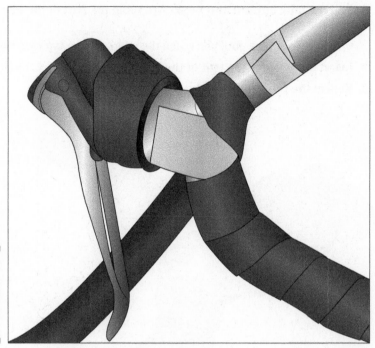

Figure 15-7:
Pull the tape
down and
toward the
shifters.

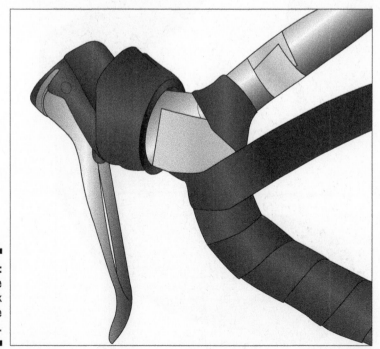

Figure 15-8:
Wrap the
tape back
around the
handlebars.

8. **Pull the tape upward and begin wrapping the part of the bar above the shifters.**

   Continue wrapping until you reach the middle of the bar (see Figure 15-9).

9. **Insert the plug for the end of the handlebar (see Figure 15-10).**

10. **Repeat the procedure for the other side of the handlebar.**

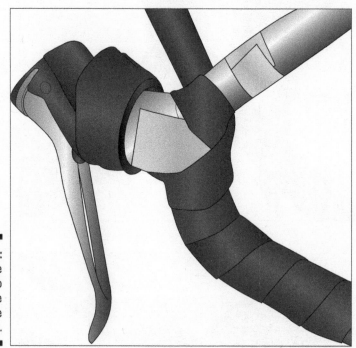

Figure 15-9:
Pull tape
upward to
wrap the
top of the
handlebars.

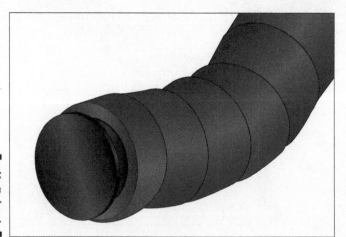

Figure 15-10:
Plug the
handlebar
end.

Getting Your Head around This: The Headset

The headset is the part of the bike that connects the stem and the fork to the frame and provides the mechanism that allows you to steer the bike.

There are two major styles of headsets:

- ✔ **Threaded:** The threaded headset screws onto the threads at the top of the column attached to the fork steering tube. This is the traditional type of headset found on a majority of older bikes.

- ✔ **Threadless:** The threadless headset is not threaded onto the column on top of the fork. Instead, it's held together by the compression of an internal bolt that runs through the top cap into a wedge in the fork steering tube. Depending on the style, it's either pressed into the head tube or sits on top of the fork steering tube and is held in place by a top cap. The threadless headset is found on almost all midrange to high-end bikes these days.

Inspecting the headset

Headsets are designed to last a long time, but even the best headsets can wear out, especially if they aren't cared for. One way to check whether your headset has issues is to test it for looseness. Here are three checks you can try:

- ✔ Straddle the frame of your bike with your hands firmly clenching the brakes. Try rocking the bike back and forth.

- ✔ Stand astride the front wheel facing your bike with the wheel pinched between your legs and your hands on the handlebars. Try wiggling the handlebars back and forth.

- ✔ Lift the front wheel off the ground and strike the tire with your hand, while listening for vibrations.

With the bike in a stand, grasp the fork and the frame and try to flex the fork to see if there is any play in the headset. Lift the front wheel off the ground and turn the handlebars back and forth. If they feel tight and don't move smoothly, you may have tightened the headset too much. With the wheels off the ground and the back wheel higher than the front, the front wheel should swing like a pendulum freely back and forth.

If, with any of these procedures, you feel play in the stem, it could mean that you need to either adjust or replace the headset.

Here are some other signs of headset problems:

✓ The handlebars and fork rattle when you ride.

✓ The handlebars don't turn smoothly.

✓ You have trouble riding in a straight line.

Adjusting your headset

Although headsets don't need to be adjusted very often, over time all the turning you do on your bike and all the bumps and jolts the headset receives from the road may cause the headset to loosen. If you inspect the headset following the steps in the preceding section and find looseness, follow these steps to adjust it.

Threadless headsets

Threadless headsets usually don't require adjustment very often, especially when compared to threaded headsets, but you may need to make an adjustment occasionally. Here's how:

1. **Loosen the stem clamp bolt or the bolts holding the stem in place.**

2. **Tighten (clockwise) or loosen (counterclockwise) the bolt in the center of the top cap.**

3. **After you've made the adjustment, retighten the stem clamp bolt or bolts.**

Do not over-tighten the top cap. It isn't designed to hold the fork in place — it's designed only to keep a slight load on the bearings for the adjustment procedure until the stem clamp bolts are tightened, holding everything in place.

4. **Check the adjustment using the procedures from the preceding section, "Inspecting the headset."**

Threaded headsets

To adjust a threaded headset, you generally need two specialized headset wrenches that fit your bike.

If you have a large, adjustable wrench for the top lock nut, you can get by with one headset wrench for the adjusting nut or cone.

The headset sizes are almost always 32 or 26. Some adjustable cones use round surfaced edges, which you can use your hands or lock jaw pliers to adjust.

To adjust a threaded headset, follow these steps:

1. **Loosen the locknut on the top of the headset by turning it counter-clockwise about one turn.**

2. **Below the locknut, locate the adjustable cup or cone.**

3. **If you are tightening the headset, turn the adjustable cup or cone clockwise in 20-degree increments. Turn it counterclockwise to loosen it.**

   After each turn, secure the locknut and check the headset adjustment (see "Inspecting the headset," earlier in this chapter).

   It may take several adjustments until you get it right. Continue until there is no looseness and the bearings are not being pressed against too tightly. If you aren't sure, err on the side of being a little tighter.

Overhauling your headset

If adjustments don't alleviate looseness or other issues with the headset, you may need to overhaul it. Headsets can take a lot of abuse, especially if you ride on challenging terrain or in bad weather, so an overhaul that replaces bearings and packs them in fresh grease can go a long way toward improving and extending the life of your bike's steering system.

Threadless headsets

Overhauling a threadless headset is sometimes easier if you remove the handlebars. Do this by removing the bolts in the stem that hold the handlebars in place. It also helps to remove the front wheel from the fork (see Chapter 7). Depending on what type of brakes you have, you may need to remove these as well (see Chapter 8).

Here's how to overhaul a threadless headset:

1. **Using an Allen wrench, unscrew and remove the bolt and top cap in the top of the stem (as shown in Figure 15-11).**

2. **Loosen the clamp bolt or bolts holding the stem in place (see Figure 15-12).**

   Be sure to keep a hand on the fork if your bike is off the ground.

3. **Slide the stem off the fork steering tube (as shown in Figure 15-13).**

   As you do this, make sure you hold onto the fork so that it doesn't fall on the ground.

4. **Remove the parts of the headset, including any washers or spacers (as shown in Figure 15-14).**

   Keep track of the order in which you remove things so you can put everything back together more easily.

5. Pull the fork out of the frame (as shown in Figure 15-15).

If the fork is stuck, you may have to tap it with a mallet, being careful not to damage the top of the steering tube.

Figure 15-11:
Loosening
the top cap.

Figure 15-12:
Undoing the
clamp bolt.

Figure 15-13:
Removing
the stem.

Figure 15-14:
Removing
spacers.

6. **Remove the bearings (see Figure 15-16).**

There is a top and bottom or an inside and outside of the bearing race. Take note of the bearing race positioning before removing the bearings. If you don't reinstall them properly, you won't be able to adjust the headset and you'll damage both the bearings and the headset.

7. **The bearings will likely be contained in a race with their surfaces exposed or sealed in a cartridge (see Figure 15-17 for both types):**

   • If the bearings are exposed, inspect them. Bearings that are pitted or do not have a shiny surface should be replaced.

   • If your bearings are sealed in a cartridge, check to see that they turn smoothly. If they don't, replace them.

8. **Clean and inspect all parts.**

9. **When you're ready to reinstall the headset, coat both cups with a layer of grease.**

10. **Insert one of the races into the bottom cup.**

11. **While holding the bottom race into place with one hand, insert the fork with the other hand.**

    This procedure is sometimes easier if you turn the bike over.

12. **When the fork is inside the head tube, slide the other race over the fork steering tube and down into the top cup of the head tube.**

13. **Slide any washers or spacers over the fork steering tube in their original order.**

Figure 15-15:
Removing the fork.

Figure 15-16:
Bearings in
the headset.

Figure 15-17:
Two styles
of bearings.

14. **Attach the top cap and screw it into place with the Allen bolt.**

15. **Follow the procedure for headset adjustment in the "Threadless headsets" section under "Adjusting your headset."**

16. **Center the stem and secure it by tightening the clamp bolt or bolts.**

If you replace a headset with the same model, you'll be able to install it yourself in most cases — you won't have to press the head-tube cups into the frame because you can reuse the ones currently in place. However, if you change headsets, you'll need your local bike shop to install it. Special tools along with skill and expertise are required for removing headset parts from a bike frame and installing new ones.

Threaded headsets

When you overhaul a threaded headset, you'll likely observe the reason for its name — the threaded steerer tube that sits at the top of a fork. You'll also see that a threaded headset is unique with its expander bolt, something that helps keep it in place when tightened.

To overhaul a threaded headset, follow these steps:

1. **Use an Allen wrench, or adjustable wrench if needed, to loosen the socket head bolt, which sits at the top of the stem.**

   Turn it just a few times to loosen it. Do not completely remove this bolt. It's connected to an expander wedge at the bottom of the stem, which keeps the stem in place. Sometimes the bolt may be buried deep inside the stem and require a longer Allen wrench (see Figure 15-18).

2. **After the bolt is loosened, place a small block of wood on it and give it a firm blow with a hammer to jar the wedge loose.**

   If the stem has not been removed for a while it may take more than one blow and/or some penetrating lubricant.

3. **Lift the stem out of the steering tube connected to the fork (as shown in Figure 15-19).**

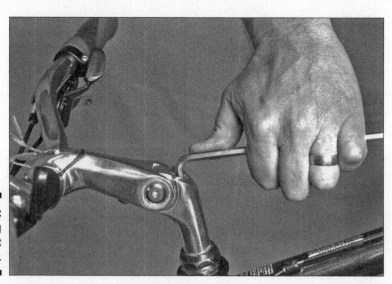

Figure 15-18:
Loosening the socket head bolt.

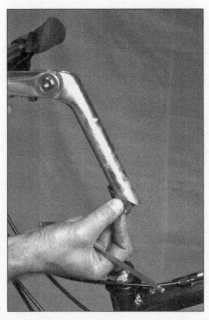

Figure 15-19:
Removing
the stem.

4. **Remove the headset locknut by turning it in a counterclockwise direction (as shown in Figure 15-20).**

Figure 15-20:
Undoing the
locknut.

5. **Slide off any washers or anything else that sits underneath the locknut you just removed.**

6. **Unscrew the adjustable cup or cone that sits against the top of the head tube.**

   As you do, hold on to the fork with one hand so that it doesn't fall to the ground.

   There is a top and bottom or an inside and outside of the bearing race. Take note of the bearing race positioning before removing it. If you don't reinstall it properly, you won't be able to adjust the headset and you'll damage the bearings and the headset.

   Be careful with the bearings that sit in the top and bottom of the head tube. If they're contained within a race, you're in good shape; if they're loose, they may fall out when you remove the adjustable cup or slide out of the fork. In the case of loose bearings, remove the top set before you slide out the fork. Then turn the bike upside down to remove the fork and the bottom set.

7. **Inspect the bearings to see if they're pitted or worn.**

   If they are, they should be replaced.

8. **Clean and inspect all parts.**

9. **When you're ready to reinstall the headset, coat both cups with a layer of grease.**

10. **Insert one of the retainers into the bottom cup.**

11. **While holding the bottom retainer into place with one hand, insert the fork with the other hand.**

    This procedure is sometimes easier if you turn the bike over.

12. **After the fork is inside the head tube, slide the other race over the fork steering tube and down into the top cup of the head tube.**

13. **Screw on the adjustable cup or cone until it presses down slightly on the bearings.**

14. **Slide any washers, locknut, and anything else over the fork steering tube in their original order.**

15. **Follow the procedure in the "Threaded headsets" section under "Adjusting your headset."**

16. **Insert the stem and, when it's at the correct height, turn the bolt clockwise.**

    This will expand the wedge at the bottom of the stem and hold it in place.

    When you adjust the height of the stem, don't set it higher than the safety limit marking engraved into the side of the stem. It may have faded over time, so you need to look carefully to find it.

Part IV
Keeping Your Bike on the Road

The 5th Wave   By Rich Tennant

PHILIP NYE—CYCLE CHIROPRACTOR

"I can feel tension and fatigue in the handlebars.
Let's get it on the couch and I'll manipulate
the frame until the wheels are aligned."

1n this part . . .

1f we had to pick just one part of this book to recommend, it would be this one. If you follow the advice in
these chapters and make a commitment to regular bike
maintenance, you won't need to spend as much time
with the other chapters of this book, because your bike
will be maintained in good working order. In this part, we
cover everything you need to know about maintenance,
including preventive maintenance (such as regular lubrication and cleaning), monthly maintenance, and yearly
overhauls — all steps that are designed to help you
enjoy years of trouble-free biking.

Chapter 16

An Ounce of Preventive Maintenance

● ●

In This Chapter

▶ Performing a safety inspection of your bike before you ride

▶ Assembling a tool kit for daily rides and extended trips

▶ Minimizing wear and tear and preventing accidents

▶ Cleaning and lubricating your bike after a ride

▶ Stowing away your bike for winter (or until your next ride!)

● ●

*I*f you're like us, you once had a bike that you never took care of — probably when you were a kid. Dennis had a BMX-style bike in his teens that he almost killed himself on, pushing it to the limits on dirt trails and bike jumps that he and his friends engineered after school. Despite all the punishment Dennis dished out on that bike, it valiantly held up to give him several pleasurable years of riding.

Modern-day bikes are designed with durable components that can take a lot of wear and tear, but this doesn't mean that you should neglect your bike the way you did when you didn't know any better. The old adage that an ounce of prevention is worth a pound of cure is especially true when it comes to your bike. If you follow the guidelines in this chapter for preventive maintenance, not only will you extend the life of your bike, but you'll have fewer repairs to make, you'll be safer, and you'll get more enjoyment out of riding.

In this chapter, we explain some simple steps you can take before, during, and after riding to care for your bike and extend its life. Cleaning and lubricating your bike is at the top of the list, but don't stop there. You can do a quick inspection before you ride, follow some basic rules while riding to minimize wear and tear on your bike, and properly store your bike when your ride is over. We cover all these steps in this chapter.

Before You Ride

If you're like a lot of bikers, when you finally have some time for a ride, the last thing you want to be thinking about is repair and maintenance. You grab your helmet and gloves and you're out the door, ready to roll.

But you can improve your bike's performance, prevent major headaches, and improve your own safety by doing a few simple things before you ride. In this section, we fill you in.

Assembling an emergency tool kit

Assembling an emergency tool kit is essential if you plan on doing anything more than taking a trip around the block. You'll want to bring along a basic set of tools so that when the inevitable breakdown happens, you won't be stranded on the side of the road.

When you're shopping for tools, look for ones that are light, so that they won't weigh you down, especially on longer trips. Size is also a consideration especially because you'll want to stow away your tools in a pouch under your seat or tucked away in a bike bag. You don't want to try biking if you have a large crescent wrench sticking out from under your seat. Your best bet is to visit your local bike shop to find small, lightweight tools to take with you when you bike.

Look at multipurpose tools — they provide a lot of functionality in one small, convenient package. Also, some bike shops offer kits with everything you need already assembled.

Putting together a basic tool kit

For starters, we recommend that you include the following tools in your emergency tool kit. (After you have some biking experience, you may decide to change or add to it.)

- ✓ **Small frame-mounted tire pump:** If you've been doing any biking already, you probably already have a tire pump — but you may not have a small one that you can mount on your frame. If you don't already have one of these small, frame-mounted pumps, put this at the top of your list.

- ✓ **Tire patch kit:** Patching a flat tire is an unavoidable part of biking, and a tire patch kit is essential. A patch kit includes patches, glue, and a tool to rough up the surface of the tube to improve adhesion.

- ✓ **Spare inner tube:** If your tube explodes, you'll have to replace it with a new one, so carrying a spare inner tube with you is important.

- **Tire levers:** Unless you have an a racing bike that uses tubular tires, you'll need tire levers to remove and install a tire.

- **Allen wrenches:** You'll need these for adjusting various parts of your bike. Most Allen wrenches come in a kit or as a part of a multipurpose tool with the most popular sizes found on a bike.

- **Screwdrivers:** You'll need both a flathead screwdriver and a Phillips screwdriver for adjusting derailleurs and other parts of your bike. You may need a regular-size screwdriver and a smaller one depending on your bike.

- **Spoke wrench:** You need a spoke wrench that fits the spoke nipples on your bike. To determine what size spoke wrench you need, visit your local bike shop and ask for help.

- **Pliers:** You'll need pliers for pulling cables.

- **Multipurpose tool:** Many bike shops offer a multipurpose tool, which includes screwdrivers, Allen wrenches, a chain tool, and other types of tools.

- **Rag:** You'll use clean rags to wipe your hands after some messy repair jobs. You can also use a rag when you're checking tires for flats, handling chains, and so on.

- **Small light:** If you have to stay out later than expected, it's good to have a light that you can clip to your bike when it gets dark. You may want to have an LED light permanently mounted or clipped to your bike. A rear blinking light is a good idea, too. Lights are inexpensive, and the front light at least is a legal requirement.

Adding tools for an extended trip

As biking becomes more popular, many riders are discovering the enjoyment in taking extended trips on their bikes. If you're planning a bike trip that will last for more than a day or two, you need to add some additional tools and parts to your emergency tool kit (see the preceding section).

Which tools you should take depends on where you're biking and for how long. If you'll be passing through a lot of small towns, chances are pretty good that you can find a local bike shop to help you in a jam. Dennis has taken extended trips through Europe where he's been able to pack very few tools because of the popularity of biking and the large number of local bike shops along the way. Once, on the outskirts of Limerick, Ireland, he had a minor accident and ruined some spokes. A passerby stopped to help and eventually took Dennis and his bike to a bike shop in town. After Dennis's bike was repaired, the friendly passerby invited him back to his house where his family gave Dennis a warm bed and a traditional Irish breakfast the next morning. Although we don't recommend having an accident to meet people, this was one of the highlights of Dennis's time in Ireland.

Although, in many cases, you'll be able to find help if you break down on the side of the road, you're better off being ready to handle the repair on your own. For extended trips, we recommend having everything from the preceding section, as well as the following additional tools:

- ✔ **Spare tire:** A number of companies make tires that can be folded and packed away. Surprisingly enough, folding tires are often actually better-quality tires, just with a foldable Kevlar bead instead of a stiff wire bead.

- ✔ **Extra tubes:** If you ride across something on the road that blows out a tube, there is always a chance that you'll hit it with your back tire as well, so keep two, just in case.

- ✔ **Chain tool:** A longer trip increases your chances of having issues with your chain, and you'll need this tool to take it apart and reconnect it.

- ✔ **Chain links and rivets:** If you have issues with your chain, you may need to replace links. Have extra rivets or connecting links available for when you reconnect the chain.

- ✔ **Spare spokes:** In our experience, spoke problems are one of the top three or four issues that you'll encounter on an extended trip. Keep at least two spare spokes on hand. Be sure to confirm what sizes you need.

  On some bikes, the size of the spokes can differ on the front and rear wheels and even within the same wheel.

- ✔ **Spare cables:** If you're on an extended trip, your bike will likely be packed down with extra weight, which puts additional strain on your cables. Pack a replacement cable for the brakes and one for the derailleur.

- ✔ **Lubrication:** You'll want to keep the parts of your bike — especially the chain — properly lubricated during your trip.

- ✔ **Duct tape:** This is the all-purpose MacGyver tool. If you have to hold something together on your bike until you get to the next town, duct tape may do the job.

Giving your bike the once-over: A pre-ride inspection

Next time you head out for a ride, take a moment to do a quick inspection of your bike. It'll only take a few minutes and you just might prevent a bigger problem from happening. Trust us: You don't want to be discovering that you have an issue with your brakes as you're going full-speed down a hill.

In the following sections, we cover all the things you should check before each and every ride.

Wheels

The quick-release levers on the wheels should be securely positioned in the closed position. Open and close the levers once to confirm that they're tight. If you find that they're loose, open the lever, turn the nut opposite the lever a quarter-turn and re-close the lever. When you're sure that the levers are secure, move the wheel side to side check for looseness. Next, lift the wheel off the ground and give it a spin to see that it doesn't wobble and that the rim doesn't contact the brake pads at any point.

Tires

Check the air pressure of your tires with a pressure gauge and compare it with the recommended pressure listed on the sidewall. Under-inflated tires will drastically increase the rolling resistance, thereby increasing the amount of energy needed to pedal the bicycle. Properly inflated tires also better absorb any impact and protect the wheel from damage.

While you're checking the pressure, visually inspect the tires, looking for any cracks, cuts, or tears.

Brakes

Give the brake levers a strong squeeze to ensure that the brakes firmly grip the wheels — you shouldn't have to pull the levers more than halfway to the handlebars. Next, examine the brake pads and make sure they have sufficient rubber. Also pay attention to their position relative to the rim — they shouldn't be too high (because they'll rub a hole in the tire) or too low (because they could slip down into the spokes). There should be 1mm to 2mm of space between the pads and the rim.

Handlebars

Straddle the front wheel pinching it between your thighs. Grip the handlebars and try to twist them side to side. Try the same procedure, but this time straddle the frame, squeeze the brakes, and try to rock the bicycle back and forth. If there's play in the handlebars or stem, it could mean either that the clamp bolts need to be tightened or you have a loose headset, which could be dangerous at high speeds.

Pedals and cranks

Just as you checked for looseness with the handlebars (see the preceding section), you'll want to do the same with the pedals and cranks. First, grab a crank in each hand and try to shake them. If there is looseness, fixing it may be as simple as tightening the crank bolts, or you may have issues with the bottom bracket. Confirm that the pedals spin freely but that you can't pull them away from the cranks.

While You Ride

One of the best ways to extend the life of your bike doesn't require a special tool or a fresh application of lube. All you have to do is be careful when you ride.

Although modern bikes are designed to withstand a significant amount of punishment, try to avoid riding in a way that puts additional strain on your bike or, even worse, increases the likelihood of an accident. Here are some steps you can take while riding, to prolong the life of your bike:

- ✓ **Pay attention to the road in front of you.** Your goal is to avoid obstacles like rocks, potholes, and other hazards, which, if impacted, could result in a bent rim or other problem.

- ✓ **Instead of jumping or riding across a curb, dismount and walk your bike.**

- ✓ **Shift into your lowest gear before you reach the steepest section of a climb.** Trying to shift when you're barely moving puts a lot of strain on the chain and derailleurs. If the chain springs off the largest cog, into the spokes, the damage will be even greater.

- ✓ **If you have to go over a bump, raise yourself off the saddle and use your arms and legs as shock absorbers as if you were a horse jockey.** This lessens the impact of the blow.

When riding, you should listen to your bike. If it makes awkward noises or grinds in certain operations, it's time to diagnose the ailment before it gets worse and destroys internal parts.

After You Ride

Even though you may be ready to relax and kick back with a cold one after your ride, if you take care of a few issues (like cleaning and lubricating your bike), your bike will last longer.

Cleaning your bike

Unless you're a part of the U.S. Olympic team and are training on an indoor track, your bike is going to get dirty. If you're like us and you love the outdoors, you probably don't mind dirt. Hopping on a mountain bike and plowing your way through mud-covered mountain passes and rolling streams may bring back the joy of childhood and your mother chasing you through the house as you left muddy footprints behind.

Your bike feels much differently about dirt and grime, though. Dirt acts as an abrasive and, as it works its way into the internal parts of your bike, it starts wearing out bearings and other components. Even if your bike isn't covered in mud and grime, dust can build up inside the chain, gears, bearings, and other parts. A bike that you haven't washed for a while because you think it's fairly clean may be wearing out unnecessarily with each turn of the crank.

If you could do only one thing in this book to care for your bike, it would be to wash your bike frequently. If you ride in wet, muddy, or dusty weather, we recommend that you clean your bike immediately at the end of your ride. If you ride your bike in normal conditions, you probably can get away with cleaning it every week or two (maybe longer, if you live in a dry climate).

If your bike appears fairly clean after riding, all it may need is a quick wipe-down. Use a damp cloth or paper towels to wipe off any dust or dirt that may have accumulated on the frame, the fork, the handlebars, and the cranks.

If your bike is a dirty or hasn't been cleaned in a week or two, it's time to do a serious cleaning. Here are the supplies you need to clean your bike:

- ✔ Bucket
- ✔ Dishwashing soap, car cleaner, or a cleaner from your local bike shop
- ✔ Sponge
- ✔ Brushes (such as a toothbrush, bottle brush, and a bathroom cleaning brush, or a specialized brush designed to clean hard-to-reach places on your bike, such as between the sprockets)
- ✔ Degreaser
- ✔ A clean rag
- ✔ Car wax

If you have a bike stand, use it to clean your bike. You'll be able to rotate the cranks to clean the chain and you'll have easier access to other parts of the bike, such as the rear derailleur.

To clean your bike properly, follow these steps:

1. **Fill a bucket with warm water and a cleaning agent.**

2. **Wet your bike with a hose without a spray nozzle.**

   Avoid spraying water directly at your bike, especially toward the hubs or bottom bracket. This may force water and dirt into your bearings and break down the grease in which they're packed.

3. **Use a brush or sponge and soapy water, and brush off as much caked-on mud or dirt from the bike as you can.**

   Brush in between the sprockets to remove any dirt trapped inside (see Figure 16-1).

4. **Spray degreaser on the freewheel, derailleur, chain, and chain ring (see Figure 16-2).**

   Allow a couple of minutes for the degreaser to penetrate the parts, and then brush it off with a brush.

5. **Use a brush or sponge to wash down the entire bike.**

   Make sure you dig out dirt between the cogs and wherever else it hides. A specially designed brush (available as most bike shops) is useful for this procedure (see Figure 16-3).

6. **Rinse the bike with a hose.**

7. **Dry the bike using a clean rag.**

   You can use a rag or a strip of cloth to wipe away water from between the sprockets (see Figure 16-4), beside the hubs, and around the derailleurs.

Figure 16-1:
Using a
brush to
clean the
sprockets.

Figure 16-2:
Degreasing
various
parts of
a bike.

Figure 16-3:
Digging out
dirt between
the cogs.

Figure 16-4:
Using a
cloth to
clean
between the
sprockets.

8. **If you have time, apply car wax to the frame and remove it using a clean rag.**

9. **Lubricate your bike following the steps in the next section.**

When you remove grease on your bike by cleaning it, you'll need to lubricate its parts afterwards. Washing and lubricating your bike go hand in hand — if you wash your bike, you should be prepared to follow it with a lube job.

Giving your bike a lube job

When you clean your bike, you'll likely remove a lot of lubrication and your bike will be thirsty for a fresh dose of oil and grease.

If you're a typical recreational rider, you may only have to give your bike a quick lube job every week or two. But if you're riding in wet weather or you're taking long bike trips, you should oil your bike more frequently. Just like the pre-ride inspection (earlier in this chapter), a lube job is quick and easy — you can do it in a few minutes, and it'll provide many benefits for your bike.

Many of the parts of a bike that require oil are not fully exposed, which makes it harder to get the oil into the right place. For this, we recommend using a spray can with a thin, straw-like extension. You'll be able to insert the extension into small, hard-to-reach areas such as inside the brake levers.

Here are the parts of your bike you'll want to lubricate after cleaning:

✔ **Brakes:** Spray some oil into the brake pivot points to keep them in working order and to prevent rust (see Figure 16-5). Be careful not to get any on the brake pads or rims, because this will impact your bike's braking capacity. Also, give a shot of lube to the spot where the cable is attached.

✔ **Brake levers:** Apply oil to the brake-lever pivots (see Figure 16-6). Pull back on the brake lever and spray the exposed cable. Be sure to cover the cable adjusters with lube to protect them from rust.

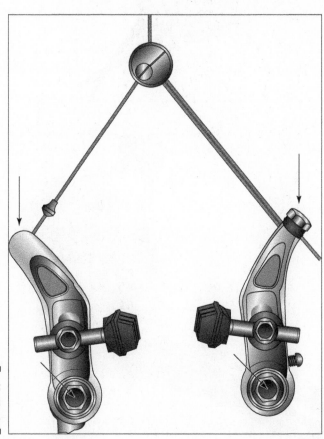

Figure 16-5:
Lubricating
the brakes.

✔ **Derailleurs:** There are several pivot points where the front and rear derailleurs move. Cover each of these with a quick shot of lube. On the front derailleur, lubricate the pivot point (see Figure 16-7) On the rear derailleur, be sure to spray both of the pulley wheels (see Figure 16-8).

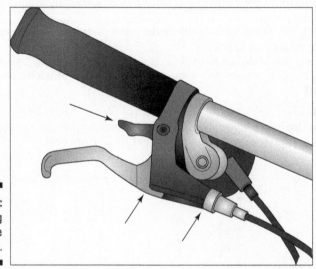

Figure 16-6:
Lubricating
the brake
levers.

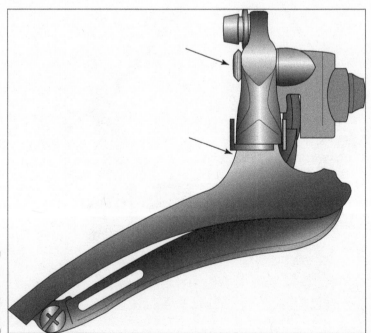

Figure 16-7:
Lubricating
the front
derailleur.

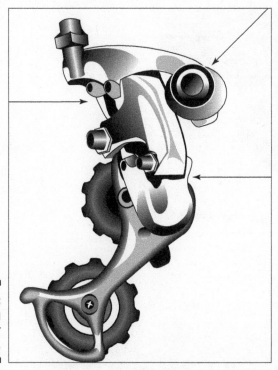

Figure 16-8:
Lubricating
the rear
derailleur.

✓ **Chain and sprockets:** Of all the parts to lubricate on a bike, the chain is the most important. A poorly lubricated chain will wear out quickly and can shorten the lifespan of your chainrings and sprocket. Apply an even amount of lube to the chain while you're turning the cranks (see Figure 16-9). You want to make sure that the oil does more than coat the surface but works its way into the individual chain links. If you notice that there is buildup of dirt and grime on the chain, clean it first with a degreaser and then apply a fresh coat of lubrication. When you're finished with the chain, apply a few drops of lube to the sprockets (see Figure 16-10).

✓ **Cables:** Give a light spray of oil to where the inner cable exits from the cable housing (see Figure 16-11). If you have a couple of minutes, remove the cable from the stop and give a spray into the cable housing.

After you're done lubricating your bike, be sure to use a rag and wipe any excess oil off your bike to prevent it from attracting dirt and grime.

Figure 16-9:
Lubricating
the chain.

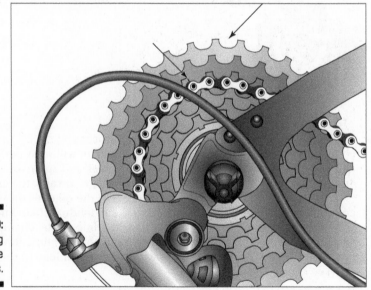

Figure 16-10:
Lubricating
the
sprockets.

Figure 16-11:
Lubricating
cables.

Storing your bike

How you store your bike is an important factor in its maintenance. Protecting your bike from the elements should be the most important consideration in storing it. Even for short-term storage such as overnight or for a few days, you should try to bring it indoors whenever possible. If you leave it outside, it'll be more exposed to wind, rain, and dirt, all of which can have a negative effect on your bike.

If you must store your bike outside for any period of time, consider buying a bike cover or even a tarp. This will provide some protection from rain and from dust and dirt blowing into its parts.

If you live in a part of the country that has a less-than-forgiving climate, you may want to store your bike for a longer period of time. If you're planning on taking your bike off the road for an extended period of time and keeping it in storage, take the following steps to preserve its condition:

✔ **Give it a complete cleaning and lube job.** This is the most basic step you can take before storing your bike.

✔ **Overhaul the hubs, bottom bracket, headset, and derailleurs; pack all the bearings in fresh grease; and true the wheels.** If you do all this before you put your bike in storage, it'll be ready to roll as soon as that first warm day of spring arrives.

✔ **Give your tires and tubes a break by letting the air out.**

✔ **Release the brake and shifter cables to take pressure off the springs.** Some people argue that most modern metals won't weaken from the continuous tension, but we like to take this step anyway. If you'd rather not take this step, you should at least open the quick-release mechanism for the brakes and shift the chain onto the smallest front sprocket and smallest rear cog — this is usually the derailleur position with the least spring tension.

Store your bike indoors to protect it from the elements. This will help limit moisture and prevent rusting of internal parts. Also, avoid storing your bike where it could be knocked over — the rear derailleur is vulnerable and could be damaged in a fall.

Consider hanging your bike from a hook on the wall or ceiling — either by the wheels or by the frame. Not only will you save some space but you'll protect the tires from supporting weight in the same position for a long period of time. Dennis thinks a bike hanging on the wall is a decorative touch for a room, although not everyone (including his wife) agrees with him on that.

Chapter 17

Regular Bike Maintenance

In This Chapter

▶ Performing monthly maintenance on your bike

▶ Doing an annual overhaul of your bike

*O*wning a bike has its privileges. Zipping around turns, wind rushing through your hair, passing cars in traffic, leaving the world and all your cares behind you as you ride off into the countryside — it doesn't get much better than this! Of course, owning a bike also entails responsibilities. Unless you have unlimited money and don't mind buying a new bike every year or two, caring for and maintaining your bike is important.

Maintenance is also critical if you care about personal safety. Unless you're an 18-year-old risk taker, you probably aren't willing to take the chance that making a sharp turn, dodging a pothole, or slamming on the brakes will land you in the emergency room. Keeping your bike in good working order by following the monthly and yearly maintenance steps outlined in this chapter will go a long way toward making your riding experience a safe and enjoyable one.

Whether you're enthusiastic about maintenance or you view it as a chore, take the time today to schedule it. Write it on your calendar, put it in your PDA, do whatever it takes to remind yourself to do it. Otherwise, it's likely to get lost in the shuffle of your busy life, no matter how good your intentions.

We start this chapter by telling you what you need to do every month to maintain the health of your bike. Monthly maintenance is all about keeping your bike clean and lubricated and inspecting your bike for potential safety issues. You can do this monthly maintenance check in 30 minutes or less. We end the chapter with the annual tune-up and overhaul, which requires more time but will dramatically extend the life and safety of your bike.

Monthly Maintenance

Once a month, set aside half an hour or so to give your bike the once-over. Specifically, there are nine steps that you should take every month — everything from checking the tires to cleaning.

One way to stay on top of your monthly maintenance is to choose a day of the month that you can easily remember. For example, if your birthday is June 13, do your maintenance on the 13th day of every month.

Surveying your bike for structural damage

Examine your bike for signs of stress and structural damage. Visually inspect each part of the frame for cracks or other visible signs of wear and tear. For the hard-to-see parts of the frame, such as the underside, rub your hands along the surface to feel for bumps or ripples. Pay particular attention to areas where the frame is welded. On aluminum frames, in particular, look for any hairline cracks or weak points.

Hold the wheel between your legs and turn the handlebars side to side. If there is movement in the handlebar or stem, you may need to tighten the clamp bolts on the handlebars, tighten the stem bolt, or adjust your headset (see Chapter 15).

Kicking the tires

Lift each tire off the ground and give it a spin to see if it's spinning in alignment. As the wheel spins, keep your eyes fixed on the brake pad as it rotates, looking for any wobble. If you see any wobble, it's probably time to true the wheel (see "Truing the wheel," later in this chapter).

You'll be able to examine the alignment better if you have a bike stand. You can also turn the bike upside down, being careful to protect the shifters. Or have a friend lift the tire off the ground while you spin the wheel and examine it.

Also, inspect the tires for signs of wear, such as cracks, cuts, tears, or bulging. If you have a badly worn tire, it should be replaced immediately (see Chapter 6). Examine the tread and remove any debris or objects that may be lodged inside.

Finally, check for tightness in the spokes. Check two spokes at a time, grabbing them between your thumb and finger to test for what should be an even tension around the wheel. In the rear wheel, one side may have a slightly different tension then the other, but these should be uniform for each half. If you find any spokes that have too much or too little tension, make an adjustment with a spoke wrench (see Chapter 7).

Cleaning your bike

Even though we recommend in Chapter 16 that you give your bike a proper cleaning after every ride (if you ride in especially muddy or dirty conditions) or at least weekly, let's face it: Most people probably won't do it that often. If you don't have the time to clean your bike after every ride or once a week, you really do need to do it during your monthly inspection.

Dirt is your bike's worst enemy. Over time, it works its way into your bike's parts, causing them to wear out faster.

Turn to Chapter 16 for instructions on how to properly clean your bike.

Cleaning your bike is easier the more frequently you do it. If you wait until it's caked in mud and covered in grime, it'll take you a lot longer to get the job done. If you stay on top of cleaning after every ride (or at least once a week), you'll be able to finish the job much faster.

Giving your bike a lube job

You probably wouldn't dream of driving your car without changing the oil every three months or 3,000 miles. And you should take the same approach with your bike.

Your bike has many movable parts that require lubrication to reduce friction and stay in good working order. A lube job is especially important if you've been riding frequently, if you've been riding in wet or dry conditions, or if you've just cleaned your bike.

Turn to Chapter 16 for instructions on how to properly lube the moving parts and pivot points on your bike.

Tightening up

The monthly checkup is a good time to inspect the tightness of your cables. While you're examining the cables, also look for kinks or fraying, which may signal that they need to be replaced.

Check all the fasteners on your bike for looseness. Don't forgot to include any accessories like racks or bottle cages in your list. If you leave a fastener loose, it may fall out and, in its place, rust may appear.

Finally, check the cranks and crank bolts or nuts for tightness. While inspecting the cranks, grab a crank arm in each hand and try to wiggle them to check for looseness. If there is play in the cranks, the nuts or bolts may need to be tightened or you may have a problem with the bottom bracket (see Chapter 13).

Checking the brakes

Of all the parts on a bike that you don't want to give out when you're riding, the brakes are at the top of the list. Make sure you inspect them monthly, checking for wear in the brake pads and replacing them as needed. (If you need to replace brake pads or make adjustments to the brakes, see Chapter 8.)

Confirm that the cable clamp has the cable securely in place.

Give your brake levers a firm squeeze to confirm that the brakes evenly and firmly grab the rim.

Check the brake pads for even wear. (You may need to take the wheel off for this.) If any debris is lodged in the pads, remove it with the tip of a key or a knife.

While you're looking at the brakes, rub down the rims with rubbing alcohol. Clean, grease-free rims will increase your braking power and extend the life of your brake pads.

Examining the chain, cogs, and chainrings

Over time, a chain will stretch as it wears and, eventually, it'll need to be replaced. A stretched chain will cause the chainrings and cogs to wear out more quickly.

How do you know if your chain is stretched? Pull a chain link away from the chainring, and see if you can expose a gap between the chain and the chainring. If you can, the chain is stretched. You can also measure the chain to confirm that 12 links measure 12 inches. If the link measures between $12^1/_8$ to $12^1/_4$ inches, it's time to replace the chain (see Chapter 10).

Some companies offer a special tool that accurately indicates the amount of chain stretch.

Also, examine the teeth of the chainrings and cogs for excessive wear. If the teeth are no longer symmetrical and look like an ocean wave or as though they've been filed down on one side, it's time to replace the part.

Protecting your saddle

If you have a leather saddle, use a leather treatment to clean the leather and replenish its natural oils. These oils help the leather repel dirt and water, both of which can break down the integrity of the leather. Although a number of products are on the market, Brooks Proofide is a wax-based treatment that is very popular with bikers. (For more information on saddles, see Chapter 9.)

Inspecting the suspension

If you have suspension on your bike, inspect all suspension pivot and linkage bolts for correct tightness. Proper tightness is critical in order for the suspension to work properly. Follow the directions in your owner's manual and consider using a torque wrench or taking your bike to your local bike shop for adjustment.

Also, inspect the suspension forks. If they use oil, examine them for leaks and follow your owner's manual for how often the oil should be changed. If they're air-sprung, check the air pressure. (For more information on suspension, see Chapter 12.)

Annual Maintenance

After cleaning and lubricating your bike regularly, the next most important thing you can do to extend the life of your bike is to give it a yearly overhaul. You wouldn't think of driving your car year after year without taking it in for service — you have to think about your bike the same way, especially if you've invested money in a quality bike and you want to have many years of comfortable, accident-free biking.

Annual maintenance is not difficult if you follow the directions in this section — however unlike preventive and monthly maintenance, it does take some time. Overhauling a bike is not something you can do in 30 minutes, especially the first time. To do it right, you should set aside an afternoon when you can focus on your bike and nothing else.

Deep-cleaning the chain

Even if you've been fastidiously cleaning your chain on a regular basis, once a year you should give it a deep cleaning by removing it and soaking it in a solvent like Finish Line Citrus Degreaser or another environmentally safe product.

Try putting the solvent of your choice, along with the chain, in a soda bottle, giving the bottle a few shakes, and letting it sit for a few hours. Soaking your chain will enable the solvent to penetrate into the links, giving you deeper clean than if you had used a chain cleaning tool. When it's finished soaking, brush off the chain and rinse with water. Dry off the chain with a towel, and let it air-dry for a few hours. Don't apply lubricant until the solvent has completely evaporated.

For more chain cleaning tips, check out Chapter 10.

Truing the wheels

Over the course of the year, your wheels are going to absorb a lot of impact. The accumulation of bumps and jolts that are normal when you ride may start to loosen spokes causing your wheels to start to wobble. To counteract this, at least once a year have your wheels trued. Truing is the process of adjusting the tension in the spokes so that the wheel spins straight.

Wheel truing is a lot like golf: The basic concept is easy, but it takes a lot of practice to master. The process of truing is best left to an expert, but you should be able to make a few minor spoke adjustments to eliminate some of the imperfections in the wheel — all you'll need is a spoke wrench.

Although professionals use a special truing stand that provides greater precision, enabling them to correct up-and-down and side-to-side wobbles, you can leave your wheels in the frame when you true them. Just make sure you remove the tires so that you can see any distortions in the rim.

For instructions on how to true a wheel, turn to Chapter 7.

Replacing cables and housing

Considering the important role that cables play on your bike, especially when it comes to braking and stopping, we recommend that you think about replacing the cables and the housing in which they sit every year — or, at a minimum, give both a very thorough inspection. If you notice any kinks, rusting, fraying, or a buildup of dirt and grime, it probably is time to install new ones. If you do install new ones, we recommend that longer-lasting stainless steels cables be used. Follow the instructions in Chapter 8 and Chapter 15 to install cables for brakes and derailleurs, respectively.

Most bikes use one type of cable housing for shifters and another for brakes. Cable housing for shifting should not be used for brakes, because it may not be able to handle the higher force applied during severe breaking.

When you go to your local bike shop to purchase cables, remember to bring along the old cable. This way, you'll find the right cable for your bike and won't buy more length of cable than is necessary.

If, after inspecting the cables, you feel they don't need to be replaced, give them a proper cleaning. Remove the inner wire and flush the cable housing with a light oil, and remove cable grit with a rag while the cable is removed from the housing. Clean the inner wire with the same solvent before inserting it back into the cable housing.

Most cable housings have an inner plastic or Teflon liner, which means that the cable doesn't have to be lubricated. If you aren't sure about your cable housing, ask your local bike shop.

Overhauling the hubs

In order to extend the life of your hubs, it's good practice to overhaul them at least once a year — especially if they've been exposed to a lot water, which can cause them to rust from the inside.

One way to test whether an overhaul is needed is to elevate the wheel off the ground and give it a good spin. It should rotate freely, with the valve coming to a stop at the bottom, because this is the heaviest part of the wheel. Another test is to lift the wheel, grabbing the wheel with one hand and grabbing the frame with the other. If there is play in the wheel when you move it side to side, this is another sign that an overhaul, or at least an adjustment, is in order. Another test is to rotate the axle with your fingers with the wheel stationary; the hub should feel butter smooth.

If you have traditional hubs with bearings held in place by a cup and cone, you'll want to inspect the bearings, replace them if needed, and repack the bearings in fresh grease.

If you have cartridge bearing hubs, you're in luck. These require less maintenance because the bearings are sealed inside the cartridge. With some sealed cartridges, you can squirt degreaser into the cartridge followed by an injection of fresh grease as part of your servicing, although this is probably not something you need to do on a yearly basis unless you're riding in severe conditions such as crossing a river.

You can find step-by-step instructions for overhauling the hubs in Chapter 7.

Overhauling the headset

Wear and tear will cause a headset to come loose over time, which may cause the steering to feel wobbly or the breaking to vibrate the bike. Looseness in the headset also causes the bearings inside the headset to be impacted each time you hit a bump, which will lead them to deteriorate faster. If you think the headset may be loose, turn to Chapter 16 and follow the steps for checking for looseness in the handlebars.

Yearly maintenance is a good time to inspect, clean, adjust, and overhaul the headset. As is the case with all parts that rely on bearings, you'll want to clean and degrease each part, if possible; replace and pack the bearings in fresh grease; and then reinstall the parts following the instructions in Chapter 15.

Don't try to install a new headset on your bike unless you know what you're doing. Most bike shops have special tools that they use to fit a headset.

Overhauling the pedals

The sign that it's time for a pedal adjustment are similar to those of other parts that rely on bearings to spin smoothly. If pedals don't rotate effortlessly, or they wobble or feel loose, you should overhaul them. You'll have your tools, cleaners, and lubricants out during your annual maintenance, so it's a convenient time to take care of the pedals.

As with hubs, pedals have traditional cup-and-cone or cartridge bearings. If you have cup-and-cone bearings, you'll want to replace the bearings before packing them in fresh grease. With cartridge bearing systems, which are found on most clipless pedals, you'll only have to add fresh grease every few years.

You can find the steps for overhauling pedals in Chapter 13.

Overhauling the bottom bracket

The bottom bracket is the last bearing-dependent component you have to deal with in your annual maintenance. The bottom bracket is designed to stand up to all the hours of rigorous pedaling that your legs can put out, but even so, it's a good idea to overhaul it once a year.

You may want to leave this task to your local bike shop, especially because it calls for some special hand tools, may entail a lot of force to loosen, and requires the application of the proper amount of torque when tightening. If that isn't a hurdle for you, follow the instructions in Chapter 13 for inspecting, cleaning, lubing, and reassembling the bottom bracket.

Cleaning the rear derailleur

Where dirt and grime builds up most on a rear derailleur is on the two jockey wheels. The focus of your annual cleaning of the rear derailleur should be on cleaning the overall derailleur, without disassembling it, and cleaning the two jockey wheels.

Whenever you remove the rear derailleur, try to do so without breaking the chain. You can do this by removing the bolt holding the bottom pulley wheel in place and loosening the bolt holding the top pulley. This will allow you to separate the S-shaped cage and slide out the chain. After the chain is removed, you can detach the entire derailleur for a thorough degreasing and lubrication before you reattach it.

For details on cleaning your rear derailleur, refer to Chapter 14.

Replacing the brake pads

The only thing between you and your next emergency stop is a thin rubber pad, so we highly recommend changing your brake pads every year. Brake pads are easy to inspect, cheap to purchase, and simple to install, so don't wait for the annual maintenance period to change them if they're worn — keep an eye on them year-round and take caution to make sure pads are properly fit and securely mounted.

As soon as the grooves that are cut into the pads start wearing down, replace them.

For instructions on changing brake pads, turn to Chapter 8.

Replacing the handlebar grips or tape

After a year's worth of riding, your bike may start looking a little ragged. The annual maintenance of your bike is your chance not just to get it back in working order but to give it back some of that glow that's lost after many hard miles of working for you.

Replacing dirty or torn handlebar grips or tapes is a simple way to improve the appearance of your bike. You can add a different color of tape or change the style of grips to meet your fancy.

To replace handlebar grips or tape, turn to Chapter 15.

Waxing the frame

Another nice touch when it comes to improving the look of your bike, while protecting its finish and preventing rust, is to wax the frame. If you're overhauling many of your bike's components at the same time, you'll have detached most of the parts from the frame, making cleaning and waxing the frame a simple task.

Although there are waxes designed specifically for higher-end paint finishes on more expensive bikes, car wax works just fine.

Checking your accessories

The annual maintenance check is a good time to inspect accessories for your bike. Verify that your emergency tool kit has everything it needs (see Chapter 16). For example, if you've patched a number of flats over the year, you may need to buy another patch kit. If you've used your spare inner tube, you should replace it.

If you have lights on your bike, replace the batteries. Do the same for your onboard computer. It's better to replace batteries now than discover that they don't work when you're caught out on the road after dark.

Part V
The Part of Tens

The 5th Wave   By Rich Tennant

In this part . . .

In this part, we tell you some practical things you can do to improve safety, comfort, and performance on your next ride. For safety, we offer an inspection checklist of things you should look for before you ride. To increase riding comfort, you find ten steps to make sure your bike fits your body size and riding style. Finally, if you're looking for an extra performance edge, we provide ten recommendations for cutting weight and improving riding efficiency.

Chapter 18

Ten (Or So) Steps to Take before You Ride

In This Chapter

▶ Recognizing the rules of the road

▶ Adjusting the handlebars and saddle

▶ Checking your tire pressure, brakes, and wheels

▶ Donning helmet and gloves

▶ Making sure people can see you

▶ Bringing your toolkit and emergency gear

One of the themes of this book is that repair and maintenance is not just about keeping your bike in great shape and extending its life, but also making sure you stay safe. Taking a couple of minutes before you ride to prepare for your trip and to inspect your bike will go a long way in increasing the odds that you and your bike return home in one piece. In this chapter, we cover the ten (or so) top steps you can take to reduce strain on your body and improve safety while your ride.

Take a Road Safety Skills Class

The League of American Bicyclists offers road-skills classes throughout the United States to make bicyclists aware of the hazards they face sharing the roadways. The classes teach you how to avoid collisions with automobiles and dodge road hazards. You can find a class near you at www.bikeleague.org/programs/education. Contact the League of American Bicyclists at 1612 K St. NW, Suite 800, Washington, DC 20006-2850 (phone: 202-822-1333; e-mail: bikeleague@bikeleague.org; Web: www.bikeleague.org).

Adjust the Handlebars

If you're going to be spending any amount of time on your bike, you should try to make it as comfortable an experience as possible. You can do a number of things to improve the riding experience, and one of these things is to adjust the handlebars.

For road bikes, the old-school approach to positioning the handlebars was to have the handlebar ends run parallel to the top tube in the frame. Although being bent over like the Hunchback of Notre Dame may be good for aerodynamics, having your weight supported on outstretched arms is not very comfortable for everyday riding.

To position your handlebars for a more enjoyable ride, set them such that they leave your back at a 45-degree angle (see Figure 18-1). You may need to rotate the handlebars within the clamp that holds them or change or adjust the stem as described in Chapter 15. With the proper adjustment, you can ensure that the weight of your upper body will be distributed between your torso and your arms.

Figure 18-1:
The proper
handlebar
angle.

Another consideration for the handlebars is the position of the brake levers. You want to be able to squeeze the levers while your hands are resting comfortably on the handlebar. If you have to reach or curl your wrists to use the brakes, they aren't positioned properly.

Adjust the Saddle

Just as important as adjusting the handlebars is finding the right position for your saddle. If your saddle is set too high or too low, you'll lose efficiency as you pedal and may even cause strain or injury to your body. We can't tell you how often we see people riding with an improperly positioned saddle — in many cases, a saddle set too low with the person's legs in a bow-legged position, which causes strain on the knees.

You know that your saddle is set to the right height if you can just barely place your toes and the balls of your feet on the ground when you sit on the saddle (see Figure 18-2). Go for the maximum leg extension without locking out your knees or bobbing your hips in order to reach low. Pain in the back of the kneecaps results from seats too low; pain in the front, from seats too high. Your leg should be bent at a slight angle when your foot is on the pedal at its lowest position.

Figure 18-2:
The proper
saddle
height.

Another adjustment you can make is the fore and aft (how far back or forward the seat is positioned). If your seat is too far to the rear, you'll be stretching to reach the bars, which puts strain on your back and knees. (See Chapter 9 for how to adjust fore and aft.)

Check Tire Pressure

Before you set off for a ride, make sure you check your tire pressure. If your tires aren't properly inflated, riding will be less efficient and you'll be at greater risk of damaging your rims and getting flats.

When checking tire pressure, it isn't enough to pinch the tires to feel whether they're firm — tires that are under-inflated feel very similar to those with the proper amount of pressure. The most accurate and surefire way of checking tire pressure is to use a tire-pressure gauge. When filling tires with air, pump them to the recommended pressure listed on the sidewall of the tire.

Check the Brakes

Checking your brakes takes only a few seconds, and it can be one of the most important things you do before setting off on a ride.

Start by visually inspecting the brake pads for wear; confirm that there are still grooves cut into the pads. When these grooves wear away, it's time to change the pads. Also, check to make sure that the brake pads are not rubbing against the wheels. There should be between 1 to 2 millimeters of space between the pads and the rim.

After visually inspecting the brake pads, give the brake levers a strong squeeze. The pads should firmly grip the wheel. (See Chapter 8 for instructions on making adjustments to the brakes.)

You should also be able to apply the breaks without having to pull the lever more than halfway back to the handlebars — any more than that, and you could be putting yourself in a dangerous position when it comes time to brake.

Look for Looseness

The rattling of components or extra movement in parts of your bike could be a sign that something is starting to come apart. If you ignore these signs, you could end up causing damage to your bike or find yourself on the end of a bike that decides to disassemble itself while you're riding it.

To test your bike for looseness:

✔ Lift the front wheel up 2 to 3 inches, and drop it back down. Do the same to the rear wheel using the seat to lift it. Listen for anything rattling.

✔ Check for looseness in the stem and handlebars by putting the front wheel between your legs and moving the handlebars from side to side (see Figure 18-3).

Figure 18-3:
Checking
for loose-
ness in the
handlebars
and stem.

✔ Examine the rest of the frame by straddling the frame with both legs and trying to move the bike forward and backward while squeezing the brakes. If the bike moves during either of these two tests, it could indicate looseness. If anything shakes or rattles, it could mean that an attachment like a water-bottle cage or a rack for carrying *panniers* (bags) is loose.

✔ Check the crank arms by grabbing one in each hand and trying to wiggle them from side to side. If there is some play in the crank arms, it could be time for a bottom bracket adjustment.

Check the Wheels

Take a moment to check the wheels before you depart on your next trip. Wheels are the only parts of the bike that are in contact with the road; ensuring that they're secure and in good working order will help ensure that you *yourself* don't come in contact with the road.

To inspect the wheels:

✔ Examine the quick-release levers to confirm that they're securely fastened in the closed position. Open and close the levers once to confirm that they're tight. If you find that they're loose, open the lever, turn the nut opposite the lever a quarter-turn, and re-close the lever. Continue this procedure until properly tightened.

✔ Grab the frame with one hand and, with the other hand, give each wheel a shake from side to side to check for looseness (see Figure 18-4). There should little or no amount of play in the hubs. Any significant movement could be a sign that there is an issue with the wheel.

✔ While you're grabbing the wheel, pluck its spokes. Like a string on a fine-tuned harp, they should respond with a consistent twang indicating they're of similar tension.

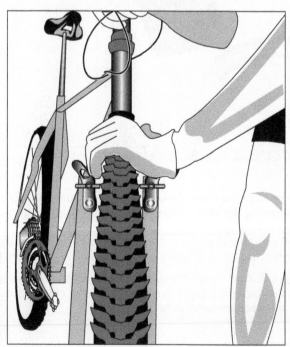

Figure 18-4: Checking for looseness in the wheels.

✔ Lift the wheel off the ground and give it a spin to see that it doesn't wobble and that the rim doesn't contact the brake pads at any point. If the wheel doesn't spin straight, it may need to be trued. Contact with the brake pads could also mean that the wheel isn't properly seated in the dropouts. (See Chapter 7 if you have to make adjustments to your wheels.)

Grab Your Toolkit

Although the probability is that your next ride will be uneventful, don't let that be a reason to hop on your bike without grabbing your toolkit. Murphy's Law has a devious way of striking in the least expected moment, so don't tempt fate by leaving your toolkit behind. (For more details on creating a tool kit and what it consists of, turn to Chapter 16.)

Most important for your toolkit is a patch kit to repair flats, tire levers to remove tires, and some Allen wrenches, screwdrivers, and spoke wrenches. For safety, remember to pack a rag or some moist wipes with your kit so your greasy hands don't slip off the bars after a roadside repair. Plus, you won't gross out your friends when you stop for a snack and have to put food in your mouth.

Wear Your Helmet and Gloves

Wearing a helmet is one of the smartest things you can do to improve safety while you bike. A stylish, light, adjustable, comfortable, and ventilated helmet doesn't cost much money — and it protects your cranium (which is pretty much priceless).

If you've been in an accident that caused an impact to your helmet, or if you've had the helmet for more than a few years, consider replacing it. The helmet's foam, which acts as a shock absorber, breaks down over time or after an accident and becomes less effective.

When Dennis isn't riding, a pair of biking gloves sits inside his helmet. Gloves significantly reduce vibration, which comes from the bike being in contact with the road. Gloves may not make much difference on a short ride, but you'll be thankful that your hands aren't numb after a couple hours on your bike. Gloves will also protect your hands in the event of a crash when the instinct is to use your hands to brace a fall. Gloves come in all shapes and sizes; Dennis likes the comfort of those with gel in the palms.

Improve Your Visibility

We can't emphasize enough how important it is to make yourself visible to others, especially if you're going to be riding on the road. Drivers are faced with many distractions — cellphones, GPS devices, iPods, food, screaming kids — and if you blend into the background, you increase the chances that you'll be on the wrong end of a close encounter with a 4,000-pound bundle of steel and rubber.

Here are some ways you can improve your visibility:

✔ Wear brightly colored clothing — even during daytime biking.

✔ Make sure that your wheels and pedals have reflectors.

✔ Use reflective arm and leg bands.

✔ Keep a bright white front light and a flashing LED rear light for when you're caught out during dusk or for nighttime riding.

Make sure you check the batteries in your lights. Although battery-powered lights are bright, they fade fast. Keep a spare set of batteries in your house so you never leave home without lights that work.

Stock Your Emergency Gear

Although most of your bike rides will be pleasantly uneventful, you never know when an emergency may strike. You can end up getting lost, having an accident, getting caught in a sudden storm, or becoming fatigued. Be prepared for the unexpected by having an emergency pack of supplies available.

Before you head out, always fill your pannier bag with the following items:

✔ Your cellphone

✔ Identification (such as your driver's license)

✔ Money

✔ Energy bars

✔ A rain jacket

✔ Sunglasses

If you don't want to have to carry your wallet with you on your rides, check out RoadID (www.roadid.com), where you can buy a wrist band with your name and emergency-contact information printed on it, as well as a shoe pouch (in which you can put money, your house key, an ID, and so on). You can get a wrist band or a shoe pouch for about $20 each (as of this writing).

Chapter 19

Ten Considerations in Fitting Your Bike

In This Chapter

▶ Looking at the length of the crank arm

▶ Choosing the right gearing

▶ Paying attention to all things saddle

▶ Finding the right frame size

▶ Handling handlebars

*I*n the course of maintaining and repairing your bike, you need to consider how any adjustments you make might affect the way your bike fits you. The better a bike is fitted or tailored to your body size, the more enjoyable your riding experience will be. A properly fitted bike leads to more efficient riding, more power delivered to the pedals, greater comfort, and less chance of soreness or injury.

When you first purchase a bike, you should work with a fit specialist at the bike shop to make sure that the bike you buy fits your body. But you can — and should — also focus on fit as you maintain and repair your bike.

Fit is not an exact science. Yes, there are some high-tech measurement and sizing machines, fitting systems, charts, and formulas. But put two experts in a room, and they'll come up with a different set of measurements. Our best advice is to follow the basic principles and tips in this chapter and throughout this book and consult with your local bike shop. If you do that, you should be able to get a fairly good fit with your bike — and your back, shoulders, arms, legs, and hands will thank you for miles to come.

Considering Crank Arm Length

The crank arm determines the circumference in which the pedals rotate. The larger the crank arm, the larger the circumference in which you'll be pedaling. A longer crank arm gives you more leverage when you pedal. Riding with a longer crank arm is kind of like being in a lower gear, an important benefit if you're doing a lot of climbing. On the other hand, a shorter crank arm comes in handy if you pedal at a high cadence (for example, if you're racing).

With longer crank arms it's important to make sure the bottom bracket has enough clearance. If you buy a bike with a crank arm that's too long, the crank arm may hit the ground when you're cornering.

Your height will impact the length of the crank arm you chose. In most cases, taller bikers should have longer crank arms, and shorter bikers should have shorter crank arms.

A number of different crank arm lengths are available. It's common to see lengths of 165mm to 180mm in 2.5mm increments, with the most common lengths being 170mm and 172.5mm. If you're in the NBA, you'll be glad to know that a few manufacturers will sell you a crank of 185mm or more. Work with your local bike store to find the crank the best suits you.

Going for Gearing

Choosing the appropriate gearing may not be fitting a bike in the traditional sense, but it is an important factor in how well a bike fits the way you ride. By selecting a bike with the gearing that meets your fitness levels, how you pedal, and the terrain on which you ride, you can make a significant and positive impact on your riding experience.

Most newer bikes have seven to ten cogs in the rear and two to three chainrings in the front. Multiply these two numbers together and you have the total number of gears for your bike. If you're in shape and you don't do a lot of climbing, you're probably fine with seven to eight cogs and two chainrings. Some riders like to have a third chainring in case a climb is necessary or fatigue sets in at the end of a long ride (though that third chainring does add extra weight and three chainrings won't shift as effortlessly as two); third chainrings are also useful for mountain biking and touring.

If you're planning on doing a lot of mountain biking or touring, talk to your local bike shop to make sure you have the right gearing. They can give you advice not just about the total number of gears but about the size of the individual cogs and chainrings, important factors in gearing. (For a more detailed discussion of gearing, turn to Chapter 2.)

Resisting the Temptation to Tilt Your Saddle

Some people are tempted to tilt the saddle downward in an attempt to find a more comfortable position and relieve pressure on the groin. Resist the temptation! The problem with this position is that it causes you to slide forward against the handlebars, which puts additional weight and stress on your arms, wrists, hands, and shoulders. In the other extreme, a saddle tilted upward can cause discomfort, especially for men — and we don't need to explain why!

In general, we recommend that you try to keep your seat flat and parallel to the ground. To check the straightness of your seat, place a level on top of the seat, and make adjustments as necessary.

Setting the Saddle Height

Saddle height is an important factor in fitting your bike. A saddle set too high reduces the amount of power available for pedaling and causes you to stretch for the pedals on the down stroke and rock back and forth on the saddle, which can cause soreness. A saddle set too low doesn't allow you to use your leg muscles efficiently, puts extra strain on the knees, and can lead to injury.

We notice many riders whose saddles are not at the proper height, sometimes significantly so. Odds are, a rider whose saddle isn't set to the proper height made some adjustments over time that affected the saddle height but didn't know exactly where to set it. In Chapter 18, we give you step-by-step instructions for choosing the proper saddle height for your bike.

After you've set the correct height for your saddle, mark the seat post with tape or a small score in the metal so you can easily return it to that position if the post comes loose or you have to remove it.

Looking at the Saddle Fore and Aft

The fore and aft are how far forward and backward the saddle is on your bike. If the saddle is too far forward, you lose leverage when you pedal; if it's too far back, you could be putting strain on your back. As with most parts of the bike, the fit depends on how you're going to be using your bike. If you're racing, you'll want to have the saddle in a more forward position along with the handlebars, which will put you in a more bent-over, aerodynamic position, and allow you to deliver more power to the pedals. If you're not racing, though, the best position will have the saddle nose behind the bottom bracket.

To find the proper fore and aft position, sit on your bike with the pedals parallel to the ground while someone supports you. Hang a string with a weight tied to the end of it from your kneecap down past the pedal. The line from your knee-cap should pass through the center of the pedal where the axle threads into the crank arm (see Figure 19-1). If the string is in front of the pedal, move the saddle forward. If the string is in back of the pedal, move the saddle backward.

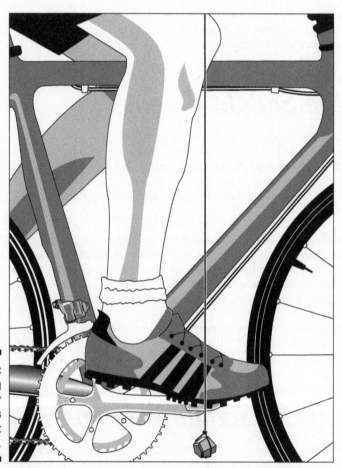

Figure 19-1:
Use a string
to set your
saddles
fore and aft
position.

After you make the adjustment, give your bike a test ride to make sure you feel comfortable. Remember that after you first change the position of the saddle, you may feel a little strange. Give it some time before you make a final decision on where it should be.

Choosing the Right Saddle Type

Unless you're a racer competing in sprints, you're going to be spending the majority of your time biking with your bum on a saddle. The saddle is one of the three points of contact your body has with the bike (the pedals and handlebars are the other two), and the saddle is where a lot of your weight is.

Some saddles are designed to support the specific anatomy of men, while others are designed for women, so make sure you choose the right one. Saddles for men are normally longer and narrower and sometimes have cutout sections or extra padding to help prevent numbness. For women, saddles are shorter and wider toward the back to better accommodate a woman's wider pelvis. (Children use smaller sized saddles than adults do.) Figure 19-2 shows the differences between saddles for men and women.

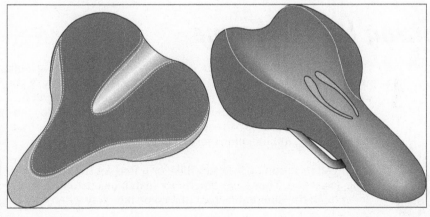

Figure 19-2: Saddles for men (right) and women (left).

Saddles come in a variety of different materials. Leather saddles conform to the shape of your butt, although they require special care, especially in wet weather. Other saddles are made with gel or foam padding with many different coverings that are more resistant to the elements.

You may think that a bigger, softer saddle would equal a more comfortable ride. Unfortunately, bigger and softer does not translate into comfort. Weight from your body should come into contact with the seat through two bones at the lower part of your pelvis. If you have a properly fitted seat, when you get off your bike, you should see two indentations centered on each side of your seat. If the seat is too soft, your entire butt is in contact with the seat causing pressure on tissue and nerves that are not designed for this. Although a firmer seat may cause your pelvic bones to be sore after the first ride or two, in the long run, you'll find that it provides the most comfortable ride. As crazy as it sounds, the more you ride, the smaller the seat you'll want.

For comfort, wear biking shorts, which are designed without seams in the crotch area — seams can chafe and rub the soft tissue in the crotch. Biking shorts also include extra padding or chamois, which provides extra comfort, wicks away moisture, and keeps bacteria at bay. Just make sure you wash your biking shorts after each ride. Also, don't forget to remove your underwear when you wear them — the goal is to have no seams and less material to bunch up and cause chafing.

If you have problems with rubbing and chafing in the groin area, consider applying a skin lubricant such as Vaseline. Some lubricants, such as Chamois Butt'r, are designed specifically for bikers.

Sizing Up the Frame

Frame size is the most important consideration when fitting a bike. Unlike most other factors, the frame is one thing you can't modify. If you end up with a bike that has a frame too small or too large, you won't be able to adjust the saddle and handlebars enough to compensate for the improper dimensions. Plus, an incorrectly sized frame can be dangerous, making starting, stopping, and handling more difficult.

When you're shopping for a new bike or frame, let the staff at your local bike shop assist you. They have experience matching customers to bikes, and they understand the different factors that come into play when choosing a frame.

The bike-shop staff will want your inseam size. This is the length from the floor to the top of your crotch. They'll take this number and subtract 10 to 12 inches from it, based on how tall you are, which will give them an estimation of the frame size you need. ***Remember:*** This is just an estimation — every bicycle will fit a little differently, depending on the manufacturer, model, type of bicycle, your riding style, and so on.

Frames are generally measured from the center of the bottom bracket to the top of the seat tube (see Figure 19-3), although manufacturers have different variations of this measurement. After the bike-shop staff has a general idea of the frame size, they'll have you try out various bikes with this size. To confirm the size, they'll have you straddle the bike with both feet on the ground and the frame between your legs. In this position, there should be at least an inch or two of space between the top tube and your crotch, more if it's a mountain bike.

Figure 19-3:
How frame
size is
measured.

Focusing on Frame Dimensions

If your local bike shop determines that you need a certain size frame, they'll still need to have you sit on the bike to confirm that the frame's dimensions suit your body type. Two 20-inch frames can vary significantly based on the dimensions in which they were manufactured. A shorter version of a 20-inch frame will provide greater performance and handling; in this case, the seat tube will be more upright, requiring you to sit in a more aerodynamic, bent-over position. Another 20-inch frame may have a longer base to provide stability and comfort and a more sloped seat-tube angle for a more upright ride, both of which provide benefits when touring.

As a general rule, when you're seated on a bike with your hands on the handlebars and feet on the pedals, the handlebars should block your view of the front hub. Another rule of thumb is that in your natural reach, your arms should make a 90-degree angle to your torso. On road drop handlebars, of the three holding positions, the middle lean (hands over brake levers) should obscure the hub with the handlebars.

In general, you shouldn't be stretched out like Lance Armstrong or sitting upright like you're getting a haircut. There should be a slight bend in your elbows and they shouldn't be locked out or pressed into your ribs.

If the top tube is slightly too long or short, this can be compensated for by adjusting the stem length. The stem can be raised or lowered; with adjustable stems, the angle can be adjusted as well.

Positioning Your Handlebars

The handlebars are one of the three points where your body comes into contact with your bike, so you need to take the time to set them in the position that's most comfortable for you.

Before adjusting your handlebars, make sure you've found the appropriate height and angle for your saddle. If you don't have the saddle in the proper position, you won't be able to set the handlebars correctly.

For most everyday riders, the handlebars should be even with or slightly higher than the seat. When you sit on the bike and grab the uppermost part of the handlebars and straighten your arms, your back should be at a 45-degree position. If you're looking for a more aerodynamic position, the bar should be an inch or two lower than the saddle. In this position, the angle of your back will be less than 45 degrees.

The height of the handlebars is sometimes limited by the type of stem you have. On some threadless stems, spacers can be used to adjust the height. If this doesn't provide enough of a change, you can replace the stem with an adjustable one that provides more range to move the handlebars.

For road bikes with dropdown handlebars, the other adjustment to consider is the angle. The traditional approach was to have the bottom of the handlebars line up parallel to the top tube. But if you don't want to be bent over in a position better left to yoga classes, a more appropriate angle is for the bottom of the handlebars to be closer to parallel with the seat stays, as shown in Figure 19-4.

Figure 19-4:
The proper
handlebar
angle.

Getting a Handle on Handlebar Style

Like many other parts of the bike, there are a plethora of different styles of handlebars on the market. You can find handlebars for road racing, mountain biking, touring, and everyday riding. Of these different types, two shapes are predominant — the drop-down road-bike style and the flat mountain-bike style.

Regardless of the style of handlebars you choose, choose a width that comes close to matching the width of your shoulders. This width will keep your arms parallel while you ride and your chest open for efficient and relaxed breathing.

Your hands should be in a relaxed position when you grab the brakes. Your wrists should not be angled down over the handlebars when squeezing the brakes. An awkward angle for your wrists will cause pressure on the nerves and lead to an uncomfortable numbing sensation in the hands and wrists.

Frequently change the position of your hands when you ride. One way to increase the number of positions for riding is to add bar-ends to your flat, mountain-bike-style handlebars. Not only do bar-ends give you an alternative position, but they can be beneficial for climbing. Just remember that your hands will be farther away from the brakes, which could be a problem if you have to stop suddenly.

Chapter 20

Ten Ways to Improve the Performance and Comfort of Your Bike

. . . .

In This Chapter

▶ Taking your bike to the next level

▶ Making all your friends jealous with your upgrades

. . . .

*O*ne of the joys of owning and working on a bike is the chance to upgrade its parts. Just like car tuning, tuning your bike can help you improve both comfort and performance while you ride. Odds are, doing a complete overhaul of your bike is probably not in your price range, especially considering that some higher-end components can be pretty pricey. But if you're going to be repairing and maintaining your bike, you may want to add on a high-performance part once in a while. In this chapter, we present ten options to consider if you're thinking about upgrading.

Upgrading Your Wheels and Tires

One way to significantly impact your bike's performance is to upgrade the wheels and tires. If you can drop the weight of the wheels and tires even slightly, you'll notice a definite difference when you bike.

Many options are available for upgrading your bike's wheels. Major wheel manufactures offer products with a variety of rim styles made of different materials. Wheels are also available with an assortment of spoke designs. Because of the improved quality of spokes, wheels are being built with fewer spokes but with comparable strength and durability.

If you upgrade your tires, you'll realize another performance gain: Higher-quality tires provide reduced weight and less rolling resistance, which makes a dramatic difference in performance. Better-quality tires are designed with more threads inside the rubber, which holds the tire together, allowing for greater air pressure, less contact surface, and a fast ride.

The tread pattern on the tires also has an impact on ride comfort. The less tread on your tires, the less rolling resistance and the better performance you'll experience.

Most wheels allow you to change the width of your tires. Tire width impacts performance — narrower tires give you a faster ride because of their decreased rolling resistance, and wider tires are more comfortable because they absorb more road shock (although wider tires have more tread on the road and more rolling resistance). To determine the width of your tire, look at the dimension written on the sidewall of your tires; specifically, look for the second number. A marking of 700x25 means the tire has a circumference of 700cm and a width of 25cm. If you plan on changing the width of your tires, work with your local bike shop to make sure you find tires that work with the dimensions of your frame.

The other important consideration when choosing tires is durability. If you're touring and riding a significant number of miles with fully-packed pannier bags, you'll want a very durable tire that can handle the weight. A more durable tire will also lead to fewer flats along the way. Many of the tires specially designed for durability have a Kevlar belt or other material designed for protection.

If you want protection from flats but don't have the money to upgrade your tires, you can fill your bike's tubes with a puncture sealant. The liquid inside the tube will automatically fill any punctures that may occur. In addition to puncture sealant, you may want to opt for thorn-resistant tubes (which are thicker than normal tubes) and tire liner (a protective stripe of Kevlar that you place between the tire and tube). The downside to this flat protection, however, is significant added rotational weight — but if you absolutely hate flat tires, you won't mind trading some performance for convenience.

Ramping Up Your Rear Derailleur

The rear derailleur is the biggest factor in shifting performance. Top-end derailleurs have stronger springs and tighter bushings and pivot points that allow for easier and faster shifting. These derailleurs are designed with jockey wheels with higher-end bearings, which cause less resistance and smoother chain movement, which, in turn, improves chain life and derailleur life.

Pair a top-of-the-line rear derailleur with an upgraded shifter, and you'll multiply the impact of that derailleur and find that you can change gears with barely a flick of the finger.

Beefing Up Your Bearings

Bearings in the wheels and bottom brackets are designed to reduce friction as you roll on down the road. Higher-quality bearings are made with greater precision and reduce friction due to their smoother surfaces and longer life. Many higher-end bearings are designed with rubber seals to keep contaminants out. The latest breakthrough in bearings are those made of ceramic, a material that is amazingly smooth with almost no resistance.

Pumping Up Your Pedals

Many casual riders think that clipless pedals are difficult to use and are only for professional riders. Unfortunately, this misconception causes a lot of riders to miss out on a significant performance gain. Studies have shown that clipless pedals can improve performance by up to 30 percent, by increasing the efficiency of the pedal stroke. With clipless pedals, you don't have to expend any energy keeping your foot centered on the pedal during the upstroke of the pedals. As a result, you can pedal in complete circles, in a pattern of push down, pull back, pull up, and push forward — a much more efficient mode of pedaling.

As for the misconception that it's difficult to disengage clipless pedals, especially in the event of an emergency, nothing could be farther from the truth. After trying clipless pedals, you'll discover that releasing your foot from the pedal is a very natural movement.

Some pedals have an adjustment for the amount of energy required to release the cleat and shoe from the pedal. This adjustment allows new riders to use a loose setting while adjusting to the pedals. Then, when they're comfortable using clipless pedals, they can tighten that adjustment to allow for hard pedaling without the fear of releasing the clips.

Casual commuters who want to increase their pedal efficiency may find power straps and conventional toe straps useful. Also, double-sided pedals, which have a normal platform on one side and a clipless pedal on the other, are great for people who like to ride their bikes with whichever shoes they're wearing at the time.

A Shoe-In: Choosing the Best Shoes for the Job

Shoes are another factor in pedaling efficiency. Many everyday riders use running, cross-training, or basic tennis shoes when riding. These shoes are designed to absorb the impact from running and walking in order to improve comfort. But on a bicycle they absorb a lot of the energy before it gets to the pedals, causing your pedaling to be less efficient. On the other hand, cycling shoes have a very stiff sole and are designed to transfer all your energy to the pedals to get you down the road as efficiently as possible.

Some biking shoes are so stiff that they look like they were cast out of iron. Others shoes are designed with the cleat recessed up into the sole and flexible materials that allow you to walk normally — these are popular with touring or mountain bikers, because they allow you to ride and then get off and walk around town or hike up an un-rideable trail. In contrast, road biking cleats are mounted directly to the sole and are hard to walk in. They're like having high heals on, because the shoes are designed with the toes set higher than the heals.

Be careful walking in road-biking cleats — they're very slippery on flat surfaces.

Saddle Up! Taking Your Saddle to the Next Level

A top-notch saddle not only can improve the comfort of your ride but increase your pedaling efficiency. There are many options on the market — enough to fit many different body types. Some saddle manufacturers even make a tool to measure your tail-bone position so you can get the most tailored and comfortable fit. However, the only way to be sure that you'll be comfortable on a saddle is to try it. Some bicycle stores have test seats to try out in the store; others allow you to try a seat on your own bicycle for a limited time to get a feel for it.

Upgrading Your Handlebars

Handlebars come in many different sizes and styles, so there's no excuse for not finding a set that fits you. A correctly sized handlebar can greatly improve riding comfort. As a general rule, your handlebars should be as wide as your shoulders. This allows for improved breathing while you ride, while giving you greater control of the bike.

With drop bars or racing-style handlebars, you have options as to the shape. Some have a flat spot for your hands in the middle of a curved drop section to give your hands support when riding. Some have a flat platform on the top section of the bars to give your palms more of a surface ledge to rest on.

Also available are triathlon or aero bars, which are attachments added to the handlebars that have hand grips and elbow rests. They allow you to ride in a bent-over position with your arms and elbows tucked in close to your body to reduce wind resistance.

If you have flat or upright handlebars, you can add bar ends to the handlebars to give you another hand position. Bar ends are small 2- to 5-inch extensions that mount to the end of the handlebars and drastically improve your comfort on longer rides, allowing you to change your body position and shift your weight to get more comfortable.

Boosting Your Brake Levers

Like the handlebars and other parts of the bike, brake levers come in different sizes and styles. Some levers are designed for improved comfort with a larger surface area for your hands when you're riding on the *hoods* (the part above the brake levers that serve as another place to rest your hands). Most bikes for women have brake levers that are smaller, with a shorter reach for people with smaller hands. Bicycles with flat or upright bars have brake levers that are adjustable for people with smaller hands as well.

The angle of the lever can also make a significant difference in comfort and performance. The levers should be positioned at an angle so that your hands rest in a natural and comfortable position.

Taking Your Clothing up a Notch

While clothing doesn't qualify as a bike component, it is an important factor in improving your riding experience. Cycling shorts are made of stretchable material that moves with you as ride your bike. Many biking shorts have panels of material to hold their shape and prevent the material from bunching up. Shorts with eight panels are popular, but basic shorts with four panels will usually suffice. The chamois or crotch liner in cycling shorts greatly improves comfort and performance. Its design helps reduce impact on key pressure points and wicks away moisture. Another advantage of cycling shorts is the fact that you don't wear any undergarment, which eliminates extra material and eliminates seams that can cause chaffing.

If you're looking for a different look or style, try bib overalls designed for cyclists. Bibs are preferred by many bikers because of the increased comfort with the elimination of the waistband.

Biking jerseys are another must in the wardrobe of any biker. Designed with special fabric, they wick away perspiration and dry quickly. They fit snug to your body, which reduces wind resistance. And they have pockets in the back for easy access to your iPod or energy bar.

A major factor when it comes to clothing is also visibility. To safely ride on the road, even during the middle of the day, you need to be extremely visible. Wear a neon-colored windbreaker, a bright cyclist jersey, or a reflective vest.

If you commute or go on long-distance rides, wear layers: arm and leg warmers, windbreakers, and sometimes a base layer, and a cover layer of jerseys. Another extremely basic and handy clothing item is a pant-cuff tie or clip, to keep your pant legs from being stained by your chain if you're riding in street clothes.

Embracing Your Inner Geek with a Cycling Computer

A cycling computer is a great addition for your bike. Most computers tell all sorts of interesting stats about your ride, such as how fast you're going, how far you've gone, your average speed, your max speed, and the time of your ride. Some computers even give you temperature and altitude readings. Others allow you to download the information to a personal computer so that you can track your riding statistics over time.

A cycling computer is like having a personal coach along for the ride. You can set goals for distance and time, and then it's off to the races. The computer tracks your progress as you bike, and you may find yourself racing against the clock.

Index

• A •

accessories
  annual maintenance, 298
  bike pump, 11, 39–40, 74, 77
  buying, 76–77
  checking, 17, 298
  clothes, 77, 308, 323–324
  computer, 77, 324
  gloves, 77, 307
  helmet, 77, 307
  lights, 77, 298, 308
  lock, 77
  overview, 17
  shoes, 77, 322
adjustable bottom bracket
  installing, 228–229
  overview, 223–224
  removing, 227–228
advanced repairs, 14–15. *See also*
      professional repairs
aero handlebars, 323
after-ride maintenance, 12
air suspension, 202
alignment, 65–66
Allen wrench, 10–11, 38–39, 275
aluminum frame, 195
angle
  brake lever, 323
  handlebar, 302–303, 316–317
  head-tube, 103
  saddle, 147, 150–151
  seat-tube, 192–193
annual maintenance
  accessories, checking, 17, 298
  bottom bracket, overhauling, 17, 297
  brake pads, replacing, 17, 297
  cables, replacing, 16, 295
  chain, deep cleaning, 16, 294
  frame, waxing, 17, 298

  handlebar grips or tape, replacing, 17, 298
  headset, overhauling, 17, 296
  housing, replacing, 16, 295
  hubs, overhauling, 17, 295–296
  overview, 16–17, 293–294
  pedals, overhauling, 17, 296
  rear derailleur, cleaning, 17
  wheels, truing, 16, 294
arm band, reflective, 308
axle, removing, 109–110
axle nuts, 86

• B •

bar ends, 254, 323
basic repairs, 13–14
basic tools
  Allen wrenches, 38–39, 275
  cleaners, 43
  degreasers, 43
  hammer, 39
  lubricants, 41–43
  multipurpose tool, 275
  patch kit, 40
  pliers, 275
  pressure gauge, 40–41
  pump, 39–40
  rag, 275
  screwdrivers, 38, 275
  small light, 275
  spoke wrench, 275
  tire levers, 41, 275
  tire patch kit, 274
  tire pump, 274
  wrenches, 37–38
battery, 308
bearings, 22–24, 321
bent rim, repairing, 54–55
bibs, 324
bike lights, 77, 298, 308
bike manufacturers, 73

bike parts
  bearings, 22–24, 321
  bottom bracket, 223–229
  brakes, 34, 119–142
  cables, 27–29
  crankset, 215–223
  derailleur, 30–31, 231–248
  drivetrain, 34, 207–230
  frames, 34, 191–201
  gears, 29–30
  handlebars, 252–260
  headset, 261–270
  illustration, 21, 22
  overview, 19–20
  pedals, 207–214
  quick-release lever, 32–33
  steering system, 34, 251–270
  suspension, 34, 201–206
  threads, 24–27
  wheels, 34, 99–118
bike pump, 11, 39–40, 74, 77
bike shops
  accessories, 76–77
  buying bike, 71–75
  cost of doing business, 71
  customer service, 71
  expertise of staff, 71
  family-friendly, 71
  overview, 69–70
  recommendations, 70
  repairing bike at, 78–79
  staff, 70
  turnaround time, 71
  women-friendly, 71
  year-round service, 70–71
bike stand, 10, 49–51, 279
bikes types, 73–74
biking accessories
  annual maintenance, 298
  bike pump, 11, 39–40, 74, 77
  buying, 76–77
  checking, 17, 298
  clothes, 77, 308, 323–324
  computer, 77, 324
  gloves, 77, 307
  helmet, 77, 307

lights, 77, 298, 308
lock, 77
overview, 17
shoes, 77, 322
biking shorts, 147
BMX bike, 74
bolts, 104
boot, tire, 93–94
bottom bracket. *See also* crankset
  adjustable, 223–224, 227–229
  annual maintenance, 297
  axle style, 230
  buying tips, 230
  cartridge, 224–226
  installing, 224–229
  overhauling, 14, 17, 297
  problems with, 63
  removing, 224–229
  size, 230
  threads, 230
bottom-bracket tools, 46
bottom-bracket drop, 103
bottom-bracket shell, 192
brake cables
  avoiding bends, 28
  broken, 63
  ferrule, 27–28
  housing, 27–28
  lubricating, 28, 285, 287
  overview, 27–28
  replacing, 16, 138–142, 295
  spare, 276
brake levers
  angle, 323
  checking, 304
  lubricating, 283
  position of on handlebars, 303
  upgrading, 323
brake pads
  adjusting position of, 130–131
  annual maintenance, 297
  changing, 13, 17, 297
  inspecting, 123–124, 304
  removing, 125–128
  resurfacing, 124

brakes
  adjusting, 130–135
  cables, 138–142
  cantilever, 86, 120–121, 128, 137
  centering, 133–135
  center-mount, 120, 122, 129–130,
    134–135, 138
  disk, 34, 120–121, 123
  hub, 34, 121
  inspecting, 123–124, 304
  installing, 128–130
  loosening, 85–86
  lubricating, 283
  monthly inspection, 15, 292
  overview, 119
  pre-ride inspection, 11, 277
  quick-release, 137–138
  removing, 125–128
  rim, 34, 120
  side-pull, 86, 103
  squeaking, 136
  tensioning, 132
  types of, 34, 120–122
  V-brakes, 86, 103, 120, 122, 128–129, 137
brightly colored clothing, 308
broken chain, repairing, 57
broken spoke, replacing, 55–56
Brooks leather saddles, 144
Brooks Proofide, 293
brushes, 279
bucket, 279
butting, 200, 254
buying
  accessories, 76–77
  bottom bracket, 230
  cartridge bottom bracket, 230
  cassettes, 176
  crankset, 230
  fasteners, 230
  gears, 30
  lubricants, 164
  new bike, 72–75
  pedals, 208–209
  threaded fasteners, 26–27
  tools, 36–37
  used bike, 75–76
bypassing rear derailleur, 60–61

• C •

cable cutters, 140
cables, brake
  avoiding bends, 28
  broken, 63
  ferrule, 27–28
  housing, 27–28
  lubricating, 28, 285, 287
  overview, 27–28
  replacing, 16, 138–142, 295
  spare, 276
cage, 31
calipers, 117
Campagnolo, Tullio, 32
Campagnolo-type chain
  overview, 156–157
  reassembling, 170–172
  removing, 168
Cannondale Web site, 73
cantilever brakes
  installing, 128
  overview, 86, 120–121
  quick-release mechanism, 137
car wax, 279
carbon-fiber frame, 196
cartridge bottom bracket
  buying tips, 230
  overview, 224
  reinstalling, 226–227
  removing, 224–226
cassettes. *See also* cogs; freewheels
  buying tips, 176
  cleaning, 176–177
  free hub, 175
  gears, 175
  inspecting, 176
  installing, 187
  lubricating, 177
  overview, 175–176
  removing, 175, 179–182
  replacing, 14
  splined, 179–181
cellphone, 11, 308

center-mount brakes
  centering, 134–135
  installing, 129–130
  overview, 120, 122
  quick-release mechanism, 138
chain
  annual maintenance, 294
  broken, repairing, 57
  Campagnolo-type, 156–157, 168, 170–172
  cleaning, 163–165
  cutting, 168–169
  deep cleaning, 16, 294
  dirt, 158
  heavy-duty cleaning, 165–167
  jammed, extracting, 58–59
  lubricating, 163–165, 285–286
  measuring, 161–162, 169
  monthly inspection, 15, 292–293
  overview, 155–156
  problems with, 158–163
  reassembling, 170–172
  removing, 168–169
  repairing, 13
  replacing, 13, 167–172
  reusable rivets, 156
  safe riding practices, 12
  Shimano-type, 156–157, 168, 170–172
  SRAM PowerLink–type, 156, 168
  stiff links, 158–160
  types of, 156–157
  wear and tear, 160–163
chain cleaning tool, 165–166
chain links, 11, 276
chain stay, 103, 192
chain tool, 11, 44, 59, 276
chain whip, 45
chainring
  fitting bike, 310
  monthly inspection, 15, 292–293
  removing, 221–222
  teeth, 30
  wear and tear, 161–163
chromoly, 254
citrus degreaser, 10
cleaners, 43
cleaning
  after ride, 278–282
  cassettes, 176–177

chains, 16, 163–167, 294
  derailleur, 17, 297
  freewheels, 176–177
  monthly maintenance, 15, 291
  rear derailleur, 17, 297
  sprocket, 280
  steps, 279–282
  supplies, 279
  wheel, 101
clincher tires, 100
clipless pedals, 208–209
clothing, 77, 308, 323–324
cogs
  cassettes, 175
  freewheels, 175
  lock ring, 175
  monthly inspection, 15, 292–293
  number of teeth, 176
  removing, 183–184
  wear and tear, 161–163
coil suspension, 202
comfort, saddle, 147
compression, 202
computer, cycling, 77, 324
cone wrench, 44
cottered crankset, 216–217
cotterless crankset, 216–221
cradle, 160
craigslist, 76
crank, loose, 63
crank arms
  length, 310
  overhauling, 14
crank extractor, 10, 218–219
crank puller, 44
crankset
  bottom bracket, 223–229
  buying tips, 230
  chainrings, 221–223
  cottered, 216–217
  cotterless, 216–221
  crank arms, 230
  installing, 216–221
  one-key release, 217
  one-piece, 215–216
  overview, 215
  pre-ride inspection, 277
  removing, 216–221

cruiser bike, 74
cruising saddle, 145–146
cup-and-cone hub, 108
customer service, bike shop, 71
cutting chain, 168–169
C-wrench, 227
cycling computer, 77, 324
cycling shorts, 323

● *D* ●

damping, 202
deep cleaning chains, 16, 294
degreasers, 43, 279
dents, in rim, 106
derailleur. *See also* front derailleur; rear
    derailleur
  adjusting, 239–241
  cable, 246–248
  cleaning, 17, 297
  installing, 236–239, 245–246
  lubricating, 284–285
  overview, 30, 231–232
  removing, 59, 233–235
  repairing, 13, 59–61
  safe riding practices, 12
diameter, wheel, 100
dimensions, frame, 315–316
direct-pull brakes, 120
dishing, 79
disk brakes, 34, 120–121, 123
down tube, 192
driver's license, 308
drivetrain
  crankset, 215–223
  overview, 34, 207
  pedals, 207–214
drop bars, 252–253, 323
drum brakes, 121
dual-pivot brakes, 134
duct tape, 11, 66–67, 276
durability, tire, 320

● *E* ●

eBay, 76
elastomer suspension, 202
emergency, preparing for, 11

emergency gear, 308
emergency repairs
  bent rim, 54–55
  broken chain, 57
  broken spoke, 55–56
  derailleur, 59–61
  duct tape, 66–67
  flat tires, 57
  jammed chain, extracting, 58–59
  overview, 53
  torn tires, 57
  walking home, 63
emergency tool kit
  Allen wrenches, 275
  multipurpose tool, 275
  pliers, 275
  rag, 275
  screwdrivers, 275
  small light, 275
  spoke wrench, 275
  tire levers, 275
  tire patch kit, 274
  tire pump, 274
energy bars, 11, 308
extended trip tools
  chain links, 276
  chain tool, 276
  duct tape, 276
  extra tubes, 276
  lubrication, 276
  rivets, 276
  spare cables, 276
  spare spokes, 276
  spare tire, 276
extra tube, 276

● *F* ●

family-friendly bike shops, 71
fasteners
  buying tips, 26–27
  female parts, 25
  loose, 25–26
  male parts, 25
  monthly inspection, 16, 292
  overview, 24–25
  tightening, 25–26
ferrule, 27

Finish Line Citrus Degreaser, 294
fitting bike
  crank-arm length, 310
  frame dimensions, 315–316
  frame size, 314–315
  gearing, 310
  handlebar position, 316–317
  handlebar style, 317
  overview, 309
  saddle, 311–314
flared handlebars, 254
flat bars, 253
flat tires
  attaching wheel, 96
  causes of, 84
  consecutive, 97
  finding puncture, 90
  inspecting tire, 93
  installing spare tube, 85
  loosening brakes, 85–86
  overview, 13, 85
  patching tube, 85, 91–93
  preventing, 97–98
  reinstalling tube and tire, 94–96
  removing, 87–90
  repairing on road, 57
  using tire boot, 93–94
  wheel, removing, 86–87
foldable tire, 11
fourth-hand tool, 129
frame. *See also* suspension
  aluminum, 195
  annual maintenance, 298
  bottom-bracket drop, 103
  bottom-bracket shell, 192
  butting, 200
  carbon fiber, 196
  chain stays, 103, 192
  damaged, 63
  dimensions, 315–316
  down tube, 192
  head tube, 192
  head-tube angle, 103
  inspecting, 196–199
  maintenance of, 199–201
  materials, 195–196
  mountain bike, 103

overview, 34, 191
painting, 200
preventing rust, 199–200
repairing, 14
road bike, 103
seat stays, 192
seat tube, 192
seat-tube angle, 192–193
size, 314–315
steel, 195
stiffness, 195
strength, 195
titanium, 196
top tube, 192
waxing, 17, 201, 298
weight, 195
Frame Saver, 199
free hub
  defined, 175
  removing body, 185–186
freewheel tool, 46
freewheels. *See also* cassettes; cogs
  cleaning, 176–177
  disadvantage of, 174
  free-hub body, removing, 185–186
  inspecting, 176
  installing, 186
  lubricating, 177
  overview, 174
  removing, 178–179
  replacing, 14
front derailleur
  adjusting, 59
  installing, 245–246
  lubricating, 284
  overview, 31, 241–242
  removing, 59, 242–244
front light, 77, 308
front wheel
  attaching, 96, 106–107
  removing, 87
Fuji Web site, 73

Gary Fisher Web site, 73
gauge, 11

gear shifters
  installing, 250
  overview, 248–249
  removing, 250
gears. *See also* derailleur
  buying tips, 30
  chainrings, 30
  fitting bike, 310
  overview, 29
  ratio, 30
  safe riding practices, 12
  sprocket, 30
  total number of, 30
gender, saddles appropriate to,
    146–147, 313
gloves, 77, 307
glue, 11
grips, replacing, 17, 298

• *H* •

hammer, 10, 39
handlebar shifters, 247
handlebars. *See also* shifting system
  adjusting, 302–303
  angle, 302–303, 316–317
  annual maintenance, 298
  bar ends, 254
  brake levers, position of, 303
  butting, 254
  drop bars, 252–253
  flare, 254
  flat bars, 253
  grips, replacing, 17, 298
  material, 254
  positioning, 316–317
  pre-ride inspection, 11, 277
  riser bars, 253
  style, 317
  sweep, 254
  tape, replacing, 17, 298
  taper, 254
  taping, 255–260
  upgrading, 322–323
  width, 254
head tube, 192
headset. *See also* shifting system

adjusting, 262–263
annual maintenance, 296
fitting, 14
inspecting, 261–262
installing, 78
overhauling, 17, 263–270, 296
overview, 261
pre-ride inspection, 11
threaded, 261–263, 268–270
threadless, 261–268
headset tool, 47
head-tube angle, 103
heavy-duty cleaning, chain, 165–167
height, saddle, 147, 152–153, 304, 311
helmet, 77, 307
hex key, 10
H-limit screw, 62
home repairs
  benefits of, 35
  bike stand, 49–51
  lighting, 49
  overview, 35–36
  space needed, 48
  specialized tools, 43–47
  storage, 49
  tools, 36–43
  ventilation, 48
  workbench, 49
housing, replacing, 16, 295
hub. *See also* wheel
  adjusting, 114
  annual maintenance, 295–296
  cup-and-cone, 108
  lubricating, 101
  overhauling, 13, 17, 108–111, 295–296
  overview, 107
  quick release, 100, 107
  reassembling, 111–114
  sealed-bearing, 108
  width, 100
hub brakes, 34, 121
hybrid bike, 74

• *1* •

icons used in book, 5
identification, personal, 11, 308

inflating tire, 101
inner tube, 11
inspection, after-accident
  alignment, checking, 65
  looseness, checking for, 64–65
inspection, pre-ride
  brakes, 277
  checklist, 11
  crankset, 277
  handlebars, 277
  overview, 276
  pedals, 277
  storing bike, 287–288
  tires, 277
  wheels, 277
installing
  adjustable bottom bracket, 228–229
  bottom bracket, 224–229
  brakes, 128–130
  cantilever brakes, 128
  cartridge bottom bracket, 226–227
  cassettes, 187
  center-mount brakes, 129–130
  crankset, 216–221
  derailleur, 236–239, 245–246
  freewheels, 186
  front derailleur, 245–246
  gear shifters, 250
  headset, 78
  pedals, 213–214
  rear derailleur, 236–239
  saddles, 147–149
  spare tube, 85
  tube and tire, 94–96
  V-brakes, 128–129
  wheels, 106–107

• J •

jammed chain, extracting, 58–59
jerseys, 324
jockey pulley, 31

• K •

Kevlar tires, 97–98
Kona Web site, 73

• L •

League of American Bicyclists, 301
leather saddle, 15, 145, 313
leg band, reflective, 308
length, chain stay, 103
Lifu tool, 36
lights, 77, 298, 308
linear-pull brakes, 120
L-limit screw, 62
lock, 77
lock ring, 175
looseness, 63–65, 304–305
lower jockey wheel, 31
lubricants
  buying tips, 164
  for extended trip, 276
  oil, 10
  overview, 41–43
  wax-based, 164
lubricating
  after-ride maintenance, 12
  brake levers, 283
  brakes, 283
  cables, 28, 285, 287
  cassettes, 177
  chains, 163–165, 285–286
  derailleur, 284–285
  freewheels, 177
  monthly maintenance, 15, 291
  preventive maintenance, 282–287
  sprocket, 285–286

• M •

maintenance. See also specific
    maintenance entries
  after riding, 12
  overview, 9–10
  regular, 289–298
  before riding, 11
  tips, 51
  while riding, 12
maintenance, annual
  accessories, checking, 17, 298
  bottom bracket, overhauling, 17, 297
  brake pads, replacing, 17, 297

cables, replacing, 16, 295
chain, deep cleaning, 16, 294
frame, waxing, 17, 298
handlebar grips or tape, replacing, 17, 298
headset, overhauling, 17, 296
housing, replacing, 16, 295
hubs, overhauling, 17, 295–296
overview, 16–17, 293–294
pedals, overhauling, 17, 296
rear derailleur, cleaning, 17
wheels, truing, 16, 294
maintenance, monthly
brakes, 16, 292
chainrings, 16, 292–293
chains, 16, 292–293
cleaning bike, 15, 291
cogs, 16, 292–293
lubrication, 15, 291
overview, 15–16
saddles, 16
structural damage, 15, 290
suspension, 16, 293
tightness, checking for, 16, 292
tires, 15, 290–291
wheels, 15, 290–291
maintenance, preventive
after-ride, 278–288
cleaning bike, 278–282
emergency tool kit, 274–276
lubricating bike, 282–287
overview, 273
before riding, 274–277
while riding, 278
manufacturers, 73
material
frame, 195–196
handlebar, 254
saddle, 144–145, 313
men, saddles for, 146–147
mini bike pump, 77
money, 11, 308
monthly maintenance
brakes, 16, 292
chainrings, 16, 292–293
chains, 16, 292–293
cleaning bike, 15, 291
cogs, 16, 292–293
lubrication, 15, 291

overview, 15–16
saddles, 16
structural damage, 15, 290
suspension, 16, 293
tightness, checking for, 16, 292
tires, 15, 290–291
wheels, 15, 290–291
mountain bike
frame, 103
overview, 74
parts of, 22
multipurpose tool, 275

• *N* •

nipple, 115
nipple spanner, 47
nuts, 104

• *O* •

one-key release crankset, 217
one-piece crankset, 215–216
one-piece saddle clamp, 148
on-the-road repairs
bent rim, 54–55
broken chain, 57
broken spoke, 55–56
derailleur, 59–61
duct tape, 66–67
flat tires, 57
jammed chain, extracting, 58–59
overview, 12–13, 53
torn tires, 57
walking home, 63

• *P* •

painting frame, 200
pant-cuff tie/clip, 324
Park Tool Web site, 36
parts
bearings, 22–24, 321
bottom bracket, 223–229
brakes, 34, 119–142
cables, 27–29
crankset, 215–223
derailleur, 30–31, 231–248

parts *(continued)*
  drivetrain, 34, 207–230
  frames, 34, 191–201
  gears, 29–30
  handlebars, 252–260
  headset, 261–270
  mountain bike, 22
  overview, 19–20
  pedals, 207–214
  quick-release lever, 32–33
  road bike, 21
  steering system, 34, 251–270
  suspension, 34, 201–206
  threads, 24–27
  wheels, 34, 99–118
patch kit, 11, 40, 274, 298
pedals. *See also* crankset
  annual maintenance, 296
  buying tips, 208–209
  clipless, 208–209
  installing, 213–214
  loose, 63
  overhauling, 14, 17, 211–212, 296
  overview, 207–208
  pre-ride inspection, 277
  removing, 209–211
  toe clips, 208
  upgrading, 321
  worn-out, 209
Pedro's Web site, 36
performance. *See* upgrading bike
Performance tool, 36
pinched flat, 84
plastic saddle, 144
pliers, 10, 11, 39, 275
pre-ride inspection
  brakes, 277
  checklist, 11
  crankset, 277
  handlebars, 277
  overview, 276
  pedals, 277
  storing bike, 287–288
  tires, 277
  wheels, 277

pre-ride tips
  brakes, checking, 304
  emergency tool kit, 274–276
  gloves, 307
  handlebars, adjusting, 302–303
  helmet, 307
  improving visibility, 308
  looseness, checking for, 304–305
  road safety skills class, 301
  saddle, adjusting, 303–304
  stocking emergency gear, 308
  tire pressure, checking, 304
  tool kit, 307
  wheels, checking, 306–307
pressure, tire
  checking, 11, 304
  low, 84
pressure gauge, 40–41
Presta valve, 87–88
preventive maintenance
  after-ride, 278–288
  cleaning bike, 278–282
  emergency tool kit, 274–276
  lubrication, 282–287
  overview, 273
  pre-ride inspection, 276–277
  before riding, 274–277
  while riding, 278
professional repairs
  frame, 78
  installing headset, 78
  overview, 14–15
  suspension, 79
  truing wheel, 79
pump, 11, 39–40, 77, 274
puncture. *See also* flat tires
  finding, 90
  sealant, 320
purchasing. *See* buying

quick release brakes, 137–138
quick release hub, 100, 107
quick release lever, 32–33, 104
quick-release wheel, 86, 104–106

• **R** •

race (bike part), 24
racing saddle, 145–146
racing-style handlebars, 323
rag, 275, 279
rain jacket, 11, 308
Raleigh Web site, 73
rear derailleur
  adjusting, 61, 239–241
  bypassing, 60–61
  cleaning, 17, 297
  installing, 236–239
  lubricating, 285
  overview, 31–32, 232
  removing, 61, 233–235
  stiff links, 159
  upgrading, 320–321
rear light, 77
rear wheel
  attaching, 96, 106–107
  removing, 87, 106
rebound, 202
recumbent bike, 74
reflective arm/leg band, 308
reflective vest, 324
reflector, 308
repair shop
  bike stand, 49–50
  lighting, 49
  overview, 10
  space, 48
  storage, 49
  ventilation, 48
  workbench, 49
repairs. See also specific repair entries
  advanced, 14
  basic, 13–14
  overview, 9–10, 12–13
  tips, 51
repairs, at home
  benefits of, 35
  bike stand, 49–51
  lighting, 49
  space, 48
  storage, 49
  tools, 36–47

ventilation, 48
workbench, 49
repairs, on-the-road
  bent rim, 54–55
  broken chain, 57
  broken spoke, 55–56
  derailleur, 59–61
  duct tape, 66–67
  flat tires, 57
  jammed chain, extracting, 58–59
  overview, 12–13, 53
  torn tires, 57
  walking home, 63
repairs, professional
  frame, 78
  installing headset, 78
  overview, 14–15
  suspension, 79
  truing wheel, 79
reusable rivets, 156, 170–172
riding bike. See on-the-road repairs; pre-ride inspection; pre-ride tips
rim
  dents, 106
  repairing, 54–55
rim brakes, 34, 120
riser bar, 253
rivets, 11, 156, 170–172, 276
road bike
  frame, 103
  overview, 73
  parts of, 21
road safety skills class, 301
RoadID Web site, 308
roadside emergency, preparing for, 11. See also on-the-road repairs
rounding, 79
rust, 199–200
rust inhibitors, 200

• **S** •

saddle
  adjusting, 13, 151, 303–304, 311–313
  angle, 147, 150–151
  comfort, 147
  cruising, 145–146

saddle *(continued)*
  design, 314
  functions, 145–146
  gender factor, 146–147, 313
  height, 147, 152–153, 304, 311
  installing, 147–149
  leather, 144–145
  material, 144–145, 313
  monthly maintenance, 15, 293
  moving around, 147
  overview, 143–144
  plastic, 144
  racing, 145–146
  removing, 147–149
  tilting, 311
  types of, 313–314
  upgrading, 322
  vinyl, 144
saddle clamp, 148
safe riding practices, 12, 102
saliva technique, for finding punctures, 90
Schrader valve, 87–88
Schwinn Web site, 73
screwdriver, 10–11, 38, 275
sealed-bearing hub, 108
seat. *See* saddle
seat post, 154
seat stay, 192
seat tube, 192
seat-tube angle, 192–193
sharp objects, 84
shifting system
  derailleur cable, 246–247
  derailleur overview, 231–232
  front derailleur, 241–246
  gear shifters, 248–250
  overhauling, 14
  rear derailleur, 232–241
Shimano STI-style shifter, 247
Shimano Web site, 156
Shimano-type chain
  overview, 156–157
  reassembling, 170–172
  removing, 168
shoe pouch, 308
shoes, 77, 322

shopping. *See* buying
shops, bike
  accessories, 76–77
  buying bike, 72–75
  cost of doing business, 71
  customer service, 71
  expertise of staff, 71
  family-friendly, 71
  overview, 69–70
  recommendations, 70
  repairing bike at, 78–79
  staff, 70
  turnaround time, 71
  women-friendly, 71
  year-round service, 70–71
shorts, 147
side-pull brakes, 86, 103
sit-bone width, 147
small light, 275
snakebite puncture, 84
socket bolt, 217–218
spare cable, 276
spare spoke, 276
spare tire, 276
spare tube, 85
specialized tools
  bottom bracket, 46
  chain tool, 44
  chain whip, 45
  cone wrench, 44
  crank puller, 44
  freewheel, 46
  headset, 47
  spoke wrench, 47
Specialized Web site, 73
Spin Doctor, 36
splined cassettes, 179–181
spoke key, 47
spoke wrench, 11, 47, 117, 275
spokes
  broken, 55–56
  extended trip tool kit, 11
  replacing, 55–56, 115
  spare, 276
  tensioning, 101
  truing wheel, 114–118

sponge, 279
sprocket
  cleaning, 280
  lubricating, 285–286
  teeth, 30
squeaking brakes, 136
SRAM PowerLink-type chain, 156, 168
staff, bike shop, 70–71
stands, 10, 49–51, 279
steel frame, 195
steering system
  drop bars, 252–253
  flat bars, 253
  handlebars, 252–260
  headset, 261–270
  overhauling, 14
  overview, 34, 251
  riser bars, 253
stiff links, 158–160
stiffness, frame, 195
storage
  of bike, 287–288
  workshop, 49
stores
  buying a bike, 71–75
  cost of doing business, 71
  customer service, 71
  expertise of staff, 71
  family-friendly, 71
  overview, 69–70
  recommendations, 70
  staff, 70
  turnaround time, 71
  women-friendly, 71
  year-round service, 70–71
strength, frame, 195
structural damage, 15, 93–94, 290
sunglasses, 11, 308
suspension. *See also* frame
  air, 202
  coil, 202
  compression, 202
  damping, 202
  elastomer, 202
  front sag, adjusting, 204–205
  maintaining, 14, 206

monthly inspection, 15, 293
  overview, 34, 201
  preload, 202
  rear sag, adjusting, 203–204
  rebound, 202
  repairing, 15, 79
  seat post, 154
  tuning, 202–205
sweep, handlebar, 254

• T •

tape, replacing, 17, 298
tapered handlebars, 254
taping handlebars, 255–260
teeth, sprocket, 30
tension pulley, 31
tensioned spokes, 101
tensioning brakes, 132
test ride, 74–75
thorn-resistant tube, 320
threaded fasteners
  buying tips, 26–27
  female parts, 25
  loose, 25–26
  male parts, 25
  overview, 24–25
  tightening, 25–26
threaded headset
  adjusting, 262–263
  overhauling, 268–270
  overview, 261
threading, bottom bracket, 230
threadless headset
  adjusting, 262
  overhauling, 263–268
  overview, 261
tilting saddle, 311
tire boot, 93–94
tire lever, 11, 41, 88–89, 275
tire patch kit, 11, 40, 274, 298
tire pressure
  checking, 11, 304
  low, 84
tire pump, 11, 39–40, 77, 274

tire tools
  patch kit, 11, 40, 274, 298
  pressure gauge, 40–41
  pump, 39–40
  tire levers, 41
tires. *See also* flat tires
  clincher, 100
  durability, 320
  inflating, 101
  Kevlar-reinforced, 97–98
  monthly inspection, 290–291
  overview, 83
  pre-ride inspection, 277
  removing, 87–90
  repairing on road, 57
  safe riding practices, 12
  spare, 276
  structurally damaged, 93–94
  torn, 57
  tread pattern, 320
  tubular, 100
  upgrading, 319–320
  width, 320
  worn-out, 84
titanium frame, 196
toe clip, 208
tool kit, emergency
  Allen wrenches, 275
  importance of, 307
  multipurpose tool, 275
  pliers, 275
  rag, 275
  screwdrivers, 275
  small light, 275
  spoke wrench, 275
  tire levers, 275
  tire patch kit, 274
  tire pump, 274
tool kit, extended trip
  chain links, 276
  chain tool, 276
  duct tape, 276
  extra tubes, 276
  lubrication, 276
  overview, 275–276
  rivets, 276

spare cables, 276
spare spokes, 276
spare tire, 276
tools. *See also tool kit entries*; tools,
    specialized
  Allen wrenches, 38–39, 275
  availability of, 10
  bottom bracket, 46
  bringing, 307
  buying, 10, 36–37
  chain, 44, 276
  chain links, 276
  chain whip, 45
  cleaners, 43
  cone wrench, 44
  crank puller, 44
  degreasers, 43
  duct tape, 276
  extended trip, 11
  extra tubes, 276
  freewheel, 46
  hammer, 39
  headset, 47
  lubricants, 41–43, 276
  multipurpose, 275
  patch kit, 40, 274
  pliers, 275
  pre-ride inspection, 11
  pressure gauge, 40–41
  pump, 39–40
  rag, 275
  rivets, 276
  screwdrivers, 38, 275
  small light, 275
  spare cables, 276
  spare spokes, 276
  spare tire, 276
  spoke wrench, 47, 275
  tire levers, 41, 275
  tire pump, 274
  wrenches, 37–38
tools, specialized
  bottom bracket, 46
  chain, 44
  chain whip, 45
  cone wrench, 44

crank puller, 44
freewheel, 46
headset, 47
overview, 43
spoke wrench, 47
top tube, 192
torn tires, repairing, 57
touring bike, 74
tread, 84
Trek Web site, 73
triathlon handlebars, 323
truing, 15–16, 79, 114–118, 294
truing stand, 116
tube
blowout, 85
damages to, 84
extra, 276
overview, 84
patching, 85, 91–93
spare, 85
thorn-resistant, 320
tubular tire, 100
turnaround time, bike shop, 71
two-piece clamp, 148

• U •

upgrading bike
bearings, 321
brake levers, 323
handlebars, 322–323
overview, 319
pedals, 321
rear derailleur, 320–321
saddles, 322
wheels, 319–320
upper jockey wheel, 31
used bike
buying tips, 75–76
pre-ride inspection, 76

• V •

valve, 84
valve leaks, 90

V-brakes
installing, 128–129
overview, 86, 120, 122
quick-release mechanism, 137
removing wheel, 103
vinyl saddle, 144
visibility, improving, 308, 324

• W •

washing bike, 12, 278–282
wax-based lubricants, 164
waxing, 17, 201, 298
WD-40, 42, 199
Web sites
BikeLeague, 301
Campagnolo, 156
Cannondale, 73
craigslist, 76
eBay, 76
Fuji, 73
Gary Fisher, 73
Kona, 73
Park Tool, 36
Pedro's, 36
Raleigh, 73
RoadID, 308
Schwinn, 73
Shimano, 156
Specialized, 73
SRAM, 156
Trek, 73
weight, frame, 195
wheel
annual maintenance, 294
attaching, 96
axle nuts, 86
bent, repairing, 54–55
for bike types, 101–102
bolts, 104
buying tips, 100
caring for, 101–102
cleaning, 101
dents in rim, repairing, 106
diameter, 100

wheel *(continued)*
  inspecting for problems, 102–103,
    306–307
  installing, 106–107
  monthly inspection, 15, 290–291
  nuts, 104
  overview, 34, 99
  parts of, 84
  pre-ride inspection, 11, 277
  quick-release, 86, 104–106
  reinstalling tube and tire, 94–96
  removing, 86–87, 103–106
  repairing, 13
  safe riding practices, 102
  size, 100
  spinning, 102–103
  tensioned spokes, 101
  truing, 15–16, 79, 114–118, 294
  upgrading, 319–320
  width, 100
width
  handlebar, 254
  hub, 100
  tire, 320

women, saddles for, 146–147, 313
women-friendly bike shops, 71
workbench, 49
workshop, home
  bike stand, 49–51
  lighting, 49
  space needed, 48
  storage, 49
  ventilation, 48
  workbench, 49
worn-out pedals, 209
worn-out tires, 84
wrenches, 10, 37–38

year-round service, bike shop, 70–71

BUSINESS, CAREERS & PERSONAL FINANCE

Accounting For Dummies, 4th Edition*
978-0-470-24600-9

Bookkeeping Workbook For Dummies†
978-0-470-16983-4

Commodities For Dummies
978-0-470-04928-0

Doing Business in China For Dummies
978-0-470-04929-7

E-Mail Marketing For Dummies
978-0-470-19087-6

Job Interviews For Dummies, 3rd Edition*†
978-0-470-17748-8

Personal Finance Workbook For Dummies*†
978-0-470-09933-9

Real Estate License Exams For Dummies
978-0-7645-7623-2

Six Sigma For Dummies
978-0-7645-6798-8

Small Business Kit For Dummies, 2nd Edition*†
978-0-7645-5984-6

Telephone Sales For Dummies
978-0-470-16836-3

BUSINESS PRODUCTIVITY & MICROSOFT OFFICE

Access 2007 For Dummies
978-0-470-03649-5

Excel 2007 For Dummies
978-0-470-03737-9

Office 2007 For Dummies
978-0-470-00923-9

Outlook 2007 For Dummies
978-0-470-03830-7

PowerPoint 2007 For Dummies
978-0-470-04059-1

Project 2007 For Dummies
978-0-470-03651-8

QuickBooks 2008 For Dummies
978-0-470-18470-7

Quicken 2008 For Dummies
978-0-470-17473-9

Salesforce.com For Dummies, 2nd Edition
978-0-470-04893-1

Word 2007 For Dummies
978-0-470-03658-7

EDUCATION, HISTORY, REFERENCE & TEST PREPARATION

African American History For Dummies
978-0-7645-5469-8

Algebra For Dummies
978-0-7645-5325-7

Algebra Workbook For Dummies
978-0-7645-8467-1

Art History For Dummies
978-0-470-09910-0

ASVAB For Dummies, 2nd Edition
978-0-470-10671-6

British Military History For Dummies
978-0-470-03213-8

Calculus For Dummies
978-0-7645-2498-1

Canadian History For Dummies, 2nd Edition
978-0-470-83656-9

Geometry Workbook For Dummies
978-0-471-79940-5

The SAT I For Dummies, 6th Edition
978-0-7645-7193-0

Series 7 Exam For Dummies
978-0-470-09932-2

World History For Dummies
978-0-7645-5242-7

FOOD, GARDEN, HOBBIES & HOME

Bridge For Dummies, 2nd Edition
978-0-471-92426-5

Coin Collecting For Dummies, 2nd Edition
978-0-470-22275-1

Cooking Basics For Dummies, 3rd Edition
978-0-7645-7206-7

Drawing For Dummies
978-0-7645-5476-6

Etiquette For Dummies, 2nd Edition
978-0-470-10672-3

Gardening Basics For Dummies*†
978-0-470-03749-2

Knitting Patterns For Dummies
978-0-470-04556-5

Living Gluten-Free For Dummies†
978-0-471-77383-2

Painting Do-It-Yourself For Dummies
978-0-470-17533-0

HEALTH, SELF HELP, PARENTING & PETS

Anger Management For Dummies
978-0-470-03715-7

Anxiety & Depression Workbook For Dummies
978-0-7645-9793-0

Dieting For Dummies, 2nd Edition
978-0-7645-4149-0

Dog Training For Dummies, 2nd Edition
978-0-7645-8418-3

Horseback Riding For Dummies
978-0-470-09719-9

Infertility For Dummies†
978-0-470-11518-3

Meditation For Dummies with CD-ROM, 2nd Edition
978-0-471-77774-8

Post-Traumatic Stress Disorder For Dummies
978-0-470-04922-8

Puppies For Dummies, 2nd Edition
978-0-470-03717-1

Thyroid For Dummies, 2nd Edition†
978-0-471-78755-6

Type 1 Diabetes For Dummies*†
978-0-470-17811-9

* Separate Canadian edition also available
† Separate U.K. edition also available

Available wherever books are sold. For more information or to order direct: U.S. customers visit www.dummies.com or call 1-877-762-2974.
U.K. customers visit www.wileyeurope.com or call (0)1243 843291. Canadian customers visit www.wiley.ca or call 1-800-567-4797.

INTERNET & DIGITAL MEDIA

AdWords For Dummies
978-0-470-15252-2

Blogging For Dummies, 2nd Edition
978-0-470-23017-6

Digital Photography All-in-One Desk Reference For Dummies, 3rd Edition
978-0-470-03743-0

Digital Photography For Dummies, 5th Edition
978-0-7645-9802-9

Digital SLR Cameras & Photography For Dummies, 2nd Edition
978-0-470-14927-0

eBay Business All-in-One Desk Reference For Dummies
978-0-7645-8438-1

eBay For Dummies, 5th Edition*
978-0-470-04529-9

eBay Listings That Sell For Dummies
978-0-471-78912-3

Facebook For Dummies
978-0-470-26273-3

The Internet For Dummies, 11th Edition
978-0-470-12174-0

Investing Online For Dummies, 5th Edition
978-0-7645-8456-5

iPod & iTunes For Dummies, 5th Edition
978-0-470-17474-6

MySpace For Dummies
978-0-470-09529-4

Podcasting For Dummies
978-0-471-74898-4

Search Engine Optimization For Dummies, 2nd Edition
978-0-471-97998-2

Second Life For Dummies
978-0-470-18025-9

Starting an eBay Business For Dummies, 3rd Edition†
978-0-470-14924-9

GRAPHICS, DESIGN & WEB DEVELOPMENT

Adobe Creative Suite 3 Design Premium All-in-One Desk Reference For Dummies
978-0-470-11724-8

Adobe Web Suite CS3 All-in-One Desk Reference For Dummies
978-0-470-12099-6

AutoCAD 2008 For Dummies
978-0-470-11650-0

Building a Web Site For Dummies, 3rd Edition
978-0-470-14928-7

Creating Web Pages All-in-One Desk Reference For Dummies, 3rd Edition
978-0-470-09629-1

Creating Web Pages For Dummies, 8th Edition
978-0-470-08030-6

Dreamweaver CS3 For Dummies
978-0-470-11490-2

Flash CS3 For Dummies
978-0-470-12100-9

Google SketchUp For Dummies
978-0-470-13744-4

InDesign CS3 For Dummies
978-0-470-11865-8

Photoshop CS3 All-in-One Desk Reference For Dummies
978-0-470-11195-6

Photoshop CS3 For Dummies
978-0-470-11193-2

Photoshop Elements 5 For Dummies
978-0-470-09810-3

SolidWorks For Dummies
978-0-7645-9555-4

Visio 2007 For Dummies
978-0-470-08983-5

Web Design For Dummies, 2nd Edition
978-0-471-78117-2

Web Sites Do-It-Yourself For Dummies
978-0-470-16903-2

Web Stores Do-It-Yourself For Dummies
978-0-470-17443-2

LANGUAGES, RELIGION & SPIRITUALITY

Arabic For Dummies
978-0-471-77270-5

Chinese For Dummies, Audio Set
978-0-470-12766-7

French For Dummies
978-0-7645-5193-2

German For Dummies
978-0-7645-5195-6

Hebrew For Dummies
978-0-7645-5489-6

Ingles Para Dummies
978-0-7645-5427-8

Italian For Dummies, Audio Set
978-0-470-09586-7

Italian Verbs For Dummies
978-0-471-77389-4

Japanese For Dummies
978-0-7645-5429-2

Latin For Dummies
978-0-7645-5431-5

Portuguese For Dummies
978-0-471-78738-9

Russian For Dummies
978-0-471-78001-4

Spanish Phrases For Dummies
978-0-7645-7204-3

Spanish For Dummies
978-0-7645-5194-9

Spanish For Dummies, Audio Set
978-0-470-09585-0

The Bible For Dummies
978-0-7645-5296-0

Catholicism For Dummies
978-0-7645-5391-2

The Historical Jesus For Dummies
978-0-470-16785-4

Islam For Dummies
978-0-7645-5503-9

Spirituality For Dummies, 2nd Edition
978-0-470-19142-2

NETWORKING AND PROGRAMMING

ASP.NET 3.5 For Dummies
978-0-470-19592-5

C# 2008 For Dummies
978-0-470-19109-5

Hacking For Dummies, 2nd Edition
978-0-470-05235-8

Home Networking For Dummies, 4th Edition
978-0-470-11806-1

Java For Dummies, 4th Edition
978-0-470-08716-9

Microsoft® SQL Server™ 2008 All-in-One Desk Reference For Dummies
978-0-470-17954-3

Networking All-in-One Desk Reference For Dummies, 2nd Edition
978-0-7645-9939-2

Networking For Dummies, 8th Edition
978-0-470-05620-2

SharePoint 2007 For Dummies
978-0-470-09941-4

Wireless Home Networking For Dummies, 2nd Edition
978-0-471-74940-0

OPERATING SYSTEMS & COMPUTER BASICS

iMac For Dummies, 5th Edition
978-0-7645-8458-9

Laptops For Dummies, 2nd Edition
978-0-470-05432-1

Linux For Dummies, 8th Edition
978-0-470-11649-4

MacBook For Dummies
978-0-470-04859-7

**Mac OS X Leopard All-in-One
Desk Reference For Dummies**
978-0-470-05434-5

Mac OS X Leopard For Dummies
978-0-470-05433-8

Macs For Dummies, 9th Edition
978-0-470-04849-8

PCs For Dummies, 11th Edition
978-0-470-13728-4

Windows® Home Server For Dummies
978-0-470-18592-6

Windows Server 2008 For Dummies
978-0-470-18043-3

**Windows Vista All-in-One
Desk Reference For Dummies**
978-0-471-74941-7

Windows Vista For Dummies
978-0-471-75421-3

Windows Vista Security For Dummies
978-0-470-11805-4

SPORTS, FITNESS & MUSIC

Coaching Hockey For Dummies
978-0-470-83685-9

Coaching Soccer For Dummies
978-0-471-77381-8

Fitness For Dummies, 3rd Edition
978-0-7645-7851-9

Football For Dummies, 3rd Edition
978-0-470-12536-6

GarageBand For Dummies
978-0-7645-7323-1

Golf For Dummies, 3rd Edition
978-0-471-76871-5

Guitar For Dummies, 2nd Edition
978-0-7645-9904-0

**Home Recording For Musicians
For Dummies, 2nd Edition**
978-0-7645-8884-6

**iPod & iTunes For Dummies,
5th Edition**
978-0-470-17474-6

Music Theory For Dummies
978-0-7645-7838-0

Stretching For Dummies
978-0-470-06741-3

Get smart @ dummies.com®

- Find a full list of Dummies titles
- Look into loads of FREE on-site articles
- Sign up for FREE eTips e-mailed to you weekly
- See what other products carry the Dummies name
- Shop directly from the Dummies bookstore
- Enter to win new prizes every month!

* Separate Canadian edition also available
* Separate U.K. edition also available

Available wherever books are sold. For more information or to order direct: U.S. customers visit www.dummies.com or call 1-877-762-2974.
U.K. customers visit www.wileyeurope.com or call (0) 1243 843291. Canadian customers visit www.wiley.ca or call 1-800-567-4797.

Do More with Dummies

Products for the Rest of Us!

DVDs • Music • Games • DIY
Consumer Electronics • Software • Crafts
Hobbies • Cookware • and more!

Check out the Dummies Product Shop at www.dummies.com for more information!